HISTORIC SITES AND MARKERS
ALONG THE MORMON AND OTHER
GREAT WESTERN TRAILS

HISTORIC SITES AND MARKERS ALONG THE

MORMON AND OTHER

GREAT WESTERN TRAILS

STANLEY B. KIMBALL

UNIVERSITY OF ILLINOIS PRESS
Urbana and Chicago

© 1988 by the Board of Trustees of the University of Illinois
Manufactured in the United States of America
1 2 3 4 5 C P 5 4 3 2 1

This book is printed on acid-free paper.

Library of Congress Cataloging-in-Publication Data

Kimball, Stanley Buchholz.
  Historic sites and markers along the Mormon and
other great western trails.

  Bibliography: p.
  Includes index.
  1. Trails—West (U.S.)—Guide-books. 2. Historic
sites—West (U.S.)—Guide-books. 3. Historical
markers—West (U.S.)—Guide-books. 4. West (U.S.)—
History, Local. 5. West (U.S.)—Description and
travel—1981– —Guide-books. I. Title.
F591.K48   1988   917.8'0433   87-13858
ISBN 0-252-01455-3 (cloth: alk. paper)
ISBN 0-252-01456-1 (paper: alk. paper)

This book honors the pioneer spirit of those courageous men and women who by their heroic trek across the continent established homes and civilization in the Far West.

—Adapted from a trail marker
Court House Square
Independence, Missouri

Contents

List of Maps

Trails I–XXV, 1

Trails XXVI–XXVII, 247

Trail XXVIII, 265

Trail XXIX, 277

Preface

We are in the midst of a great American western trails renaissance. Interest in historic trails has never been higher. There seems, in fact, to be a one-to-one relationship between our destruction of this part of our national heritage and our desire to learn more about it, to personally experience the power of place and the spirit of locale. Thanks to scholars, history buffs, publishers, historic societies, and the U.S. Congress, our historic trails are now becoming better known, more fully appreciated, more carefully preserved, and more clearly marked. As further evidence of the renewal of interest in western trails, there has been an annual increase in the number of markers, parks, schools, businesses, museums, exhibits, events, and tourist attractions with appropriate names and purposes. Watch for them. Additionally there has been a yearly increase in county, state, and federal road signs pointing out historic sites and markers connected with trail history.

One of the things this book attempts to do is to further our growing appreciation and knowledge of those roads west across the country that were used from about 1830—when the trans-Appalachia region was still the Far West to many and when the first wagons were attempting the Oregon Trail—to the wedding of the rails at Promentory Point, Utah Territory, in 1869.

The fifteen trails and their variants described in this book pass through fifteen states from New York to California: New York, Ohio, Indiana, Illinois, Missouri, Iowa, Nebraska, Wyoming, Utah, Kansas, Colorado, Oklahoma, New Mexico, Arizona, and California. Among the trails described here are some of the most famous in American history—the Mormon Pioneer Trail, the Oregon-California Trail, and the Santa Fe Trail. Other once-famous trails presented here include the Boonslick, the Overland–Bridger Pass, the Dragoon, the Mormon Handcart, the Trappers'–Cherokee Trail, the Fort Leavenworth–Military Road, the St.

Joseph Trail, the Nebraska City Cutoff, the Golden Road, and the Ox-Bow. In addition to these thirteen trans-Mississippi trails, two other roads west, routes that might properly be called trans-Appalachian, are considered. One crosses New York from near Binghamton to Buffalo. The other runs from Kirtland, Ohio, to Independence, Missouri.

All or parts of most of these trails have been known by different names before, during, and after the period covered by this book. Modern travelers will occasionally find road signs and markers informing them that they are driving along the Lewis and Clark Trail, the Hiawatha Trail, the Osage Trace, the Eddyville Trail, the Raccoon Forks Trail, the Omaha–Fort Kearny Road, the Council Bluffs Road, the Lodgepole Creek Trail, the Overland Trail, the Leavenworth and Pikes Peak Express Road, the Smoky Hill Trail, the Butterfield Overland Dispatch or Butterfield Overland Mail Road, *El Camino Real*, the Chihuahua Trail, the California Emigrant Road, the Southern Emigrant Trail, the Lincoln Heritage Trail, the Niagara Historic Trail, the Texas Trail, the Deadwood Trail, the Great River Road, the National Route, the touristy Old West Trail, the Pony Express Trail, Geronimo Trail, and the National Road.

This book is a comprehensive guide to more than 550 historic sites and markers scattered along some 10,000 miles of emigrant trails. By the use of the accompanying maps and commentary in the text, the trails themselves can be followed rather closely. There are a few spelling curiosities along these trails. It is Fort Caspar, but the city is Casper. It is Colonel S. W. Kearny and Fort Kearny, but Kearney city and county. The land formation is Scotts Bluff, and it is Scotts Bluff National Monument and Scotts Bluff County, but Scottsbluff city. The Indian tribe is spelled Pottawattamie in Iowa and Pottawattomie in Kansas.

Some attention ought to be given to place names scattered along these trails as reminders of the native Americans and the Spanish, French, and British Empires which at various times controlled what became the United States. Trail study helps bring back to life this important part of our colonial history. The reader and traveler will note communities, streams, rivers, mountains, peaks, deserts, springs, and other landforms bearing revealing toponyms.

Years ago this book began as a guide to historic sites and markers along Mormon trails. Since that time, for a variety of reasons, the scope of this book has been expanded greatly. Among the reasons for so doing are: the desire to offer a more comprehensive view of the trans-Mississippi / Missouri West; the ability to appeal to more readers; and the need to inform travelers, especially Mormons, that Mormons used far more western trails than just the route of their famous trek from Nauvoo, Illinois, to Salt Lake City, Utah. In fact, there are very few western trails that the Mormons did not use at one time or another.

Careful readers will note that of the 415 markers described in this work, 182 (or 44 percent) refer to the Mormons, Utah, or Salt Lake City and that 96 (or 53 percent) of these have been erected by non-Mormons. This is an indication of the growing popularity of and interest in Mormon emigrant history that I have noted since 1963 when I first started work on western trails. In every state, almost in every county, all kinds of people have been anxious to acquaint me with their local history. Most of the time their information has been correct, but too often people are so anxious to have had Brigham Young pass through or near their community (or ranch), or at least to have a nearby Mormon grave, that I have heard many legends and distorted facts and have had to be careful when demolishing these fabrications.

Some vestiges of the original Mormon orientation of this book remain. I do not, for example, follow the Oregon-California Trail beyond Fort Bridger in Wyoming. I have also included two trails, the First Mormon Road West and the route of the Zion's Camp March, the treatment of which is almost exclusively Mormon. The reader must also remember that the Mormons used every trail presented in this book, but sometimes they called them by different names and their forgotten presence on some of these trails is noted. One other caveat: Some will wonder why many trails radiating from Salt Lake City are not presented. That is because I consider such trails colonizing trails and the focus of this book is on emigrant trails.

Since the Mormons were the only organized group in American history to use all the trails studied in this book, a brief account of their early history is presented here to help explain when and why they used all these trails.

Joseph Smith, the Mormon prophet, organized the Church of Jesus Christ of Latter-day Saints in western New York in 1830 and shortly thereafter established the church in Kirtland, Ohio, and western Missouri. Until 1839, when the Mormons were finally driven from Ohio and Missouri into Illinois, there was much travel on trails east of the Missouri River.

The Mormons found only temporary refuge in Illinois. Smith was murdered in 1844 and subsequent mob activity drove them farther west. Led by Brigham Young, they crossed Iowa in 1846, reestablishing themselves in Utah in 1847. Thereafter, the Mormons used many western trails to gather from the United States and Europe to their new Zion in Salt Lake City. When the transcontinental railroad was completed in 1869 most Mormon emigrants became "Pullman Pioneers" and their use of emigrant trails declined. During the Mexican War of 1846–48 the Mormon Battalion marched from Council Bluffs, Iowa, along the Santa Fe Trail to Santa Fe, New Mexico, and then continued on to San Diego, California, making a wagon road as they went.

Because the trails considered here are of different lengths, places, importance, and because the degree to which they are marked varies so greatly, I have worked out a basic format that will accommodate a diversity of presentations. Some trails, for example, are treated site by site and marker by marker. Others are better presented county by county, and still others state by state. Because of the great differences among these trails, some accounts are but a few pages long, others much longer. Less well known trails, furthermore, are given comparatively more detailed treatment than the better-known trails.

The order of presentation of these trails could have been in several ways, by (for example) importance, chronology, or geography. The ordering selected—Mormon, Oregon-California, Overland, Colorado, Santa Fe, Missouri, and trans-Applalachia—is an attempt to combine importance (a highly debatable question), geography, and reader convenience.

The work is also organized and cross indexed so that the reader or traveler may study any particular site or marker, follow a whole trail from beginning to end, or concentrate on one state at a time. Each of the more than 550 sites or markers is fully described and located, and the full text of most markers is also given. Most of the sites are open to the public, but some are on private ground and permission as well as directions must be secured to visit them. The symbol (P) appears following the site name to indicate this.

To avoid an excess of road directions, guidance is usually not given between sites or places when reference to the maps presented in this book or to ordinary road maps provides sufficient information. When necessary, however, detailed instructions are supplied, and in some cases the reader is advised to have county maps available. Mileage, except where otherwise noted, is calculated from the center of the community (traditionally from the main post office), not from its limits.

Unfortunately, this guide suffers from a problem that plagues all such guides, which is the fact that road numbers and names change, as do the routings of roads. Furthermore, access to some sites can change for a variety of reasons. I will be grateful for information from users to help keep the text up to date. The traveler should also be aware that all too often markers are vandalized by "hunters" who apparently cannot hit anything else. Worse is the problem of the theft of bronze plaques and medallions. Slowly these stolen plaques are being replaced with anodized aluminum—which is adequate, and the metal is not worth stealing. There are also four-legged vandals out there, for cattle find some markers ideal to use as scratching posts. Then there is the problem of cedar trees. At one time, the thing to do was to plant one or more little cedar trees near newly erected markers. All well and good, but in time people forget or neglect to trim those trees, and eventually the cedars partially or completely hide the markers. Over the years I have broken off many branches in order to uncover these markers. Once, in a remote area, I found a marker I had been searching for without success when a call of nature caused me to enter a grove of cedars. Users of this guide should also be aware of the fact that too many contemporary ranch and oil company roads look more like old trails than the old trails themselves do. Be careful, because it is easy to be fooled.

A short bibliography refers readers and travelers to related books, articles, and trail guides for further reference and use. I have included cross-references where certain sites, markers, and trails are interrelated. Important forts and trail centers are mentioned in the text. Furthermore, in our increasingly historically minded present, almost every county through which these trails run boasts of some kind of local museum (usually at the county seat) that can be very helpful to the traveler. A selected list of these museums is offered in the appendix. Some chambers of commerce and Boy Scout councils also offer free information, as do many tourist establishments along the trails.

These trails extend almost from coast to coast. Since 1963 I have followed all of them and have been over the trails many times on foot, in four-wheel drive vehicles, and in small planes. Each mile, site, and marker has been plotted on appropriate maps. The sites have been numbered in four consecutive sequences keyed to maps 1–18, 19–20, 21–22, and 23–30; the relevant maps precede each group of related trails in the text. The illustrations provide a photographic record of some trails, sites, and markers; I have selected these photographs from the complete series I have taken of these places. Unless otherwise stated, all photographs are mine.

In most cases the trails can be followed successfully, with reasonable accuracy, in ordinary passenger cars with careful driving. There are, however, many very important and interesting historic sites that can be reached safely only with off-road vehicles (ORVs), in dry weather, and with the aid of detailed maps. In such areas travelers should drive off the top half of the gas tank and carry water; a compass, binoculars, and good maps are also recommended. In the text, the reader is alerted to these difficult places, and directions are given both for how to reach them and for how to work around them. Common courtesy demands that travelers who go through ranch gates close them immediately. In the few instances where one must cross an electrified fence, be sure to lower it properly. Threaded plastic insulators are provided for this purpose. When in doubt, crawl under but *never* straddle one, especially if the ground is wet.

Some symbols have been employed in this study: ORV designates the need for off-road vehicles; a solidus (/) is used to indicate line changes in many of the inscriptions; DAR refers to the Daughters of American Revolution, who have put up scores of markers; BLM refers to the Bureau of Land Management of the Department of the Interior; (P) means that the site is on private ground; and "see trail X, 5" is a cross-reference to site or marker number 5 of the trail bearing that Roman numeral in the table of contents.

No one ever produces a book alone. Over the years I have been helped by many librarians, archivists, historical societies, museums, governmental employees, trail experts, and friends. While I may have unfortunately forgotten the help of some, I would like particularly to thank Lida L. Green in Iowa; Don Snoddy of the Union Pacific Railroad Museum; Michael Beaudry and Dr. John L. Latschar of the National Park Service in Colorado; A. M. Bradbury, also of Colorado, who did research for me on several trails; Jerry Jacobs, John E. Christensen, and Floyd Armstrong of Kansas; and Ruth Olson, Director of the Santa Fe Trail Center, also in Kansas. Special thanks are due students in my seminars and travel-study classes, who have made signficant contributions to the understanding of the transportation frontier of the Old West. Several airplane pilots exercised much skill to fly me just where I needed to be on some trails.

My work would have been very limited without the help of many local people I met across the country who went out of their way to show me unusual and little-known historic markers and sites. Particular thanks are extended to farmers and ranchers who, with one notable exception in eastern Utah, never refused my requests to do research and even to camp on their private property. Without such range courtesy no good studies of trails could ever be written.

My work would have been harder and less productive without the years of support I have received from some of my associates: C. Booth Wallentine and R. Don Oscarson, in the Mormon Pioneer Trail Foundation; William Evans and Richard O. Clark of the Public Communications department of the Mormon church; Wendell J. Ashton of the *Deseret News*; Jay Todd of the *Ensign*; Lowell Durham of the Deseret Book Company; and Charles D. Tate, Jr., of *B.Y.U. Studies*.

I am especially grateful to all my trail companions with whom I have driven, hiked, and flown these trails and who have shared their observations and insights with me. I expressly remember Ken Stobaugh and Mark McKiernan on trans-Appalachian trails; Gene C. Herrin, Roger P. Blair, and Wayne B. Erickson with whom I camped during several seasons of trail research in Wyoming; and Don Couchman in Luna County, New Mexico. I also tramped the old trails with Hal Knight of the *Deseret News*, with Charles McCarry of the *National Geographic*, with Lane Johnson of the *Ensign*, with photographers Eldon Linschoten and Jed Clark; I roamed the Omaha-Council Bluffs area with Gail Holmes, as well as the whole Santa Fe area with Dr. Marc Simmons. Greg Franzwa, founder of the Oregon-California Trails Association, has shared his unmatched expertise with me on those trails. I had some memorable experiences on the Mormon Trail with Oliver Smith of the Sons of Utah Pioneers and with my son Chase. Walter Dennis, foreman of Jimmy Camp Ranch in Colorado, introduced me to some of the rarely seen sites on that ranch, and Dan Sharp guided me around some name cliffs in Oklahoma.

More particularly I must acknowledge the help of the late great Oregon Trail expert, Paul Henderson, who gave me my first field training on reading trails and who provided help and encouragement until his death in 1981; the financial support of both the Office of Research and Projects of Southern Illinois University at Edwardsville and the Public Communications Department of the Church of Jesus Christ of Latter-day Saints; and the close reading and comments on the entire manuscript by Merrill J. Mattes and Brigham Madsen. I wish to thank my excellent typist, Ruth Anne Gevers, who saw this manuscript through the computer, an intimidating experience for me; cartographers Diane Clements and Jim Bier, for their important contributions in creating the maps; Barbara E. Cohen of the University of Illinois Press for her assistance and superb editorial skills; and my wife, Violet, for the extensive help she has given me in matters of literary quality and for her constant encouragement of my efforts. She traveled a number of these trails with me and some of her photographs appear in this book.

TRAILS I–XXV

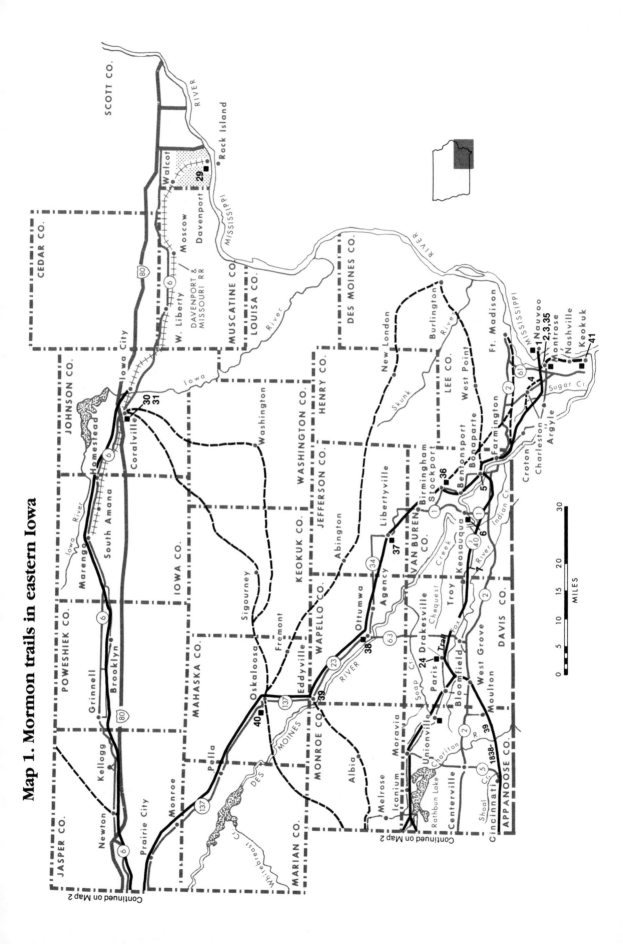

Map 1. Mormon trails in eastern Iowa

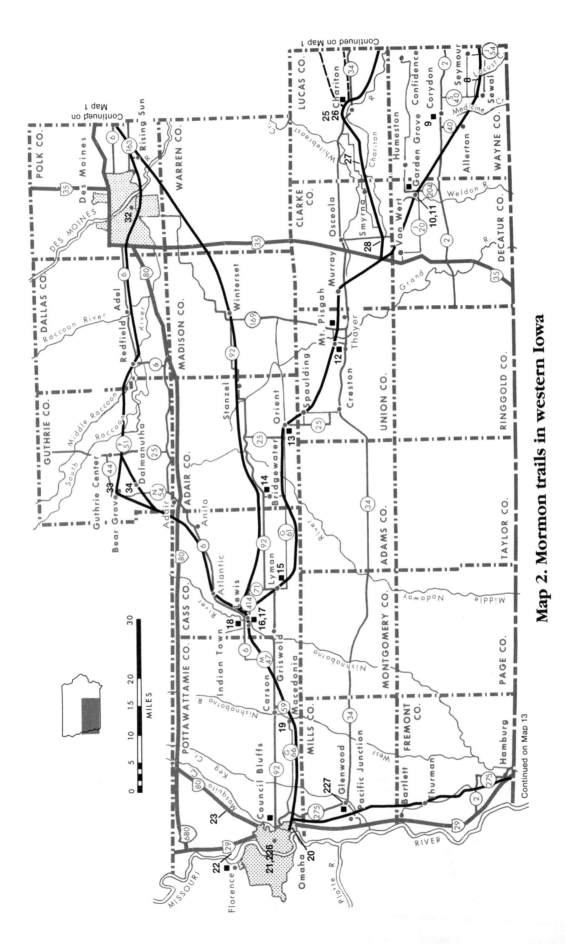

Map 2. Mormon trails in western Iowa

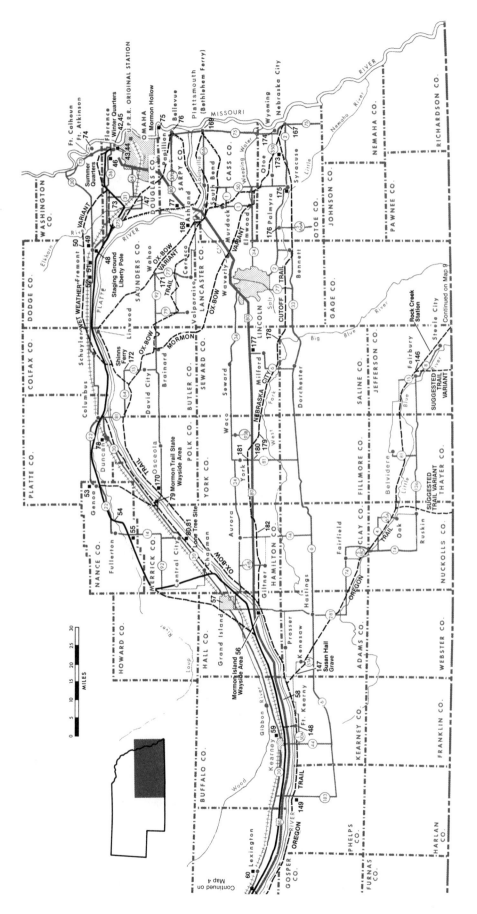

Map 3. Mormon trails in eastern Nebraska

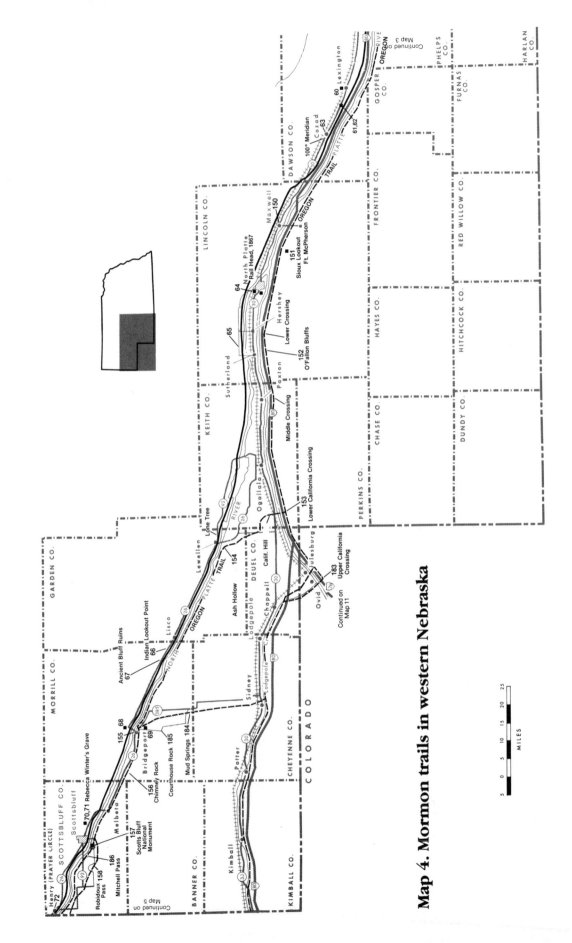

Map 4. Mormon trails in western Nebraska

MILES

5 0 5 10 15 20 25

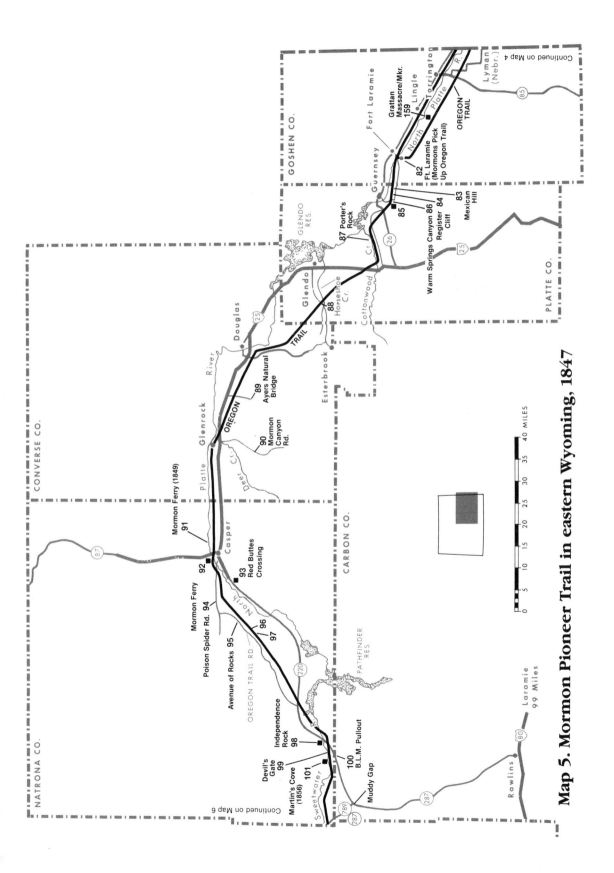

Map 5. Mormon Pioneer Trail in eastern Wyoming, 1847

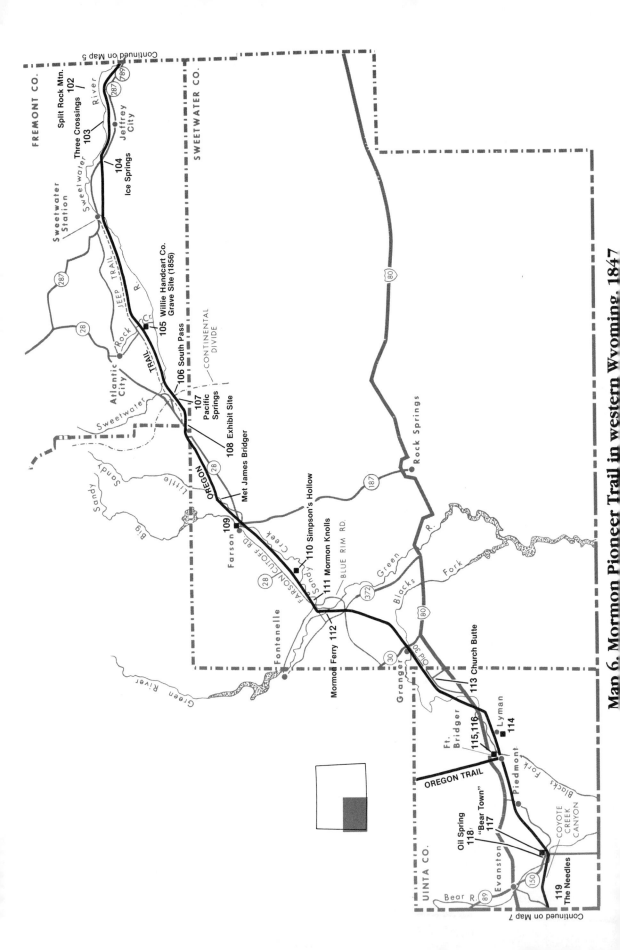

Map 6. Mormon Pioneer Trail in western Wyoming, 1847

Map 7. Mormon Pioneer Trail, 1847, and Golden Road, 1850, in Utah

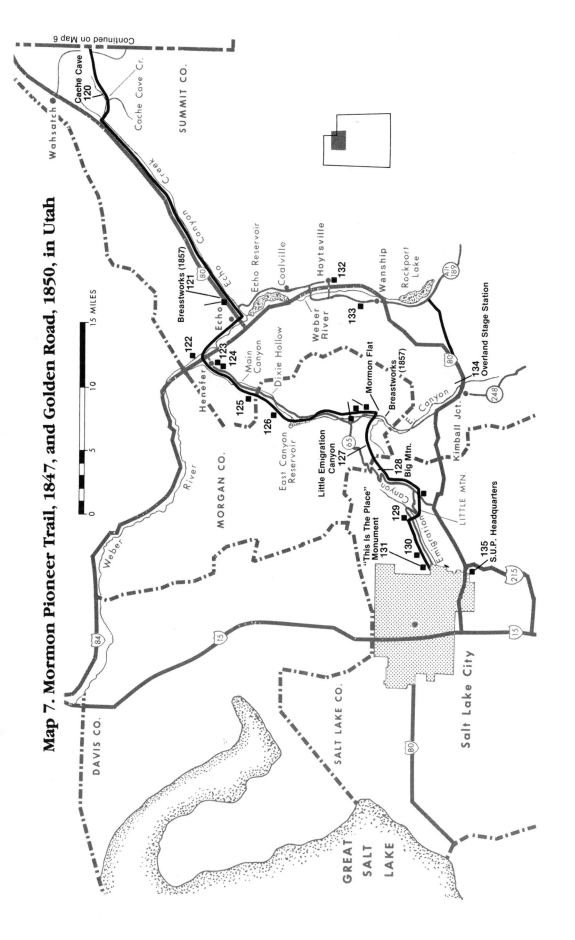

Continued on Map 6

Wahsatch

Cache Cave Cr.

Cache Cave 120

SUMMIT CO.

DAVIS CO.

Echo Canyon

Echo Creek

Breastworks (1857) 121

Echo Reservoir

Coalville

Hoytsville

132

Weber River

133

Wanship

Rockport Lake

Alt 189

Overland Stage Station

80

Echo

122

123

124

Main Canyon

Dixie Hollow

Henefer

Mormon Flat

Breastworks (1857)

134

80

248

125

126

East Canyon Reservoir

127 Little Emigration Canyon

65

128 Big Mtn.

E. Canyon

Kimball Jct.

LITTLE MTN.

MORGAN CO.

Weber River

"This Is The Place" Monument 131

129

130

Emigration Canyon

S.U.P. Headquarters 135

84

SALT LAKE CO.

15

215

15

80

Salt Lake City

GREAT SALT LAKE

15 MILES

10

5

0

MILES

Map 8. The Santa Fe Trail in Missouri and eastern Kansas

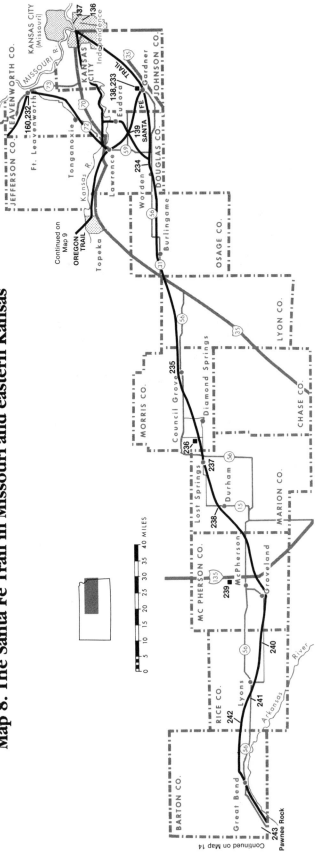

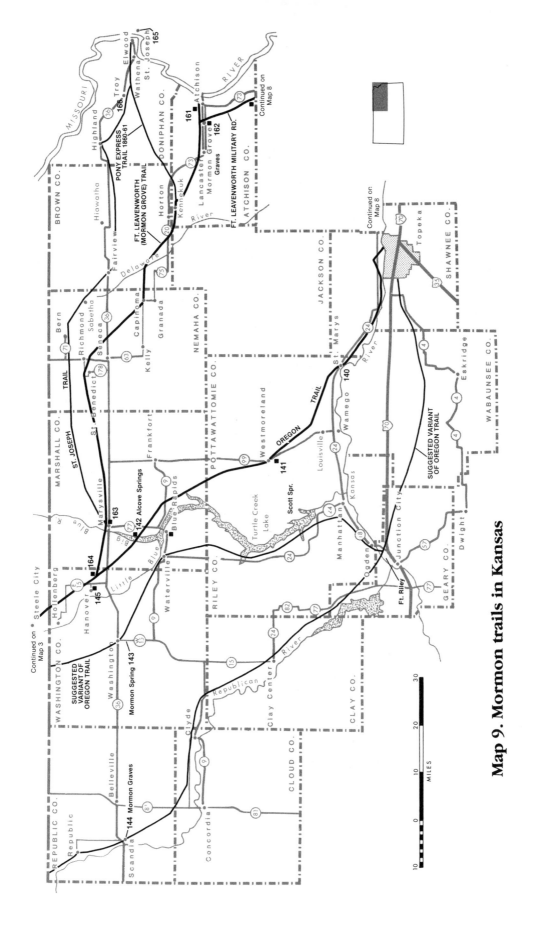

Map 9. Mormon trails in Kansas

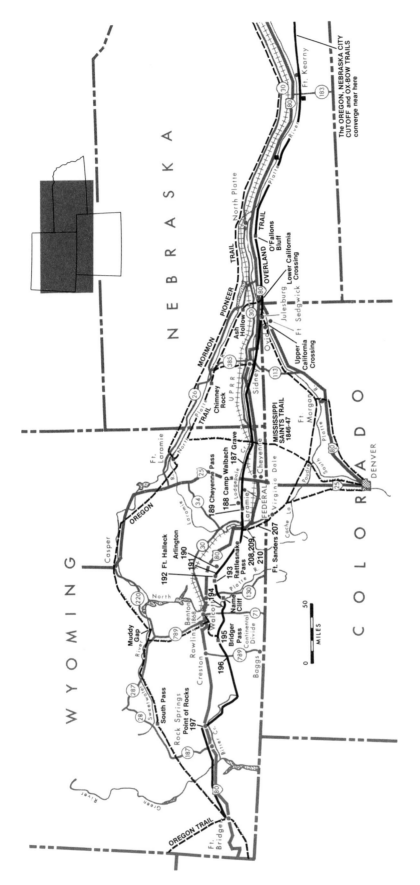

Map 10. The Overland–Bridger Pass Trail and variants in Nebraska, Wyoming, and Colorado

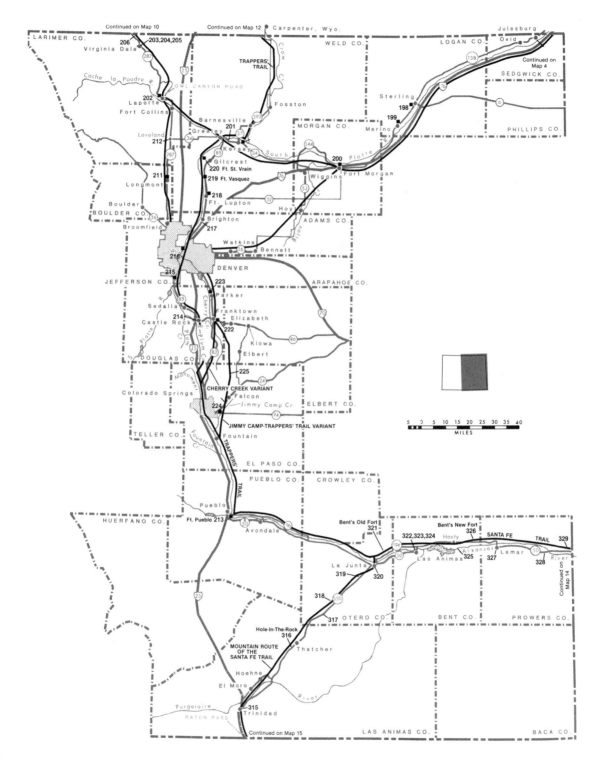

Map 11. Western trails in Colorado

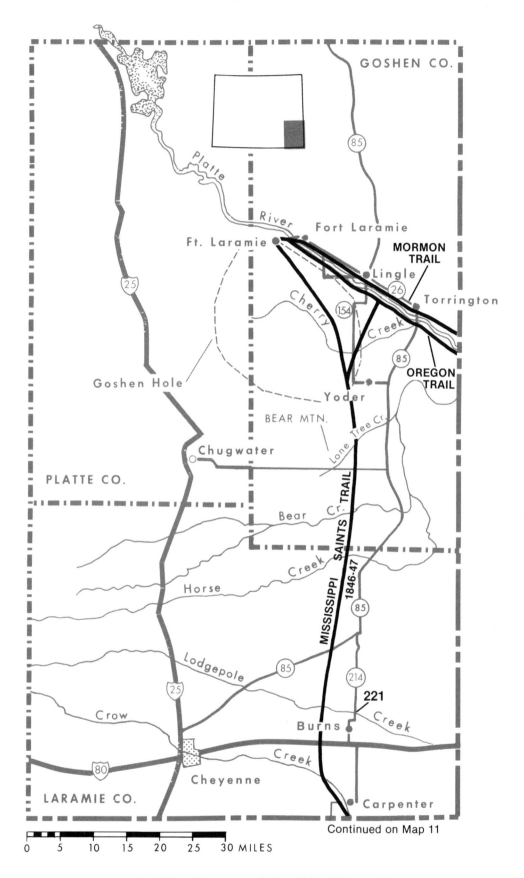

Continued on Map 11

Map 12. The Trappers' Trail in Wyoming

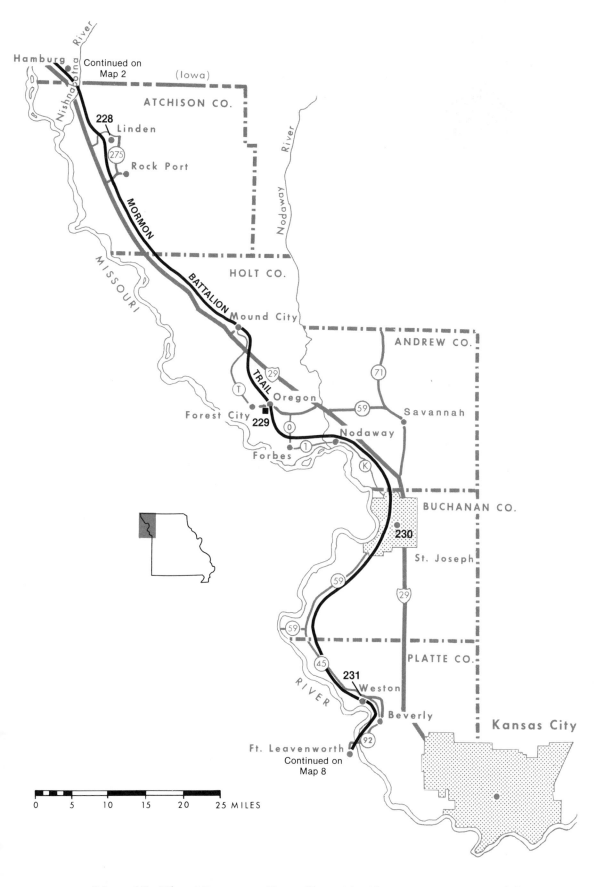

Map 13. The Mormon Battalion Trail in Missouri, 1846

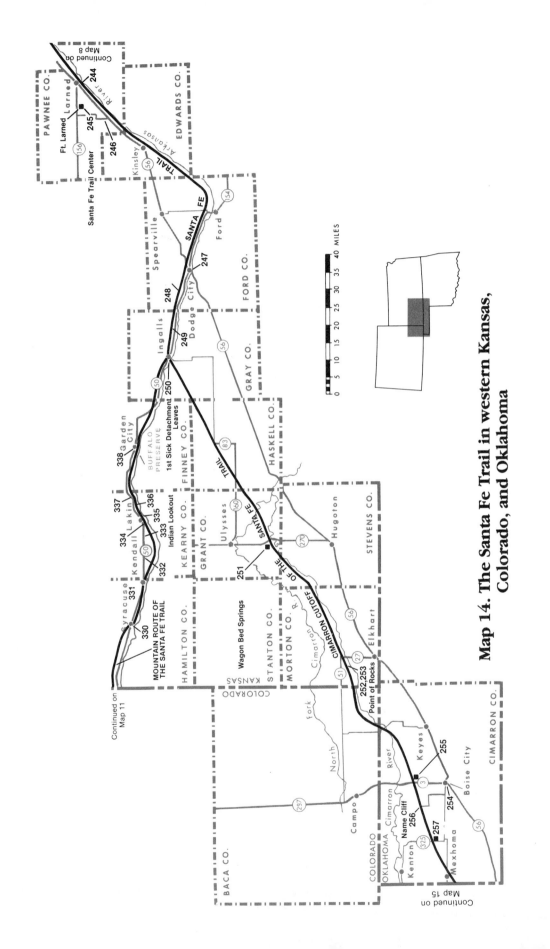

Map 14. The Santa Fe Trail in western Kansas, Colorado, and Oklahoma

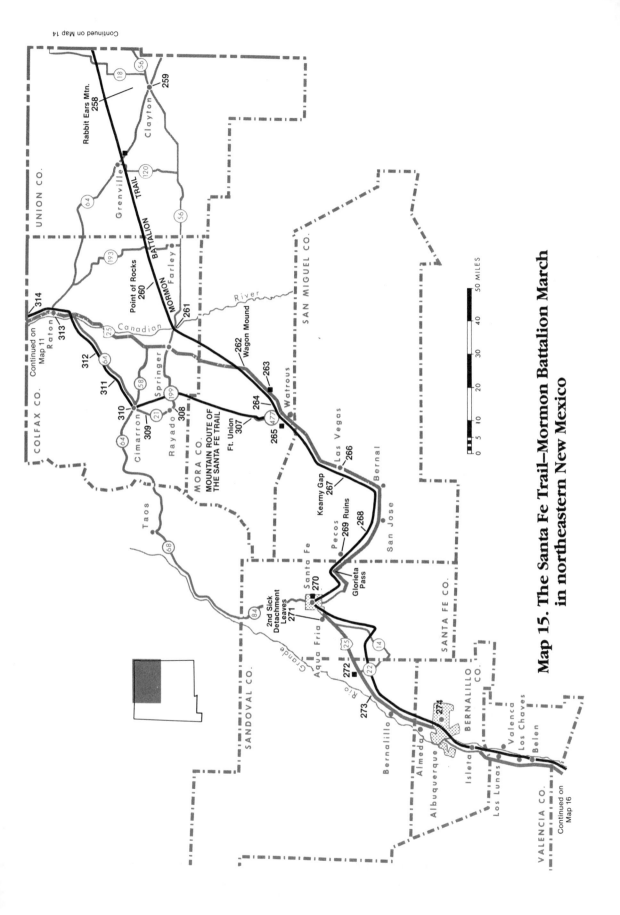

Continued on Map 14

Rabbit Ears Mtn. 258

259

Grenville

UNION CO.

64

120

193

56

Clayton

18

56

MORMON BATTALION TRAIL

Farley

Point of Rocks 260

261

Canadian River

Continued on Map 11

314

313

Raton

312

311

310

309

308

64

25

58

21

199

Springer

Cimarron

Rayado

307 Ft. Union

MOUNTAIN ROUTE OF THE SANTA FE TRAIL

MORA CO.

COLFAX CO.

64

Taos

68

SANDOVAL CO.

262 Wagon Mound

263

264

265

477

Watrous

Las Vegas

266

Bernal

Kearny Gap 267

269 Ruins

Pecos

268

San Jose

San Miguel Co.

SAN MIGUEL CO.

Santa Fe

270

Glorieta Pass

2nd Sick Detachment Leaves 271

84

Agua Fria

Rio Grande

272

22

25

14

273

274

Bernalillo

Almeda

Albuquerque

Isleta

Los Lunas

SANTA FE CO.

BERNALILLO CO.

Valenca

Los Chaves

Belen

VALENCIA CO.

Continued on Map 16

0 5 10 20 30 40 50 MILES

Map 15. The Santa Fe Trail–Mormon Battalion March in northeastern New Mexico

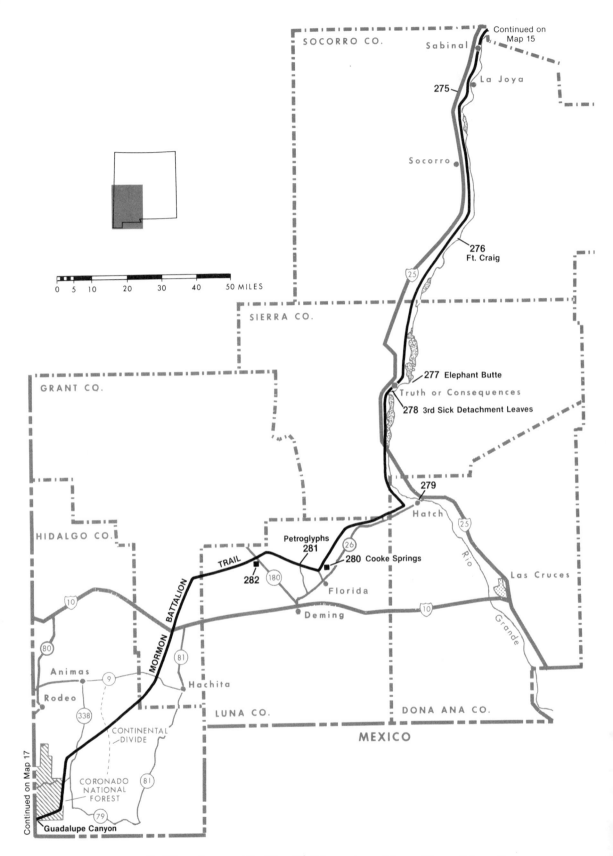

Continued on
Map 15

SOCORRO CO.

Sabinal

La Joya

275

Socorro

276
Ft. Craig

25

SIERRA CO.

GRANT CO.

277 Elephant Butte

Truth or Consequences

278 3rd Sick Detachment Leaves

279

Hatch

25

HIDALGO CO.

Petroglyphs
281

26

280 Cooke Springs

Las Cruces

TRAIL

282

180

Florida

Rio

10

Deming

10

MORMON

BATTALION

80

81

Animas

9

Hachita

Rodeo

338

LUNA CO.

DONA ANA CO.

Grande

CONTINENTAL
DIVIDE

MEXICO

Continued on Map 17

CORONADO
NATIONAL
FOREST

81

79

Guadalupe Canyon

0 5 10   20   30   40   50 MILES

**Map 16. The Santa Fe Trail–Mormon Battalion March
in southwestern New Mexico**

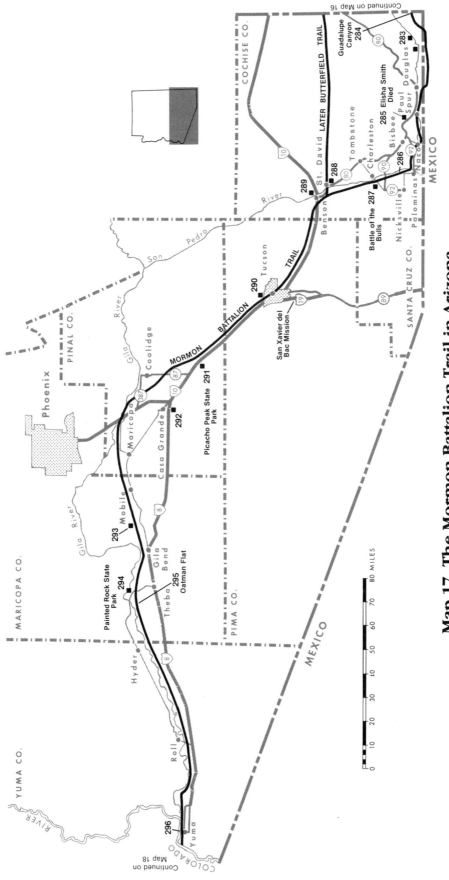

Map 17. The Mormon Battalion Trail in Arizona

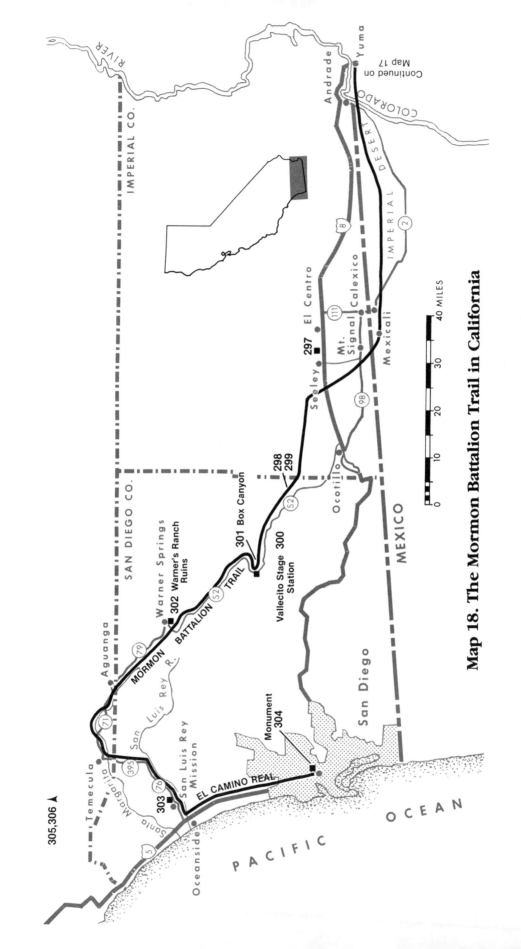

Map 18. The Mormon Battalion Trail in California

I

The Mormon Pioneer Trail of 1846 across Iowa

(see maps 1 and 2)

This is the first of the great Mormon emigrant trails and the beginning of the famous Mormon trek to the west, to their Zion in the Valley of the Great Salt Lake. This trail, orginally following territorial roads and Indian paths, meanders more than three hundred miles from Montrose, Iowa, on the right bank of the Mississippi River to what is now Council Bluffs, Iowa, on the left bank of the Missouri River, thereby crossing what might be called a Mormon Mesopotamia.

Almost all physical remains of the old roads and trails have long since given way to progress, and the gentle, rolling Iowa terrain provides few of the dramatic landmarks seen on other western trails. There are, however, over one hundred road signs marking the pioneer route across Iowa and many other historic sites and markers for the modern traveler to locate and enjoy.

Exodus to Greatness Historic Site / Marker   1

Parley Street, Nauvoo, Hancock County, Illinois

The logical, if not the geographical, beginning of the Mormon Trail of 1846 across Iowa is Nauvoo, Illinois, specifically at the Exodus to Greatness marker by the Mississippi River at the foot of Parley Street. It is a large metal plaque set in an upright concrete slab located at the approximate site where the Mormons crossed the river in their flight from anti-Mormon activities. The first crossing was on February 4, 1846, and through the following September thousands more crossed the river at various places. The marker was placed by the Mormon church and was completed on August 19, 1978.

EXODUS TO GREATNESS

Near here, the Mormon exodus to the Rocky Mountains began on February 4, 1846. In seven years, members of the

Church of Jesus Christ of Latter-day Saints, commonly called the Mormons, had built Nauvoo to a size comparable to Chicago, with approximately 11,000 population. Fleeing enemies, these refugees crossed the Mississippi River with their wagons on flatboats, except for a few days when they crossed on ice.

Under Brigham Young, they crossed Iowa to the Missouri River. On its west bank, they endured the winter of 1846–47 at Winter Quarters in tents, dugouts and log huts.

The trek from there began with the departure of Brigham Young's first company on April 7, 1847, reaching Salt Lake Valley on July 24, 1847.

Seeking freedom to worship God as they believed, more than 50,000 Mormon pioneers, mostly with ox-drawn wagons or handcarts, crossed the plains to the Rocky Mountains before the completion of the transcontinental railroad May 10, 1869.

With Salt Lake City as their base, the Latter-day Saints under Brigham Young, who died in 1877, founded more than 350 communities in the Rocky Mountains.

Before following this trail into Iowa, travelers should visit the community of Nauvoo, which has been called the Williamsburg of the Midwest. Start at the visitors' center of Nauvoo Restoration, Inc., on Kimball Street, where free films, guides, and maps are available. One should also visit the visitors' center maintained by the Reorganized Church of Jesus Christ of Latter Day Saints (RLDS) on Water Street. The easy and historic way to pick up the trail at Montrose, Iowa, from Nauvoo is by a sometimes ferry. Otherwise one must drive via Keokuk or Fort Madison, Iowa, a 20- to 25-mile detour via Highways 96 and 61.

2   Old Fort Des Moines Historic Site / Marker

River Front Park, Montrose, Lee County

The Mormon Trail of 1846 in Iowa proper begins on the Mississippi River bank, where the first Fort Des Moines was established in 1834 by several companies of Dragoons, an elite corps of infantry expecially created by the war department to serve on foot or horseback on special assignments.

The site is important in Mormon history because up to forty refugee Mormon families temporarily lived in the fort (which had been abandoned in 1837) between the time they were driven out of Missouri during the winter of 1838–39 and before settling in Nauvoo, Illinois. Among those to reside here were the families of three future presidents of the Mormon church: Brigham Young, John Taylor, and Wilford Woodruff.

The site of the old fort, now River Front Park in Montrose, is located at the river at the eastern end of Main Street. The fort is marked by a bronze plaque set into a boulder at the south end of the little park.

> This barracks well / marks / the First Fort Des Moines / and was used by / a detachment of Dragoons / stationed here Sept. 25–1834 / to June 18–1837 / Montrose Womans Civic Club, 1923.

Mormon Pioneer Trail Road Signs   3

The old trail goes straight west out of Montrose on Main Street. At the western end of the community on the north side of the road is the first of the approximately one hundred blue-and-white metal road signs placed across Iowa in 1972 by the Mormon Pioneer Trail Foundation and the Iowa Department of Highways. They are situated on modern highways that follow the old trail, or where the old trail crosses modern highways, and they approximate the placing of a similar set of wooden road signs erected by the Civilian Conservation Corps (CCC) of the Iowa Conservation Committee between 1933 and 1940. Only two of these wooden signs appear to be left, at Mt. Pisgah and Drakesville (see trails I, 12 and II, 24 below).

> Mormon Pioneer Trail / Original trail / crossed here.

Many of these 1972 road signs have been replaced with brown-and-white National Park Service signs, reading MORMON PIONEER NATIONAL HISTORIC TRAIL. They are placed at least every 10 miles on all-weather roads that either follow or approximate the old trail. These same National Park Service signs also mark the Mormon Trail across Nebraska, Wyoming, and Utah.

4   ## Sugar Creek Historic Site

6 miles west of Montrose, Lee County, on road J-72
in secs. 11 and 14, T66N, R6W

Six miles directly west of downtown Montrose, on road J-72 (the road to Argyle), is the Sugar Creek Camp, a staging ground where the fleeing Mormons organized themselves for their exodus, which commenced here on March 1, 1846. The historic site extended north and south of the modern bridge over Sugar Creek to the east of the creek. There is no marker here.

5   ## Des Moines River Ford Historic Site / Marker

Bonaparte, Van Buren County

The trail continues west via Croton, where there is a marker commemorating the "point farthest north where a Civil War battle was fought, August 5, 1861," along the Des Moines River, and up through Farmington to Bonaparte, where the Mormons forded the river. The old crossing place is near the modern bridge over the river. There is no marker here, but some local people are considering erecting one.

To follow the old route today, travelers should continue west on J-72 for 3.5 miles to Highway 394, turn north 4.5 miles to road J-62, turn west 7 miles to Croton, then north along the Des Moines River to Farmington, where one is advised to ask locally for directions to Bonaparte, 8 miles upriver via road W-46. The easy way from Farmington to Bonaparte is to cross the Des Moines River at Farmington and take a road right along the river upstream.

6   ## The Ely Ford Historic Site / Marker

Lacey-Keosauqua State Park, Van Buren County

About 12 miles west and north of Bonaparte is Iowa's largest park, 2,260 acres, along the Des Moines River near Keosauqua. In this park on the river bank is a marker and a road sign commemorating the Mormon Trail. The Pioneers of 1846 did not use this ford, but later emigrating companies did.

The marker is a metal plaque set in pink sandstone. There is no indication who placed this marker nor the year of its placement.

ELY FORD / Mormon Crossing.

To the left of the road just before reaching this marker, there is a wooden road sign reading MORMON TRAIL. The best way to locate this marker and old ford is to enter the park immediately south of Keosauqua and the Des Moines River off Highway 1, follow a twisting park road past the assistant ranger's and park ranger's buildings, taking the right-hand fork at the wye intersection, then turning to the river on the first road to the right. From the park entrance off Highway 2 take the left-hand fork of the wye intersection, then turn to the river on the first road to the right.

Mormon Graves at Richardson's Point (P) 7

About 6 miles west on road J-40 from the western exit of Lacey-Keosauqua State Park, Van Buren County; in sec. 32, T69N, R11W, north of the Oak Point Cemetery

Ask directions to the crossroads community of Lebanon; the cemetery is exactly 3 miles west of this community, and the larger town of Troy is 3 miles beyond the cemetery. During March 1846 the original group of Pioneers camped at Richardson's Point (today's Oak Point), where at least two Mormons died. In 1985 these graves were located and marked by relatives. The graves are located in the NE 1/4 of sec. 32, but travelers will have to ask directions locally and secure permission to visit them.

James M. Tanner / died: 17 Mar. 1846 / age 15 months / son of / Sidney Tanner.

Edwin S. Little / born 23 Jan. 1816 / died; 18 Mar. 1846 / son of James Little.

Locust Creek Historic Campsite 8

Wayne County, in sec. 4 or 9, T67N, R20W

From Richardson's Point the old trail follows the Fox River, crossing the Chariton River and Shoal Creek, west to Locust Creek, where on April 13, 1846, William Clayton, the camp clerk, wrote the words to the now-famous Mormon hymn "Come, Come Ye Saints."

The most direct way to reach this site from Richardson's Point is to proceed due west on J-40 for 15 miles to Bloomfield, Davis County, then take Highway 2 for 25 miles west to Centerville, Appanoose County, south 9 miles to Cincinnati, then west toward Sewal on J-54 for 14 miles to Locust Creek. A closer following of the old trail requires Van Buren, Davis, Appanoose, and Wayne counties' maps. There is no marker anywhere near Locust Creek and nothing to see. It is hardly worth the effort. Some will wish to skip Locust Creek and remain on Highway 2 all the way to Corydon.

9 The Wayne County Historical Society Museum Exhibit

Corydon, Wayne County

Although there is no marker near Locust Creek, there is the impressive "Come, Come Ye Saints" exhibit in the Wayne County Historical Society Museum at Corydon, on Highway 2 about 15 miles northwest of Locust Creek. For those who visit the Locust Creek campsite, the best way to Corydon is to take any combination of section-line roads going due north some 8 miles to Highway 2, then turn west. Ask locally for directions.

The exhibit, officially titled *The Hymn That Went Around the World*, features photographs, maps, illustrations, and a full-size replica of a family with covered wagon and oxen. This cooperative venture between the Mormon church and the Wayne Country Historic Society opened on July 14, 1973.

10, 11 Garden Grove Historic Site / Markers

Garden Grove Town Park, Decatur County, on Highway 204

Twenty-one miles northwest of Corydon via Highways 2 and 204 is the small community of Garden Grove. The Pioneers, going northwest from Locust Creek via present-day Allerton, reached this site on the East (Weldon) Fork of the Grand River on April 23, 1846, and remained there until May 12. Here they built a permanent camp for the benefit of those who would follow.

The community of today took its name from the old camp. In the small town park, west of town center, is a large boulder with a bronze plaque on it.

Dedicated 1956 / in memory of the Mormons / who founded Garden Grove, Iowa / in 1847 [1847 is wrong, it should
read 1846].

One mile straight west of the first Garden Grove marker on a county
road is a small, three-acre trailside historic park maintained by the
Decatur County Conservation Board (signs give directions). Just to the
north of the A-frame shelter is a fenced plot enclosing a metal marker
on a sandstone slab, apparently placed there by the Mormon church.

THE LATTER-DAY SAINTS AT GARDEN GROVE

Early in 1846 thousands of members of the Church of
Jesus Christ of Latter-day Saints (Mormons) left their homes
in Nauvoo, Illinois bound for the great basin in the Rocky
Mountains.

Moving westward across Iowa, their advance company
made camp here April 25, 1846 calling the site Garden Grove.

Within two weeks, 359 men under the leadership of President Brigham Young cleared 300 acres of land, planted crops,
built log houses, and cut 10,000 surplus rails for fencing and
enough logs to build 40 additional houses.

Garden Grove thus became a stopover for many emigrants
that followed later. Death overtook some, however. They were
buried here. Refreshed by their stop at this place, the Mormon
Pioneers went on to the Rockies where they founded cities
and towns and made desert to "Blossom as the Rose."

Mt. Pisgah Historic Site / Markers   12

Near Thayer, Union County, in sec. 8, T72N, R28W

The old trail continues northwest from Garden Grove via present-day
Van Wert and Murray some 40 miles to a place the Mormons named
Mt. Pisgah, after its biblical counterpart. To reach Mt. Pisgah today take
various roads from Garden Grove north to Highway 34 and turn west to
Thayer, then go 1 mile west of Thayer on U.S. 34, then north 2.2 miles
on U.S. 169 to a Union County road sign that reads "Mt. Pisgah / Morman
[*sic*] Cemetery / Historical Site / 2 miles," proceed west 1.2 miles, and
turn south 0.5 mile (right through what appears to be private property)

to the cemetery west of the gravel road. There is little left of the old campsite, which today is a small, nine-acre park with information signs and historical markers maintained by the Union County Conservation Board.

One of the signs was placed there by the state of Iowa.

MT. PISGAH–MORMON PIONEER WAY STATION

Between 300 and 800 Mormon pioneers perished here from 1846 to 1852. Having been driven from their homes by armed mobs, they stopped here on their westward trek, named it Mt. Pisgah after a Biblical mountain range, and established a way-station. Thousands of acres were cleared, buildings built, and caves dug for shelter until log cabins were constructed, but lack of food and inadequate shelter took their toll. In spite of hardships, Mt. Pisgah became a stopping place for an almost endless train of westward-bound Mormon Pioneers until 1852, when the last of the Latter-day Saints left and the site was bought by Henry Peters and named Petersville.

The original community was located on the slope and flat lands east of this spot. The cemetery extended down the hill to the west, north, and south beyond the railroad tracks. Headstones were long ago removed or destroyed by the elements, but the large monument was erected in 1888.

On the reverse side of this marker is the following:

CHIEF PIED RICHE TELLS THE SPIRIT OF MT. PISGAH

Soon after the Mormons arrived here the renowned Indian chief, Pied Riche, came to bid them welcome and tell them how the Pottawattamie Indians had likewise been driven from their homeland in what is now Michigan. "We must help one another and the Great Spirit will help us both. Because one suffers and does not deserve it is no reason we shall suffer always. We may live to see it right yet. If we do not our children will."

In 1928 the DAR placed a bronze marker set in a native boulder here.

1846 / Mt. Pisgah / Site of the / first white settlement / in Union County / erected by the / Nancy McKay Harsh Chapter / and the Iowa Society D.A.R. / 1928.

About thirty-six years after the Mormons quit Mt. Pisgah, they dedicated a suitable monument to honor their dead who rested here. This monument may have been the first marker to a historic site erected in Iowa.

This monument erected A.D. 1888 in memory of those members of THE CHURCH OF JESUS CHRIST OF LATTER DAY SAINTS who died in 1846, 1847, and 1848, during their exodus to seek a home beyond the Rocky Mountains. Interred here is William Huntington, the first presiding elder to the temporary settlement called Pisgah, Lenora Charlotte Snow, daughter of Elder Lorenzo and Charlotte Squires Snow, [and] Isaac Phineas Richards, son of Elder Franklin D. and Jane Snyder Richards.

The other sides of this monument are lined with some sixty-four names of those who died here. There is also an information kiosk with extensive text regarding the site here, and just north of here on private property (along the same road leading into the cemetery) is one of the two remaining wooden Mormon Trail signs put up by the Iowa CCC in the 1930s (see trail I, 3).

Orient Historic Site / Marker   13

Orient, Adair County, on Highway 25

Leaving Mt. Pisgah on June 1, 1864, the Pioneers passed through present-day Orient, 28 miles northwest of Mt. Pisgah. To reach Orient, return to Thayer, turn west on Highway 34 some 15 miles to Creston, then north 12 miles on Highway 25. Here on the west side of the public school ground on Highway 25 is a bronze plaque set in red sandstone.

THE MORMON TRAIL

Determined and authenticated by the Historical Department of Iowa, 1911.

This monument was erected in 1917 by the Iowa Daughters of the American Revolution in memory of the Pioneers who followed this trail and its tributaries.

. . . .

The western boundary of Iowa would be at this point had the constitution of 1844 been adopted.

14   Mormon Trail Park Sign / Ruts (P)

Near Bridgewater, Adair County, in sec. 3, T74N, R33W
Some 14 miles west of Orient on Highway 92 is Bridgewater, located 1 mile north of the old trail. This fact is commemorated by the 160-acre Mormon Trail Park and Morman [*sic*] Lake maintained by the Adair County Conservation Commission. The park is 2 miles east of Bridge-water.

Mormon Trail Park / Adair County Cons. Comm.

Some of the very few Mormon Trail ruts in Iowa may be seen near this park in sec. 4 of Washington township. Proceed south (from the western end of the park) to the first intersection, turn west on County Road G-53 for about 0.2 mile. The first house north of the road belongs to Mr. Jacob Pote. The deeply eroded ruts, on his private pasture ground, run east and west, about 0.25 mile west of his home, just north of the road. While they can be glimpsed from the road, you must ask for permission to enter the pasture for a good look. There are some ruts in sec. 9 of this township, but they are not worth the effort to find. My study of the original General Land Office survey of Iowa indicates that both sets of ruts are authentic.

15   Reno Cemetery Marker

Cass County, in sec. 16, T74N, R35W
From the ruts take any road south 2 miles to road G-61 (a county road due west from Orient) and turn west 12 miles to a tee intersection. The cemetery is at the northeast corner of this intersection. This, in fact, is all that is left of this post-Mormon community. About 200 feet east of the cemetery gate and along the fence line next to G-61 is a bronze plaque set in sandstone.

1846–1926 / In memory of / the Pioneers who traveled / the Old Mormon Trail / Erected by the Citizens / of Edna Township / Cass County, Iowa.

Cold Spring State Park Marker   16

Cold Spring State Park, Cass County

Seventeen miles west of Reno and 1 mile south of Lewis, Cass County, on a country road is the Cold Spring State Park. To reach this park take the gravel road on the west side of the cemetery for 2.1 miles north to another gravel road, go west for 10 miles (through Lyman), and turn north for 5 miles towards Lewis. Near the parking area in the camping area there was until recently a sawed-off telephone pole marker about four-foot high reading MORMON TRAIL. This pole has been replaced with a National Park Service sign near a set of four swings. About 100 feet west of this swing set is a fence separating the park from some fields. If you look carefully, the very dim traces of the old trail may be seen crossing these fields.

Lewis Markers   17

Lewis Town Park, Cass County

One mile north of the Cold Spring State Park, in the Lewis Town Park is a marker similar to the one in Orient, originally placed 1 mile west of Lewis by the DAR in 1917.

THE MORMON TRAIL

Determined and authenticated by the Historical Department of Iowa, 1911.

This monument was erected in 1917 by the Iowa Daughters of the American Revolution in memory of the Pioneers who followed this trail and its tributaries.

. . . .

At this point was Indian Town and the Junction of the trail from Raccoon Forks.

The Raccoon Forks Trail was an old Dragoon Trail, which the Mormon Handcart companies used across part of Iowa (see trail IV, 33). As is evident from the text, this marker was originally placed at Indian Town (see trail I, 18). I found it rather humorous that there is a Mormon Trail Saloon across from this DAR marker.

18   Indian Town Historic Site

Near Lewis, Cass County, in sec. 9, T75N, R37W

Going west from Lewis on Minnesota Avenue for about 1 mile is the site of old Indian Town, a Pottawattamie settlement on the west bank of the Nishnabotna River. The Mormons noted and visited this settlement. There is no longer any marker here because the marker the DAR originally erected has been removed to the Lewis Town Park (as noted in trail I, 17).

19   Mormon Trail Crossing Historic Site

Old Towne Park, Macedonia, Pottawattamie County

One mile west of today's Macedonia, along the east bank of the West Nishnabotna River, is an eight-acre undeveloped park where Macedonia was first founded in 1848, possibly by Mormons.

The easy way to reach Macedonia from Lewis is to pick up Highway 6, which is 1 mile north of Lewis, and go 16 miles west to Highway 59 and then 9 miles south.

In 1850 the flooding of the river caused some Mormons to settle here for about three months, until the water subsided. Later a wooden bridge was built and became known as the Mormon Trail Crossing.

20   Mosquito Creek Historic Campsite

Pottawattamie County, in sec. 8, T74N, R43W

From Macedonia, the Pioneers followed a Pottawattamie trail (approximated today by road G-66) about 25 miles due west to Highway 275 at a site variously called Millers's Hollow, Kanesville, and eventually Council Bluffs. The first Mormon encampment in the area was northwest of where Highway 275 crosses Mosquito Creek, near the present-day Iowa School of the Deaf. This was also the site from which the famous Mormon Battalion left for San Diego in 1846 (see trail XXIV, 226). There is no marker here, but one is being planned.

The Mormons began their exodus to Salt Lake City in 1846 from Nauvoo, Illinois, seen here in an aerial photograph. Joseph Smith's "Mansion House" is in the center of this picture. *See trail I, 1.*

C. Booth Wallentine, president of the Mormon Pioneer Trail Foundation, installs one of the first Mormon Pioneer Trail road signs across Iowa in 1972 in Wayne County. Also present are officials of the Wayne County Historical Society and the Iowa State Highway Commission. Photo courtesy of C. Booth Wallentine. *See trail I, 3.*

left, Wooden road signs such as this one, which no longer exists but was photographed at Orient, Iowa, in 1970, were placed across Iowa by the Civilian Conservation Corps between 1933 and 1940. The only two left are at Drakesville and Mt. Pisgah. Photo courtesy of the Church of Jesus Christ of Latter-day Saints. *See trail I, 3.* **below,** New signs like this one are being placed along the Mormon Trail between Nauvoo, Illinois, and Salt Lake City, Utah, by the National Park Service. *See trail I, 3.*

Ely Ford of the Des Moines River, near Keosauqua, Iowa, was not used by the Mormon Pioneers in 1846, but later emigrating companies made use of it. *See trail I, 6.*

In April 1846, the Mormon Pioneers established a camp at Garden Grove, Iowa. The date "1847" on this marker is in error. *See trail I, 10.*

There are very few pioneer trail ruts visible in Iowa today. These are located in Adair County on private land, but are visible from county road G-53. *See trail I, 14.*

Some markers along the Mormon Trail are not elaborate, but they serve to mark the westward course of the migration as well as the granite sculptural ones do. *See trail I, 16.*

Council Bluffs Historic Site / Marker 21

Bayliss Park, Council Bluffs, Pottawattamie County

Although there were eventually many campsites and temporary settlements of Mormons in Pottawattamie County, there is at the present time but one official marker commemorating the Mormon presence in the Council Bluffs area. It is a bronze marker in a large, seventeen-ton boulder placed on the north side of Bayliss Park on South Main Street in downtown Council Bluffs.

> This boulder commemorates the early travel upon the Mormon Trail through Kanesville, now Council Bluffs, and is dedicated to the memory of the throngs who crossed Iowa in advance of settlements. Here thousands of pioneers encamped awaiting pasturage on the plains and turns at the ferries to press onward into the beckoning Golden West. . . .

On the opposite side of this boulder is a bronze bas-relief depicting pioneers with covered wagons, the work of Paul Fjelde.

The Mormon Pioneer Memorial Bridge Historic Site 22

On I-680 near Crescent City, Pottawattamie County

The Mormons used two main ferrying places to cross the Missouri River into Nebraska where they finally set up their Winter Quarters for 1846–47. These two places correspond quite closely to where the South Omaha and the Mormon Pioneer Memorial bridges are located today. On the Iowa side, there are no markers at either of these crossings, but the Mormon Pioneer Memorial Bridge, the Iowa end of which is located 10 miles north of Bayliss Park on I-680, may be considered as a memorial. There is a historical marker on this bridge, but it is on the Nebraska side (see trail VI, 42).

Iowa State Historical Society Sign 23

On I-80 in a rest area about 10 miles
northeast of Council Bluffs

This 1976 sign, located near Underwood, Pottawattamie County, off the eastbound lane of I-80, tells the general history of the Council Bluffs area:

The Council Bluffs area was the scene of such important events in Iowa history as the exploration of Lewis and Clark, the Mormon Trail, the Missouri River steamboat traffic, and the railroad industry. Francois Guittau established the first white settlement here at Trader's Point in 1824. When the Mormons arrived in 1846 they called the community Kanesville. By special charter in 1853 the State Legislature changed the name to Council Bluffs. The name derived from a council held by Lewis and Clark with the Indians in 1804 on the west side of the river near here.

The first steamboat landed in the area in 1819. For the next several decades hundreds of steamboats docked at Council Bluffs bringing people and goods for their westward journey on the Oregon and California trails and to the western gold fields.

In 1856, Congress authorized four railroads to traverse Iowa from east to west. Two of these were to terminate in Council Bluffs, the Northwestern from Lyons and the Rock Island from Davenport. This emphasis has not changed, and today Council Bluffs is served by two interstate highways, 80 and 29.

II

The Mormon Pioneer Trail of 1846 across Iowa: Variant A

(see maps 1 and 2)

The segment of the original Pioneer Trail across Iowa in 1846 between Drakesville, Davis County, and Garden Grove via Locust Creek and close to Missouri (even into Missouri, for the state line was 10 miles farther north at that time) may have been used but once or twice. At Drakesville two important, shorter variants originated: one the Mormons took to Garden Grove, the other to Mt. Pisgah. At both places the variants then followed the Pioneer Trail to the Missouri River.

These variants west of Drakesville came into use soon after the Pioneers reached Garden Grove on April 24 and Mt. Pisgah on May 18, 1846. By that time grass was sufficient for later companies to take the shorter, more direct route the Pioneers had originally planned on using, but did not because they felt the need to stay close to Missouri settlements at which they could purchase feed for their teams.

Using variant A emigrants did not cross the Fox River near Drakesville as the Pioneers had done, but continued some 60 miles west following the high ridge road between the Fox River and Soap Creek via present-day Unionville and Moravia on road J-3T in Appanoose County to the Chariton River, which was forded at a place then called Dodge's Point (now inundated by Rathbun Lake) near present-day Iconium, Appanoose County. The trail continues generally west via present-day Confidence, Millerton, and Humeston in Wayne County to Garden Grove. Parts of this variant were used by the Mormons until at least 1853.

Part of this variant in Wayne County, between Confidence and Humeston, was once known as The Mormon Trail, a designation now generally forgotten.

24   Drakesville Trail Marker

Drakesville town park, Davis County

There is only one Mormon Trail marker along this variant. It is one of the Iowa CCC Mormon Trail road signs of the 1930s (see trail I, 3) and is located at the west end of the Drakesville town park on Highway 273.

III

The Mormon Pioneer Trail of 1846 across Iowa: Variant B

(see maps 1 and 2)

This variant of the Mormon Pioneer Trail, from Dodge's Point (near present-day Iconium, Appanoose County) to Mt. Pisgah, came into use at the same time and for the same reasons as variant A did. Instead of crossing the Chariton River, as variant A does, variant B follows the high ground along the Chariton River as far north as possible, to the Chariton Point, near present-day Chariton, Lucas County. Today the Chariton River can be followed only by zigzagging around on various county roads—it is not worth the effort. Travelers are advised to go directly north of Iconium for 8.5 miles to Georgetown on U.S. 34, then west 18 miles to Chariton. There the river turns west, and the Mormons followed high ridges between the Chariton River and White Breast Creek through Lucas and Clarke counties via Smyrna, intersecting the Pioneer route about 6 miles south of Osceola on today's U.S. 69. This variant is commemorated by two markers.

Chariton Point Historic Site / Marker   25

Chariton, Lucas County

This marker is located 1 mile south of the courthouse in Chariton on the west side of Blue Grass Road, also marked as County Road B and H-40. It is a bronze plaque set in a large stone.

> THE MORMON TRAIL
>
> Determined and authenticated by the Historical Department of Iowa, 1911. This monument was erected in 1917 by the Iowa Daughters of the American Revolution in memory of the Pioneers who followed this trail and its tributaries.
>
> ·
>
> [Commemorating] Chariton Point, junction of Eddyville Trail. Here Lucas County was organized in 1848.

The Eddyville Trail referred to in this marker ran from Eddyville, Wapello County, on the Des Moines River to the Chariton Point. It was used by some Mormons (see trail V, 39 and map 1).

26 Chariton Trail Historic Site / Marker

Chariton Courthouse, Chariton, Lucas County

On the southwest corner of the Lucas County courthouse in Chariton is a companion marker to the one at Chariton Point. It is a bronze plaque set in a large granite boulder.

THE MORMON TRAIL

Determined and authenticated by the Historical Department of Iowa, 1911. This monument was erected in 1917 by the Iowa Daughters of the American Revolution in memory of the Pioneers who followed this trail and its tributaries.

. . . .

Here upon the trail September 11, 1849 was located the townsite of Chariton.

27 Mormon Trace / Trail Road

U.S. 34, S-23, and H-50 in Lucas and Clarke counties

In addition to the two trail markers along this variant route, there is other evidence of the Mormon use of this trail in Lucas and Clarke counties. In Lucas County, for example, there is a Mormon Trail School District and a Mormon Trail Basketball Conference. In the 1904 *Atlas of Iowa* there is a reference to a road, marked today as U.S. 34 and County S-23 and H-50, running north of the Chariton River and west from Chariton, called the Mormon Trace Road, another designation now generally forgotten. This same H-50, extending westward into Clarke County via Smryna to U.S. 64, was designated by the same atlas as the Mormon Trail Road. There are no trail markers along these roads today.

Lost Camp Historic Site 28

6 miles south of Osceola, Clarke County,
in sec. 20, T71N, R25W

Also along variant B route is the site of Lost Camp, which was established near the junction of this trail with the Pioneer route of 1846, or approximately where variant B intersects modern U.S. 69, some 7 miles south of Osceola. Little is known of Lost Camp other than that it was a branch of the Mormon church in 1846–47. There is no marker here.

IV

The Mormon Handcart Trail of
1856–57 across Iowa
(see maps 1 and 2)

What has often been called the most remarkable travel experiment in the history of the Old West commenced in Iowa City, Iowa, in 1856. By that year it had become possible to travel by rail from the East Coast to Iowa City, and that railhead became the point of departure for the Rocky Mountains. Brigham Young had also decided to try a supposedly faster, easier, cheaper, and certainly more unusual way to bring thousands of European converts to Salt Lake City—by handcart. The carts could be pushed or pulled by hand and were designed to carry up to five hundred pounds of clothing and supplies.

Coming by rail from the East Coast via Albany, Rochester, Buffalo, Toledo, and Chicago, many Mormon immigrants crossed the Mississippi at Rock Island, Illinois, entering Iowa at Davenport, where they picked up the Davenport and Missouri Railroad for the railhead at Iowa City, about 55 miles west.

The first train crossed the river on the new trestle on April 21, 1856, and almost immediately Mormon emigration agents began shifting westering Mormons from other jumping-off places such as Westport, Missouri, and Atchison, Kansas, to Iowa City. This famous handcart trek was undertaken by 2,962 people in nine companies between 1856 and 1860, but only the first seven companies trod Iowa soil. These seven companies made the 275-mile trip across Iowa from Iowa City to Florence, Nebraska, in from twenty-one to thirty-nine days, averaging twenty-five days at a rate of 11 miles a day. The last two companies were able to ride various railroads from the East Coast all the way to Council Bluffs.

From Florence the handcart companies followed the Mormon Trail of 1847 for 1,100 miles to Salt Lake City. The handcart era ended after 1860, at which time the Mormons switched to large oxteam trains sent out from Salt Lake City to haul emigrants and freight west from the Missouri River and other points.

Davenport Historic Site / Markers   29

*Intersection of Fourth Street and East River Drive,
Davenport, Scott County*

In Davenport, there are two markers related to the Mormon Handcart Trail. They mark the western end of the (now demolished) 1856 trestle connecting Rock Island with Davenport and are located on the East River Drive just east of where Fourth Street intersects East River Drive. The formal address is 706 East River Drive. The first marker was erected in 1958 by the Mississippi River Bridge Centennial Committee. (A similar marker is located on Rock Island, by the river west of the arsenal.)

> This replica of a pier from / first railroad bridge across / Mississippi River is located / near site of original. Dedicated April 21, 1958 / commemorating centennial / of first railroad engine / to cross the span linking / east to west.

The second marker at the same site is very small and reads:

> This boulder marks the / site of the western abutment / of the first bridge across / the Mississippi River / built in 1853– 55.

From Davenport the railroad proceeded to the railhead at Iowa City via Walcot, Moscow, and West Liberty. Today motorists can follow this route quite closely along U.S. 6 between Davenport and Iowa City.

Coralville Historical Markers   30

Coralville, Johnson County

From the depot at Iowa City (which was located three blocks east of the present station), the emigrants walked 3 miles west to the staging area on Clear Creek at a small settlement known as Clark's Mills, later as Coralville. Here there are several markers. The first one is a bronze plaque on a large boulder placed just west of the intersection of Fifth Street and Tenth Avenue by the DAR in 1936.

> "Let them come on foot, with handcarts and wheelbarrows. Let them gird up their loins and walk through, and nothing shall hinder them."

THE MORMON HANDCART BRIGADE CAMP

South of this boulder on the banks of Clear Creek is the site of the "Mormon / Handcart Brigade Camp." In 1856 some thirteen hundred European immigrants, converts to the Mormon faith, detrained at Iowa City, the end of the railroad. Encamped here, they made handcarts and equipment for their journey on foot to Salt Lake City. 1936.

Also in western Iowa City and Coralville is Mormon Trek Boulevard, running north and south, honoring these pioneers, and there are some small road signs marking the Mormon Trek Trail in downtown Coralville.

31   Mormon Handcart Park / Markers

Coralville, Johnson County

In 1976 in connection with the U.S. Bicentennial Celebration a several-acre Mormon Handcart Park was developed in Coralville on ground owned by the University of Iowa through funds provided by the Mormon church. The site is located along Clear Creek and U.S. 6 near the Hawkeye Court housing complex to the west of Mormon Trek Boulevard. At this site three markers with extensive text were placed in 1979 commemorating a pioneer campsite, pioneer burial ground, and the whole site in general. The easiest way to visit this park is to drive to the intersection of Highway 6 and Second Street (known, but not marked here as Mormon Trek Boulevard), travel south (under a trestle), and take the first street to the right and follow the signs.

32   Fort Des Moines Historical Site / Marker

Riverside Drive, Des Moines, Polk County

From Coralville, the handcart companies generally followed modern U.S. 6, one of the oldest and most historic roads in the state, about 112 miles west to Des Moines, via Homestead and South Amana, two German colonies established in 1854, and on to Brooklyn, Newton, and Rising Sun, a suburb of Des Moines on Highway 163. Part of this road is also officially marked as the Hiawatha Pioneer Trail.

In present-day Des Moines, they would have passed old Fort Des

Moines, abandoned since 1846. Marking this site today is a bronze marker in a granite base located near the partially restored old fort on the west bank of the Des Moines River near the intersection of Riverside Drive and Southwest First Street.

> SITE OF OLD FORT DES MOINES / Established 1843 / evacuated in 1846 / Erected by / Abigail Adams chapter of the / Daughters of the American Revolution / assisted by / Park Commissioners / and / Early Settlers of Des Moines / Dedicated June 14, 1908.

Bear Grove Marker and Dalmanutha   33, 34

Guthrie County, in sec. 18, T79N, R32W

West of Des Moines the Mormons proceeded via Adel, Redfield, and the Middle and South Raccoon rivers, to Bear Grove, in Guthrie County. It is only a wide spot in the road today, but then it was an important coach stop and a place where the handcarters obtained needed supplies.

To reach Bear Grove today one needs Dallas and Guthrie counties' maps. Take a county road for 7 miles north from Redfield to Highway 44, go west for 15 miles to Guthrie Center, continue 6 miles farther west to a section-line road, and turn south for 2 miles. The road is not straight and there is one intersection—turn south, not west.

There is a small wooden marker in this deserted community.

> Bear Grove Store & Post Office 1852–1923.

Some handcarters went west from Redfield via Dalmanutha rather than by the way of Bear Grove. Dalmanutha is located is sec. 5, T78N, R32W and consulting a Guthrie County map is advised. To reach Dalmanutha from Guthrie Center, take County Road 25 about 4.2 miles south to a section-line road, turn west 1 mile, go south 0.5 mile, then turn west and follow a twisting county road for about 4 miles to a cemetery near an intersection, bearing west at all intersections. The cemetery is approximately where Dalmanutha used to stand.

From Bear Grove and Dalmanutha, the Mormons traveled the old Dragoon Trail (see trail V) southwest for some 30 miles to Lewis, in Cass County, at which point they intersected the Pioneer Trail of 1846 and followed it to Council Bluffs on the Missouri River. (For information about a marker to this trail and about the Mormon Pioneer Trail in Lewis, see trail I, 17.) Modern travelers should return from Bear Grove or Dalmanutha to U.S. 6 and proceed southwest for 34 miles to Lewis via Adair, Anita, and Atlantic.

V

The Dragoon Trail of
1846–53 in Iowa

(see maps 1 and 2)

The Dragoon Trail has totally disappeared from Mormon memory, and yet it was used extensively throughout the main period of the great migration across Iowa from 1846 through at least 1853. This trail is unusual in that it did not originate from buffalo tracks, Indian paths, or meandering settlers. It was purposely blazed in 1835 by the First U.S. Dragoons under Colonel Stephen W. Kearny, who had been ordered to locate a site for a new fort near the confluence of the Raccoon and Des Moines rivers, on the site of present-day Des Moines. (See trail I, 2 for an account of the first Fort Des Moines.) By 1846 the colonel's trace had become an important road into the trans-Mississippi interior, a fact not unknown to the Mormons.

In general the trail follows the highlands of the Des Moines River valley via Ottumwa, Oskaloosa, and Pella to Des Moines. From Des Moines, Mormon emigrants reached the Missouri River along trails later used by the handcart companies (see trail IV) or by way of Warren, Madison, and Adair county roads.

There are five markers placed by the DAR along this route as well as a sixth marker pertaining to this trail in River Front Park, Montrose (see trail I, 2).

Dragoon Trail Historic Site / Marker No. 1   35

Montrose, Lee County

The first DAR marker is located on the northwest corner of the main intersection in Montrose and is a metal plaque affixed to a metal pole.

> Here began the / Dragoon Trail / Blazed in 1835 by the / First U.S. Dragoons / under Colonel Stephen W. Kearny / Marked by Daughters of the American Revolution / 1938.

36   Dragoon Trail Historic Site / Marker No. 2

Near Stockport, Van Buren County, in sec. 31, T70N, R8W

From Montrose, the Dragoon Trail angles northwest via Charleston, Bonaparte, and Bentonsport. The second marker is located 3 miles south of Stockport at the northeast corner of the intersection of modern roads 269 and 16 at a settlement originally known as Brattain's Grove and later as Utica; there is no community there today. This marker is similar to the one the DAR placed at Orient, Iowa (see trail I, 13).

THE MORMON TRAIL

Determined and authenticated / by the Historical Department / of Iowa, 1911.

This momument erected in 1917 / by the Iowa Daughters / of the / American Revolution in memory of / the Pioneers who followed this / trail and its tributaries.

. . . .

At this place was Brattain's Grove, / junction of the / Dragoon and / Mormon trails.

This unique reference to the "junction of the Dragoon and Mormon trails" commemorates at least one group of Mormons who, perhaps because of high water in the Des Moines River at the regular crossing at Bonaparte, went north along Coates Creek, turning west near this marker. A century ago groves scattered on largely featureless prairies became well-known landmarks.

37   Dragoon Trail Historic Site / Marker No. 3

Libertyville, Jefferson County

The trail proceeds northwest to Libertyville. On the west side of the road in the town center is a trail marker identical to the one in Montrose, only it is set in stone.

Here passed the / Dragoon Trail / Blazed in 1835 by the / First U.S. Dragoons / under Colonel Stephen W. Kearny / Marked by the Daughters of the American Revolution / 1938.

Dragoon Trail Historic Site / Marker No. 4   38

Ottumwa, Wapello County

From Libertyville, the trail goes generally west to present-day Ottumwa. About 4 miles north of downtown Ottumwa on U.S. 63, at the entrance to the municipal golf course, this marker is on the west side of the road. All that remains of this marker is a boulder nearly hidden by trees; the plaque is gone. The inscription was the same as the one in Libertyville. Most likely the old trail passed through Dahlonega, a suburb northeast of Ottumwa, and followed high ground along the Des Moines River valley to present-day Des Moines.

Eddyville Historic Site / Marker   39

Eddyville, Wapello County

About 18 miles northwest of Ottumwa on the Des Moines River is Eddyville, at one time an important fording place on that river, founded in 1840. Some Mormons crossed here and followed what was known as the Eddyville Trail for 50 miles west to Chariton Point (see trail III, 25). There is a marker here that refers to an Indian settlement.

> Indian Village Centenary / of / Chief Hard Fish / Dedicated 1937.

Dragoon Trail Historic Site / Marker No. 5   40

Mahaska County, in sec. 32, T76N, R16W

The last of the Dragoon Trail markers is on the west side of Highway 163 5 miles northwest of Oskaloosa, across the road from a water tower.

> Here passed the / Dragoon Trail / Blazed in 1835 by the / First U.S. Dragoons / under Colonel Stephen W. Kearny / Marked by the Daughters of the American Revolution / in 1938.

From Mahaska County the trail proceeds ever northwest, via Pella and Monroe on Highway 163, to the site of the second Fort Des Moines, at the confluence of the Raccoon and Des Moines rivers (see trail IV, 32). Pella was founded in 1847 by some Hollanders seeking religious freedom. The restored part of the community should be visited.

From here the trail turns southwest across Warner, Madison, and Adair counties to Lewis, in Cass County, where it intersects the Pioneer route of 1846 (see trail I, 17). I have discovered no markers or historic sites connected with this trail between Des Moines and Lewis.

41   Keokuk Historic Marker

Rand Park, Keokuk, Lee County

There is one other marker in Iowa that might logically be connected with the Pioneer trails of 1846. It is a monument at the northern end of Rand Park, erected in 1913 by the DAR in honor of Chief Keokuk of the Sauk and Fox Indians. During 1853, when the town of Keokuk was, for one year, the jumping-off place for Mormon emigrants, there was a Mormon camp just east of Rand Park, on the bluffs overlooking the river near the intersection of Morgan and Second streets. On one side of the Keokuk monument is a bronze plaque also placed by the DAR.

> To the memory of the pioneers who entered Iowa by Keokuk, the Gate City and either settling in our state or passing farther west traveled over the well known road known as the Mormon Trail. With this tablet the Daughters of the American Revolution of Iowa officially open the marking of that early and important highway.

The first part of the famous Mormon Battalion Trail also passed through Iowa, but it is more appropriate to describe this Mormon trail in Iowa when the whole Mormon Battalion Trail is presented (see trail XXIV).

This statue by Torlief S. Knaphus, on Temple Square in Salt Lake City, commemorates the use of handcarts by Mormon Pioneers between 1856 and 1860; approximately three thousand Mormons traveled west this way. Photo courtesy of the Church of Jesus Christ of Latter-day Saints. *See trail IV*.

Some Mormons following the Dragoon Trail crossed the Des Moines River at Eddyville, Iowa, the site of this marker commemorating an Indian village. *See trail V, 39*.

Mormon oxcarts in Omaha, as they appeared in an 1860 photograph. Photo courtesy of the Union Pacific Railroad. See trail VI.

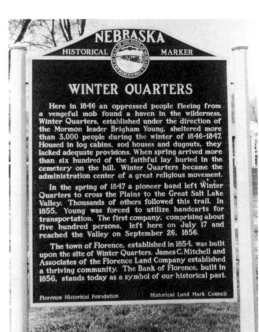

NEBRASKA
HISTORICAL   MARKER

WINTER QUARTERS

Here in 1846 an oppressed people fleeing from a vengeful mob found a haven in the wilderness. Winter Quarters, established under the direction of the Mormon leader Brigham Young, sheltered more than 3,000 people during the winter of 1846-1847. Housed in log cabins, sod houses and dugouts, they lacked adequate provisions. When spring arrived more than six hundred of the faithful lay buried in the cemetery on the hill. Winter Quarters became the administration center of a great religious movement.

In the spring of 1847 a pioneer band left Winter Quarters to cross the Plains to the Great Salt Lake Valley. Thousands of others followed this trail. In 1855, Young was forced to utilize handcarts for transportation. The first company, comprising about five hundred persons, left here on July 17 and reached the Valley on September 26, 1856.

The town of Florence, established in 1854, was built upon the site of Winter Quarters. James C. Mitchell and Associates of the Florence Land Company established a thriving community. The Bank of Florence, built in 1856, stands today as a symbol of our historical past.

Florence Historical Foundation   Historical Land Mark Council

left, Nebraska historical markers such as this one at Winter Quarters have been erected throughout the state at important spots along the old trails. Winter Quarters was established by Brigham Young following the Mormon exodus from Nauvoo in 1846. *See trail VI, 43.* **below,** This marker, with artwork by Avard Fairbanks, commemorates Mormon Winter Quarters and the cemetery nearby where more than six hundred Mormons tragically ended their trek west during their first winter here. *See trail VI, 43.*

The Platte River is a flat, shallow, braided stream that was an important source of water for westering Americans on the Mormon and Oregon-California trails. *See trail VI, 51.*

left, Many trails used overlapping routes, as commemorated by this marker located one-half mile east of Ames, Dodge County, Nebraska. *See trail VI, 52.* **below,** Some trail markers are hard to find because they are hidden behind overgrown trees, as is this marker near Lexington, Nebraska. *See trail VI, 60.*

Ancient Bluff Ruins, looking southwest, are much as they looked to Brigham Young and other Mormon Apostles who climbed them in 1847. *See trail VI, 67.*

Heber J. Grant, then president of the Mormon church, visited the grave of Rebecca Winters with some of her descendants about 1926. Photo by Paul Henderson. *See trail VI, 71.*

VI

The Mormon Pioneer Trail of 1847
across Nebraska
(see maps 3 and 4)

The most famous of all Mormon treks began on April 5, 1847, when my great-great-grandfather, Heber C. Kimball, one of the Mormon apostles, moved a few wagons about 3 miles west of Winter Quarters. It was not until April 19, however, that the whole group of Pioneers—143 men, 3 women, and 2 children—were sufficiently well organized at their appointed staging ground on the Platte River near present-day Fremont, Nebraska, to commence in earnest their 1,100 mile exodus. Mormon Pioneer National Historic Trail road signs are located every 10 miles along all-weather roads that either follow or approximate the old trail across Nebraska (see trail I, 3).

In general the trail follows the gentle, broad Platte River valley for some 475 miles to Fort Laramie, where the Pioneers crossed the Platte and intersected the Oregon Trail. They followed the Oregon Trail for 397 miles to Fort Bridger and then picked up the faint trace of the Reed-Donner party, taking it as far as the Valley of the Great Salt Lake, arriving there on July 24.

Before the Mormons could start for the Far West, however, they had to prepare for the winter of 1846–47. During that summer of 1846, the Mormons crossed the Missouri River at several places into what is now Nebraska and established two temporary camps before settling at their Winter Quarters. One was the Cold Spring Camp 4 miles west of the river in present-day South Omaha, near Ralson, at the confluence of Big and Little Papillion creeks northwest of the intersection of U.S. 275 and Sixtieth Street. Another was called Cutler's Park, which was 8 miles to the north, to the east of Mormon Bridge Road, in and near what is now Forest Lawn Cemetery. A marker is planned for this site.

Finally in September, Young made the final decision for the location of Winter Quarters, which was on the high ground of the Missouri River, where Florence, Nebraska, is today. (Technically there is no longer a

Florence; in 1916 it was absorbed by Omaha and is sometimes called North Omaha. The name, however, is historically convenient, and I use it in this book.)

42   Mormon Pioneer Memorial Bridge
Historic Site / Marker

On I-680 in Florence, Douglas County

Only one of the several Mormon crossing places of the Missouri River has been designated by an offical marker. This was done June 1, 1953, by the Utah Pioneer Trails and Landmarks Association at the time of the dedication of the Mormon Pioneer Memorial Bridge across the Missouri at Florence, which is now part of I-680. The marker may be found on the Nebraska side, just to the south of the entrance to the eastbound lane. Because of heavy traffic, it is best to park and walk to this marker.

MORMON PIONEER MEMORIAL BRIDGE

This bridge is on the Mormon Pioneer Trail from Nauvoo, Illinois, to the Rocky Mountains. Driven from their homes by mobs, many of the dispossessed Mormon people crossed the Mississippi River on the ice in February 1846. From these refugees five hundred volunteers for the Mexican War left here on the longest infantry march in recorded history. Winter Quarters were established on the west bank of the Missouri River, and a ferry was operated at this site. Six hundred of these people—Nebraska's first white settlers—died here that winter.

April 5, 1847, Brigham Young and one hundred and forty-seven others resumed the journey to select the trail and locate the place where the Mormon people could worship God in accordance with their religious belief. They reached the Valley of the Great Salt Lake July 24 and founded Salt Lake City "in the tops of the mountains." Thousands followed. They instituted modern irrigation and built an empire in the West.

Winter Quarters Historic Site / Markers   43, 44

Florence City Park, Florence, Douglas County

In the area of old Winter Quarters there are several markers, a cemetery, and a visitors' center. One, a Nebraska historical marker, is located at the southern end of the Florence park at Thirtieth and State streets.

WINTER QUARTERS

Here in 1846 an oppressed people fleeing from a vengeful mob found a haven in the wilderness. Winter Quarters, established under the direction of the Mormon leader Brigham Young, sheltered more than 3,000 people during the winter of 1846–1847. Housed in log cabins, sod houses and dugouts, they lacked adequate provisions. When spring arrived more than six hundred of the faithful lay buried in the cemetery on the hill. Winter Quarters became the administration center of a great religious movement.

In the spring of 1847 a pioneer band left Winter Quarters to cross the Plains to the Great Salt Lake Valley. Thousands of others followed this trail. In 1855, Young was forced to utilize handcarts for transportation. The first company, comprising about five hundred persons, left here on July 17 and reached the Valley on September 26, 1856.

The town of Florence, established in 1854, was built upon the site of Winter Quarters. James C. Mitchell and Associates of the Florence Land Company established a thriving community. The Bank of Florence, built in 1856, stands today as a symbol of our historical past.

At the northern end of this park there is another marker consisting of the bronze figure of an angel with two plaques set in a masonry monument. The artwork is that of Avard Fairbanks and it was erected by the Mormon church.

Winter Quarters Location of the Camps of Israel / Pioneer Mormon Cemetery ⅓ of a mile west.

Before visiting this cemetery note that along State Street in Florence are two side streets named Young Street and Mormon Street. And west of Florence, Fifty-sixth Street becomes the Mormon Bridge Road to its intersection with U.S. 36.

There are also two markers across the street from the Florence park, at 9124 North Thirtieth Street, commemorating an old Mormon mill on Mill Creek. One is an official Nebraska historical marker. The present mill at this site is, of course, post-Mormon, but the area was the center of old Winters Quarters. The house of Brigham Young was just east of the mill, which originally stood 200 feet southwest.

THE FLORENCE MILL

The Florence Mill, one of the earliest in Nebraska, was constructed by the Mormons at Winter Quarters during the winter of 1846–47. Supplying both flour and lumber, the water-powered mill enabled the Mormons to cope more readily with the adverse conditions encountered during their stay in Nebraska. In 1847–48 groups of Mormons began to leave this area for the Salt Lake Valley. As a result Winter Quarters and the mill were abandoned.

In 1856, Alexander Hunter began to operate the mill. Its products helped fill the demands created by the growing town of Florence, established in 1854 on the old site of Winter Quarters.

The second marker at this old mill site was placed in 1931 by the DAR.

1846 / On this lot stands / the old mill / built during the westward / migration of the Mormons / Purchased by / Jacob Webber in 1860 / Now owned and operated / by his descendants / 1931.

Travelers driving west on State Street one-third of a mile will come to the famous Mormon Pioneer cemetery in which are buried an estimated 600 emigrants who died in the area between 1846 and 1853. The property is owned and maintained by the Mormon church and is open to visitors.

45 Winter Quarters Cemetery Historical Site / Markers

Intersection of State and Thirty-third streets, Florence
At the east entrance to the Mormon Pioneer cemetery is a marker placed by the DAR in 1931.

PIONEER / MORMON CEMETERY / 1846–1863 [should be 1853]
/ It is estimated that 600 / emigrants were buried here / Isaac
Salder Chapter / Daughters of the American Revolution.

The bronze memorial gates to the front and rear of this cemetery
were done by Avard Fairbanks and each bears the same inscription:

I AM THE RESURRECTION AND THE LIFE

THIS MORTAL BODY IS RAISED TO AN ETERNAL BODY

In loving memory of six thousand Pioneers who died on
the plains between 1846–1869. The bodies of nearly six hundred of these brave souls were buried within this sacred en-
closure. 1936.

The dead shall hear the Son of God and they that hear shall
live. John V:25.

For they shall rest from their labors here and shall continue
their work. Doctrine and Covenants. 124:86. 1936.

Just inside and to the right of the main entrance are five bronze
plaques with extensive text regarding the Winter Quarters experiences.
The title of five are: Mormons Arrive in Winter Quarters, Preparations
for the Winter Begins, Winter Quarters on the Banks of the Missouri
River, Sickness Rages Through the Camp, and Winter Quarters Abandoned.

In the center of the north end of the cemetery is one of the finest
works of sculpture produced by the Mormon church. It is a nine-foot
tall bronze statue of two figures on a three-foot high granite base. It
was unveiled on September 20, 1930. A father and mother are standing
beside the shallow open grave of their child. The statue is encircled by
a paved area of tiles and bronze tablets bearing biblical verses. In front
of the statue is the figure of an angel beneath which is written " 'Jesus
knowing that the Father had given all things unto His hands, and that
He was from God, and went to God.' John XII:3." The lower part of this
tablet is filled with columns of names of the dead buried there. Two
columns are blank, "For the unrecorded dead." This work is by Avard
Fairbanks.

Across the street to the east of the cemetery is the Cemetery Information Center maintained by the Mormon church. Here may be seen a
film, signs, maps, and illustrations pertaining to the Mormon history of

the whole area, especially to the westward trek. There is also a picnic area, an old wagon, a handcart, and a log cabin to be seen.

There are four other historic sites and two information signs in the Winter Quarters area that should be visited (see trail VII, 73–76).

46   Mormon Pioneer Campsite / Marker

Douglas County, west of Florence

About 4 miles west of the Mormon Pioneer Memorial Bridge on Highway 36 is the first monument to the exodus across Nebraska. It is located at the intersection of Old 36 and Seventy-second Street, at the southern boundary of the North Omaha Airport. The marker was placed by the Daughters of Utah Pioneers during April 1947. Of the scores of markers erected by this society, this one is number 95.

> On April 15, 1847, in this vicinity the Mormon Pioneers en route from Nauvoo, Illinois to the Rocky Mountains made their first camp after leaving Winter Quarters on the west bank of the Missouri River 5 miles north of Omaha, Nebraska, where they spent the winter of 1846–47. Heber C. Kimball, a twelve apostle [a member of the Twelve Apostles] of the Church of Jesus Christ of the Latter-day Saints and close friend of President Brigham Young, led the first company, thus forming the nucleus for the gathering of the groups that followed. The Pioneers reached Salt Lake Valley July 24, 1847, established Salt Lake City, from which place Mormon colonization extended to all the intermountain area and the Pacific Coast.

47   The Elkhorn River Crossing Historic Site, 1847

U.S. 6, Douglas County, west of Omaha

The first major natural obstacle across Nebraska was the crossing of the Elkhorn River, which over the years the Mormons crossed at various places (see trail VII, 73). The original crossing of 1847 was just north of where a bridge on U.S. 6 crosses it today, directly west of Omaha, 10 miles west of I-680, near Waterloo. There is no marker here.

Liberty Pole Camp Historic Staging Ground Site   48

Near Fremont, Dodge County, in sec. 21, T17N, R8E

Once across the Elkhorn, the Pioneers headed for the broad and gentle valley or floodplain of the Platte River. Shortly after the various groups making up the Pioneer band successfully negotiated the Elkhorn, Young brought them together at a staging ground near present-day Fremont to organize them better for the journey. This staging ground, later named the Liberty Pole Camp (from a large cottonwood pole erected there on July 4 by the Second Company of Pioneers), it was located approximately one-quarter of a mile from the Platte River, southwest of Fremont and west of U.S. 77. The pole remained until at least 1857. There is no marker here. There are, however, three markers commemorating the Mormons passing through or near Fremont.

Mormon Pioneer Trail Markers   49

Barnard Park, Fremont, Dodge County

One marker is on the north edge of Barnard Park, on the south side of Military Avenue, between Irving and Clarkson streets. It was placed there on May 22, 1950, by the Utah Pioneer Trails and Landmarks Association, the 117th such marker put up by this group, which has since disbanded.

MORMON PIONEER TRAIL

The Mormon Pioneer Trail from Nauvoo, Illinois to the Rocky Mountains passed here April 17, 1847. In this vicinity a military-type organization was formed with Brigham Young, lieutenant general; Stephen Markham, colonel; John Pack and Shadrack Roundy, majors; and captains of hundreds, fifties and tens. In the company were 143 men, 3 women, and 2 boys.

The Pioneers reached the Valley of the Great Salt Lake July 24, 1847. Between that date and 1869, when the railroad reached Utah, approximately 80,000 [actually, more than 50,000] persons followed the old trail to the mountains. Nearly 6,000 died and were buried along the way. . . .

A second marker, put up by the DAR in 1912, is at the intersection of Military and D streets:

The Overland emigrant trails through Fremont to Oregon, California, Utah, and Colorado.

50   Mormon Migration Marker

3.2 miles north of Fremont, Dodge County
Just north of Fremont, 3.2 miles north of Highway 30, on the east side of U.S. 77 is the third marker commemorating historic trails, including a wet weather variant that passed through Fremont (see trail VII, 74).

This monument/ marks/ an old Indian Trail East to West/ Route of Major S. H. Long/ June 7, 1820/ A part of Mormon/ Migration/ 1847 to 1864/ and California Gold Rush 1849/ Erected by/ Dodge County/ June 7, 1926.

51   Great Platte River Route Historical Marker

Fremont State Recreation Area,
near Fremont, Dodge County
Four miles west of Barnard Park, on the south side of U.S. 30, is the Fremont State Recreation Area, where there is a Nebraska historical marker commemorating the Great Platte River route.

THE GREAT PLATTE RIVER ROUTE WEST

The north bank of the Platte River, from the 1830's through the 1860's, served as a major overland route to the West. It was used by fur traders, soldiers, gold seekers and other emigrants. The expedition of Major Stephen H. Long passed through this area in June 1820. Just south of the river were the last villages of the Pawnee Nation, prior to their being placed on a reservation. Fremont was named in honor of General John C. Fremont, when settled in 1856. This trail is usually referred to as the Mormon Trail, as they were the first to use it in great numbers.

The route was also known as the Omaha–Fort Kearny Military Road, and the stage line between Omaha and Salt Lake City also ran here. It became the line of the first transcontinental telegraph in 1861, and a few years later it became the route of the Union Pacific Railroad, the first transcontinental route. The railroad reached Fremont in 1866, and, in a few years, the Platte Valley of Nebraska ceased to be a frontier, becoming a prosperous farming region.

With the development of the automobile, this route became U.S. Highway 30 or the Lincoln Highway, the first transcontinental road. It was completed to San Francisco in 1913, though the portion of the road west of Fremont was not paved until 1920. Begun as a major road to the West, it was developed into and remains an important route to the East as well.

It is an almost universal misconception that the Mormons blazed the Mormon Trail on the north side of the Platte River. The original Oregon Trail from 1812 was north of the Platte to begin with and later, about 1827, after Independence, Missouri, became the eastern terminus, shifted to the south side. The Mormons of 1847 simply followed the older Oregon Trail to Fort Laramie, where they crossed the North Platte River and picked up the main route of the Oregon Trail. Among those who preceded the Mormons west along the north bank of the Platte were Robert Stuart, James Clyman, Major Stephen H. Long, Samuel Parker, and Narcissa Whitman. The Mormons found only a trail, which they made into a road and thereby earned the right to have that route bear their name.

Dodge County Historic Markers   52

One-half mile east of Ames, Dodge County

About 2 miles beyond the Fremont State Recreation Area to the north of U.S. 30 and one-half mile east of Ames is a small granite marker to some historic trails.

> Overland Trail/ 1813 to 1867/ Mormon Trail/ 1847 to 1864/ Military Road to/ New Fort Kearny/ 1856/ Site of Albion/ Lincoln P.O. and/ Timberville P.O./ From 1856 to 1868/ Erected by/ Dodge County/ May 30, 1928.

Eight miles west of Ames is North Bend, and 1 mile west of this community, to the north of U.S. 30, is a "MORMON TRAIL 1847" granite marker.

West from the Fremont area the old trail can be followed rather closely along U.S. 30 to Columbus and along Highway 22 to Fullerton. Columbus is about 40 miles west of Ames near the junction of the Loup and Platte rivers, where in 1859 a ferry was established that was used by many Mormons (see trail VII, 78). In Columbus near the entrance to Pawnee Park is a 1927 DAR marker commemorating the "North Branch / Oregon Trail."

53   Genoa Historic Site / Marker

Genoa city park, Genoa, Nance County

About 20 miles west of Columbus on Highway 22 is Genoa, which was established as a way station by the Mormons in 1857. In the small town park at the west end of the community is a Nebraska historical marker.

GENOA: 1857–1859

Genoa, named by the Mormon Pioneers, was among several temporary settlements established by the Church of the Latter Day Saints in 1857, along the 1000-mile trail from Florence, Nebraska to Salt Lake City. These settlements were to serve as way-stations for the Brigham Young Express and Carrying Company, which had the government mail contract to Salt Lake City, and as rest and supply stops for Saints traveling across the plains.

Mormons from St. Louis, Florence, and Alton, Illinois were called to establish the Genoa settlement in the spring of 1857, and the Colony arrived here on May 16. During the first year, 100 families settled at Genoa and began to fence the land and plant crops under the direction of Brother Allen, Mission president. A steam powered mill was constructed and log, frame, and sod structures were erected to house the settlers and their livestock.

In the fall of 1859, the Mormon Colony was forced to abandon Genoa when the settlement became part of the newly created Pawnee Indian Reservation. Genoa served as the Pawnee Indian Agency until 1876, when the Pawnee were removed to the Indian Territory and the reservation lands offered for sale.

Next to the Genoa marker is one regarding the Pawnee that should also be noted.

Loup Ford of 1847 Historic Site   54

Near Fullerton, Nance County, in sec. 4, T16N, R5W
The pioneer ford across the Loup River is roughly 9 miles west of Genoa. Over the years the Mormons used many fording sites above and below this original crossing. There is no marker here.

Mormon Pioneer Historic Campsite / Marker   55

Near Fullerton, Nance County
Two and one-half miles south of the center of Fullerton, across the Platte River and to the west of Highway 14 in a roadside parking area, is a Nebraska historical marker commemorating a Mormon Pioneer campsite.

MORMON PIONEER CAMPSITE
In the early spring of 1847, several hundred pioneers of the Church of Jesus Christ of Latter-day Saints (Mormon) camped near here on their historic trek to the valley of the Great Salt Lake. Driven from their homes in Illinois and Missouri, more than 3,000 of the oppressed people had wintered near the present site of Omaha, housed in log cabins, sod houses and dugouts, preparing for the journey to their new Zion in the Rocky Mountains.

The first company of pioneers, led by Brigham Young, left Winter Quarters on April 14 with 143 men, three women and two children traveling in 73 wagons. They arrived in what is now Salt Lake City on July 24, 1847. Several other companies took the trail in the months and years that followed. traveling the same route, and many of them camping at or near this spot.

Between 1855 and 1860 several thousands made the 1300-mile journey on foot, pulling their wordly possessions in handmade two-wheeled carts. The dramatic and ofttimes tragic story of these Handcart Pioneers is one of the epics of

American History. Overpowered by summer heat or caught in the cold of prairie blizzards, hundred of them lie buried in unmarked graves along the trail.

From this campsite the old trail continues generally south (modern travelers should take Highway 14 for 18 miles south to U.S. 30), again reaching the Platte a few miles east of the present community of Grand Island. From here Highways U.S. 30 and I-80 follow the old trail closely for 146 miles west to North Platte. The original Grand Island was a shifting bar in the Platte River continually redefined by the current. Westering Americans estimated its length at from forty to sixty miles in length.

56   Mormon Island State Wayside Area

Grand Island exit off I-80

A reminder of the Mormon trek through here is the Mormon Island State Wayside Area off the westbound lane of I-80, 6 miles directly south of the community of Grand Island. At one time there was an information sign in the wayside area, but it is no longer there. The name of the area commemorates the fact that some Mormons wintered on an island near here in the 1850s. At the entrance to the wayside area is a wooden sign reading MORMON ISLAND STATE WAYSIDE AREA.

57   The Mormon Trail Marker

At the Stuhr Museum, Grand Island, Hall County

On the grounds of the Stuhr Museum of early Nebraska history is a Nebraska historical marker commemorating the Mormon Trail. This important museum is south of Grand Island, east of Highway 34. (There is a five-dollar admission fee.)

THE MORMON TRAIL

Religious freedom, an American ideal, has on occasion been denied certain sects because of prejudice. Mormons were once persecuted and forced from their homes. The north bank of the Platte River served as the exodus route for thousands of members of the Church of Jesus Christ of Latter-day Saints (Mormons). Driven from Nauvoo, Illinois, Mormon leader Brigham Young led the first migration up this valley in 1847 to found the proposed state of Deseret, now Utah.

During the following two decades, thousands more gathered at Winter Quarters on the west bank of the Missouri River near present Florence, Nebraska, before beginning the trek across the plains and mountains to their land of Milk and Honey. The journey called for strength and courage, as well as faith, for tragedy often stalked their wagons and handcarts, turning this valley into a Mormon "trail of tears." Hundreds of pioneers lie buried along this trail, most in unmarked graves.

After 1860 the overland trail along the south bank of the river was lined with road ranches and stage stations, but the Mormon Trail had few such conveniences, and the pioneer settlements here in Hall County were almost the last vestiges of civilization until the travelers reached Utah.

There are five other trail markers in Hall County, erected by the Hall County Historical Society in 1923, all reading: "Old California Overland Trail extensively traveled during the Gold Rush to California in 1849 and by the Pioneers of this location in 1857." They are placed close to the Wood River and are often nearly covered by grass. The easiest one to locate is at the north end of the town of Wood River, west of Highway 11.

Gibbon Rest Area Marker   58

*Windmill Wayside Park Area off eastbound lane
of I-80 at Gibbon, Buffalo County*
In this rest area off I-80 is a Nebraska historical marker commemorating the founding of Gibbon in 1871, which refers to the fact that "Gibbon [is] on the old Mormon Trail. . . ."

Kearney Area Historic Site / Marker   59

Centennial Park, Kearney, Buffalo County
Some 40 miles farther west, at Kearney is another Nebraska historical marker in Centennial Park on Eleventh Street. It was in this general vicinity that the Pioneers first sighted and hunted buffalo.

In 1847 Brigham Young led the first migration over the Mormon Trail along the north bank of the Platte River, and in 1866 the Union Pacific Railroad pushed its main line westward to this valley, bringing pioneer settlers. However, it was not until 1871 when the Burlington & Missouri River Railroad fixed the junction point of its line with the Union Pacific that a townsite was established here. . . .

60 Lexington Mormon Trail Crossing Sign

Lexington, Dawson County

About 30 miles farther west on either U.S. 30 or I-80 the traveler reaches Lexington. Exactly 0.2 mile beyond the community's northern limits on the west side of Highway 21 is a wooden Mormon Trail Crossing sign erected by the Dawson County Historical Society. This badly weathered sign is nearly hidden by large cedars and appears to have been almost forgotten.

Mormon Trail Crossing / 1847 / Dawson County / Historical Society.

61, 62 Central Platte Valley Markers

In rest stops on east- and westbound lanes of I-80,
10 miles west of Lexington, Dawson County

Just 10 miles west of the Lexington exit are rest areas on both sides of I-80. In each is a Nebraska historical marker. The markers do not bear the same information. The text on the marker in the eastbound lane will be presented first, followed by the variant text on the marker in the westbound lane.

Here in Dawson County, much of the early history is concerned with the pioneer trails to the west. The Mormon Trail to Utah and the first transcontinental railroad passed through here on the north side of the Platte River; the Oregon Trail and the Pony Express followed the south side of the Platte.

Indian trouble was not uncommon here in the early days

of settlement. The Plum Creek Massacre occurred in 1864 when Sioux Indians attacked a wagon train, killing several men and taking prisoners at a site near here in Phelps County. Also near here, in 1867, a group of Cheyenne led by Chief Turkey Leg cut the telegraph line, derailed a locomotive, and killed several Union Pacific Railroad employees. The Army's Pawnee Indian Scouts, commanded by Major Frank North, came to the rescue and drove away the hostile Cheyenne.

Permanent settlements began to appear after construction of the railroad. One of the earliest of these was Plum Creek, later renamed Lexington. The first settlers moved there from a stage station on the south side of the river shortly before the coming of the railroad.

The text on the marker in the westbound lane is identical to the first two paragraphs on the marker in the eastbound lane. The concluding paragraph, however, is different.

CENTRAL PLATTE VALLEY

. . . .

The town of Cozad, northwest of here, lies directly on the 100th Meridian, considered an important goal in the building of the first transcontinental railroad. When the tracks reached this point in 1866, some 250 businessmen, senators, congressmen and other notables came here to celebrate. The 100th Meridian is often cited as the "line of aridity," west of which rainfall is usually insufficient to support nonirrigated agriculture.

The 100th Meridian Historic Site   63

Cozad, Dawson County

Five miles beyond the I-80 rest areas lies the little community of Cozad, the claim to fame of which is that it lies on the 100th meridian, reached by the U.P.R.R. on October 5, 1866, 247 rail miles west of Omaha. Beyond there, it was once widely believed, rainfall was too scant for ordinary agriculture. In the town, near the railroad station on U.S. 30, is a historical marker citing this information.

64   **North Platte Historic Site/Marker**

*Lincoln County Historical Society,
North Platte, Lincoln County*

Forty miles west of Cozad is the confluence of the North and South Platte rivers and the city of North Platte. In 1938 the Lincoln County Historical Society and the Utah Pioneer Trails and Landmarks Association erected a Mormon Pioneer Camp bronze marker attached to a concrete base just north of the North Platte River on the east side of Highway 70. Rather unwisely, this marker was moved recently to the grounds of the Lincoln County Historical Society at 2403 North Buffalo Street.

MORMON PIONEER CAMP

Mormon Pioneers enroute from Winter Quarters (Omaha) to the Valley of the Great Salt Lake, under the leadership of Brigham Young, camped near here May 11, 1847. While in this vicinity William Clayton made a distance measuring device which when attached to a wagon wheel, accurately recorded the distance traveled.

There is another displaced marker on the grounds of this museum. It is the Sioux Lookout Nebraska historical marker, originally located at the Sioux Lookout on the Oregon Trail 10 miles to the southeast (see trail XII, 151).

65   **Sand Hills Historic Area Ruts**

*North of Sutherland, Lincoln County,
in sec. 4, T14N, R33W*

Some of the very few, as well as some of the best, Mormon Trail ruts in all Nebraska can be reached from North Platte. A Lincoln County map is advised. Take Highway 70/97 for 3 miles north of the Platte River from North Platte where a gravel road turns west (this is just before the wye where 70 and 97 separate). The ruts are located on top of some sandhills about 21 miles to the west, immediately east of the bridge to Sutherland. (If you stay on the correct road, this will be the first bridge you come to. Do not turn south at a tee intersection after driving 14 miles. Turn north one mile, then west again.) The ruts are on top of the sandhills by the Sutherland bridge, about 100 yards to the east. This site can be reached more easily by taking U.S. 30 to Sutherland and driving 3.5 miles north to the same bridge. The ruts are worth the climb. There is no marker here.

Travelers must return to Sutherland and take U.S. 30 and U.S. 26 more than 50 miles west to come to the next historic site. Lake McConaughy now covers 24 miles of the old trail. Drive to the town of Lewellen in Garden County. Just south of the river is the famous Ash Hollow on the Oregon Trail (for a reference to the Mormons at Ash Hollow, see trail XII, 154). West from Lewellen, U.S. 26 follows the old Mormon Trail closely for 111 miles, to the Wyoming state line.

Indian Lookout Point Historic Site 66

Near Lisco, Morrill County, in sec. 19, T18N, R46W

Indian Lookout can be reached 30 miles west of Lewellen (or only 2 miles west of Lisco) just beyond the Morrill County line. To the north of U.S. 26 is the promentary many Mormons climbed to see if they could spot Chimney Rock (see trail XII, 156). It takes sharp eyes to do it. There is no marker here, but the climb is worth it.

Ancient Bluff Ruins Historic Site / Marker 67
and Trail Ruts (P)

8 miles west of Lisco, Morrill County,
in secs. 32 and 33, T19N, R47W

Five miles west of Indian Lookout Point, also to the north of the highway, are the dramatic Ancient Bluff Ruins. These magnificently eroded formations were named by English Mormon Pioneers, who thought they resembled ruined castles in their homeland. On Sunday May 23, 1847, the leaders of the Pioneers climbed the highest bluff, wrote their names on a buffalo skull, and placed it at the southwest corner. These bluffs are on private land and permission must be secured to visit them. Three-tenths of a mile east of the ranch road leading into the bluff area on the north side of U.S. 26 and very close to it may be seen a short section of well-defined trail ruts. About 1.5 miles east of these bluffs, north of the highway, is a 1985 Nebraska historical marker commemorating Narcissa Whitman, Eliza Spalding, and these bluffs.

NARCISSA WHITMAN

Narcissa Whitman, trail-blazer and martyred missionary, is one of the great heroines of the frontier West. In 1836 she and Eliza Spalding, following the north side of the Platte on horseback, became the first white women to cross the American continent.

The Protestant "Oregon Mission" was composed of Dr. Marcus Whitman, Rev. Henry Spalding, their new brides, and William Gray. They traveled from New York to Otoe Indian Agency (Bellevue, Nebraska), then joined an American Fur Company caravan led by Thomas Fitzpatrick. From the Green River rendezvous they journeyed westward with traders of the Hudson's Bay Company. In November, 1847, Narcissa, her husband, and eleven others were massacred by Cayuse Indians at their Walla Walla mission, now a National Historic Site.

The missionaries passed this point in June, 1836. In May, 1847, the Mormon Pioneers passed here en route from Winter Quarters (present North Omaha) to Salt Lake Valley, calling these formations "Ancient Bluff Ruins." Beginning with the California Gold Rush in 1849 this "Mormon Pioneer Trail" became "the Council Bluffs Road" to emigrants bound for the West Coast.

68   Bridgeport Mormon Pioneer Camp Marker

Near Bridgeport, Morrill County

Going west another 17 miles, two more Mormon trail markers may be found. The first is a bronze plaque set in a cobblestone monument, erected in 1938 by the Utah Pioneer Trails and Landmarks Association. It is located just south of U.S. 26, by the Union Pacific Railroad tracks where U.S. 26 turns sharply to the south towards Bridgeport.

MORMON PIONEER CAMP

Brigham Young and his company of Mormon Pioneers camped about 1000 feet west of this point May 24, 1847. They were enroute from Nauvoo, Illinois, and Winter Quarters, Nebraska, to the Valley of the Great Salt Lake, which they reached July 24, 1847. The Mormon Trail was on the north side of the river and the Oregon Trail on the southside.

There is a Pioneer Trail Museum in Bridgeport near the railroad station on Highway 385/92.

Oregon Trail–Old Mormon Road Marker 69

Bridgeport, Morrill County

The second marker in the Bridgeport area is at the extreme southern end of Bridgeport, near the railroad station, at the junction of Highways 88 and 92 / 385. It is a metal marker set in a monument of cobblestones and was dedicated in 1939 by the Camp Clarke Association.

> THE OLD OREGON TRAIL, 1790 Feet South, 1830–1869.
> THE OLD PONY EXPRESS ROUTE, 6 Mi. South, 1860–1861
> The First Transcontinental Telegraph Line Passed 6 Miles South, 1861–1870.
> Old Deadwood Trail, 4 Mi. North, 1847–1869.
> Old Mormon Road, 1 Mi. North, 1847–1869.
> The Burlington Railroad, Pioneer of the North Platte Valley, constructed its line in 1889.

West of Bridgeport, U.S. 26 passes the Paul Henderson grave (see trail XII, 155) and famed Chimney Rock on the Oregon Trail (see trail XII, 156). After visiting Chimney Rock (which is a must), travelers should turn north at Melbeta and again pick up U.S. 26 going towards Scottsbluff in order to visit Rebecca Winters's grave.

Rebecca Winters's Grave Information Sign 70

East of Scottsbluff, Scotts Bluff County,
in sec. 30, T22N, R54W

Rebecca Winters's famous grave, one of the few known graves of the approximately 6,000 Mormons who died crossing the plains, is located 3 miles east of downtown Scottsbluff, south of U.S. 26 in a pullout where the Belt Line Road crosses the Burlington and Northern Railroad tracks and intersects with U.S. 26 (compare it to trail XII, 147). Here is a Nebraska historical marker.

REBECCA WINTERS

Rebecca Winters, daughter of Gideon Burdick, a drummer boy in Washington's army, was born in New York State in 1802. She was a pioneer in the Church of the Latter Day Saints, being baptized with her husband Hiram in June 1833.

Membership in the Church brought persecution in Ohio, Illinois and Iowa. In June 1852 the family joined others of their faith in the great journey to Utah. It was a pleasant trip across Iowa through June, but in the Platte Valley the dread cholera struck. Rebecca saw many of her friends taken by the illness, and on August 15 she was another of its victims. She was buried on the prairie near here with a simple ceremony.

A close friend of the family, William Reynolds, chiseled the words "Rebecca Winters, age 50" on an iron wagon tire to mark the grave. The family continued on with the wagon train and settled in Pleasant Grove, Utah.

Burlington Railroad surveyors found the crude marker and changed the right-of-way to save and protect the grave. In 1902 a monument was erected by Rebecca's descendants. Rebecca Winters is a symbol of the pioneer mother who endured great hardships in the westward movement.

71   Rebecca Winters's Grave Site

Near Scottsbluff, Scotts Bluff County

One-quarter of a mile west of the historical marker along the railroad tracks is the grave itself. It was originally marked by the words "Rebecca Winters, age 50" inscribed on an old iron wagon tire, which still exists. After the discovery of the grave, the Mormon church added a headstone and a footstone and fenced the plot in 1902.

In memory of REBECCA WINTERS

Wife of HIRAM WINTERS. She died a faithfull Latter Day Saint, August 15, 1852. Aged 50 years.

While making that memorable journey across the plains with her people to find a new home in the far distant Salt Lake Valley she gave her life for her faith, her reward will be according to her works. This monument was erected in 1902, her centennial year, by her numerous descendants in Utah.

Just south of Scottsbluff, across the Platte River on the Oregon Trail, is the Scotts Bluff National Monument, where there is a museum and visitors' center with Mormon Trail exhibits (see trail XII, 157). This museum should not be missed.

Prayer Circle Bluffs Historic Site 72

Near Henry, Scotts Bluff County, in sec. 3, T23N, R58W
The low, sandy Prayer Circle Bluffs are about 1 mile east of Henry. They may be reached off U.S. 26 by following a service road along the Ramshorn Canal, but the road is very sandy. The bluffs are also visible from the highway.

It was here on May 30, 1847, that Young called a special prayer circle on behalf of the Pioneers with him, those following, and others remaining at Winter Quarters. There is no marker here.

Less than a mile from the center of Henry is the Nebraska-Wyoming state line.

VII

The Mormon Pioneer Trail of 1847 across Nebraska: Variants

(see map 3)

Over the years many variants evolved along the Pioneer route of 1847 across Nebraska. The first were occasioned by the advent of several ferries across the Missouri River between Bellevue and Winter Quarters (Florence), which gave rise to different routes to the Elkhorn Crossing. Similarly, the Mormons crossed the Loup River at different places. There were also two variants at the extreme western end of the trail in Nebraska, but these were really part of the Oregon Trail and will be described along with the rest of that trail (see trail XII, 157–158 and trail XVIII, 186).

73   Elkhorn Crossing Historic Site / Marker

On U.S. 30 near Elk City, Douglas County

A variant Elkhorn River crossing place, about 6 miles north of the Pioneer crossing (see trail VI, 47) is directly west of Winter Quarters, near where Highway 36 crosses that river. In 1932 some individuals marked this site with a small marker placed about one-quarter of a mile east of the bridge on the south side of the road.

The marker, only eighteen inches high, is difficult to locate. (Recently some friends and I took a shovel and cleared earth and debris that were hiding it.) The best way to find this small marker is to take a sighting south along the yellow dividing strip on County Road 88, which forms a tee intersection with U.S. 36 near the marker. This sighting will be about thirty-five feet west of a utility pole. The marker is about twelve feet south of the pole, about four feet from an equally small right-of-way (ROW) marker. Both markers are usually hidden by weeds.

Elkhorn River / ford and Ferry / used by / the Mormons in 1847 / and other emigrants. And the point where / the U.S.

Government / in 1857 / bridged the river / was located / 88 rods [484 yards] south / of the marker.

On the other side:

Erected by Frank Gelstor, Harry Turner / and Clarence Reckmeyer, July 4, 1932. / As you travel on west you know / all is not forgotten.

Old Fort Atkinson Historic Site / Marker   74

Fort Calhoun, Washington County

About 12 miles north of Winter Quarters on U.S. 73 the Mormons established Summer Quarters north of old Fort Atkinson, which had been built in 1820 to protect the American fur trade. It was then the nation's largest and most westerly military post and was built on the site of the Lewis and Clark Council Bluff of 1804. The Mormons not only used their Summer Quarters for haying, farming, and grazing, but also utilized the mud bricks from the fort for building; it had been abandoned since 1827. The old fort is being restored now and is a Nebraska state historical park with a visitors' center.

Westward from this fort was the so-called wet weather variant that the Mormons used during periods of high water on the Elkhorn River. This 60-mile long variant fords the Elkhorn 1 mile south of Arlington, Washington County, passes Fremont 3 miles to the north, and rejoins the main Mormon Trail at the confluence of Shell Creek and the Platte River, near Schuyler, Colfax County. North of Fremont there is a marker to this trail (see trail VI, 50).

Mormon Hollow Historic Site / Marker (ruined)   75

Fontenelle Forest, Bellevue, Sarpy County, in sec. 24, T14N, R13E

Many westering Mormons crossed the Missouri River just north of Bellevue. Some of them allegedly spent the winter of 1846–47 in Mormon Hollow, a one-half mile long, deep ravine located in Fontenelle Forest. Although no hard evidence supports this belief, it is a persistent rumor. In the hollow itself, which can be reached from Boy Scout Camp Wakonda, is a wooden sign reading MORMON HOLLOW.

At the extreme eastern end of the hollow along the Burlington and Northern railroad tracks, Boy Scout Troop 12 placed a bronze marker on a cobblestone monument in 1932. The plaque has been missing for years, but the three-foot high monument remains. It can be reached by continuing east from the sign in the ravine or by walking 0.4 mile south along the railroad tracks, south of Childes Road. (A detailed map of the forest can be obtained from the interpretive center.) Whether the Mormon story is true or not, many Mormons reached the Elkhorn by following a trail west from this place.

> Mormon Hollow / Opened by the Mormons in 1846 / Erected by / The Boy Scout Troop 12 / June 19, 1932. [This plaque no longer exists.]

76 Peter Sarpy's Trading Post Historic Site / Marker

Bellevue, Sarpy County

Located near the Missouri River in an undeveloped park area off Kountze Memorial Drive, this sign commemorates an early trading post on the Missouri River.

> In 1824 Peter Sarpy built a trading post for the American Fur Company approximately 500 feet east of this point. This was the last unofficial post office and the only ferry crossing above Westport, Missouri.
>
> In 1846 the post provided free ferry service and accommodations to several thousand Mormons. The continuous operation of this trading post from 1823 until May 13, 1857, makes Bellevue the oldest continuous settlement in the Nebraska Territory.
>
> Peter Sarpy was a member of the committee that founded Bellevue, Sarpy County, and the Fontenelle Bank on May 13, 1857. Sarpy sold the trading post to Thomas Benton and moved to Plattsmouth where he died in 1865. The trading post was torn down in 1868.

The Great Platte Valley Marker 77

Amelia Hill Rest Area on I-80,
near Gretna, Sarpy County

There were two routes from the Bellevue area to the Elkhorn River. One closely follows the left bank of the Platte River, crossing the Elkhorn near its confluence with the Platte. In this general area, about 3 miles from the confluence there is a Nebraska historical marker in the Amelia Hill Rest Area off the southbound lane of I-80.

THE GREAT PLATTE VALLEY

Here is the great Platte Valley. Highway to the West. On these nearby bluffs prehistoric Indians built their homes. The Pawnee and Oto established large earthlodge villages near here.

As you travel west in the valley you will follow the route of the Indians, white explorers, and the military trails to the western United States. In 1820, an exploring party under Major Stephen Long followed the Platte Valley to the Rocky Mountains, as did an 1826 expedition under General William Ashley. By 1830, the valley had become the major supply route for fur traders in the Rocky Mountains.

Beginning in 1847, the Mormons on their way to Utah followed a trail along the north side of the Platte. The Oregon Trail reached the Platte 150 miles west of here and followed the south side of the river. By the late 1850's, it was estimated that 90 per cent of all traffic which crossed the Plains followed the Platte.

The famous Pony Express followed the Platte Valley, as did the first transcontinental telegraph line. By 1869, the first transcontinental railroad was completed and it, too, followed the valley, opening the land along the river for permanent settlement.

At least two trail variants developed along the Loup River. The Pioneers forded near present-day Fullerton (see trail VI, 54). In 1857 a downstream ford was discovered near Genoa, which the Mormons established as a way station that same year (see trail VI, 53). From this ford the trail angles southwest along the Platte, reaching the 1847 trail a few miles east of Grand Island near a famous landmark called Lone Tree (see this trail, 80 and 81).

One year later a ferry began operating at the mouth of the Loup near modern Columbus. Since both these variants pass the site of the famous Lone Tree, I have dubbed them the Lone Tree variants.

78   Duncan Marker

U.S. 30 in downtown Duncan, Platte County

On the northeast corner of the intersection of Main Avenue and Ninth Street in Duncan is a Nebraska historical marker commemorating the founding of Duncan in 1871. It refers to the fact that "the Mormon Trail passed nearby during the mid-19th century. . . ." This is probably a reference to the trail of 1847, which runs 4 miles north of Duncan, north of the Platte River, but it also may be a reference to a variant of the 1847 trail, a route that crosses the Loup River at present-day Columbus, where a ferry was established in 1859 (see trail VI, 52). From Columbus this variant closely follows U.S. 30 through Duncan, joining the 1847 route just west of Grand Island (see trail VI, 56).

79   Mormon Trail State Wayside Area / Marker

On U.S. 30, 9 miles east of Central City, Merrick County

The Mormon Trail State Wayside Area is on the south side of the U.S. 30, 9 miles east of Central City, approximately where the trail from Columbus intersects the older trail from Genoa. There is a Nebraska historical marker in this small park.

THE MORMON TRAIL

For thousands of Mormons, the great pioneer trail along the north bank of the Platte, which paralleled the river about a mile south of here, was an avenue of escape from persecution and a roadway to a new life.

Brigham Young led the first mass migration over the Mormon Trail to the Great Salt Lake in 1847. The north bank of the Platte was chosen to avoid contact with the travelers on the heavily-used Oregon Trail that followed the south bank of the river from near Kearney westward. Among the expeditions which followed, were several so poor that pioneers walked and pulled handcarts.

The trail became one of the great roadways to the west, used by Mormons, military expeditions, gold seekers and settlers.

The completion of the Union Pacific Railroad in 1869 ended extensive use of the trail as the railroad tracks followed essentially this same route. Today, the Lincoln Highway (highway 30) follows this great roadway to the west.

The Lone Tree Markers   80, 81

On U.S. 30, Central City, Merrick County

Ten miles west of the Mormon Trail State Wayside Area, at the western end of Central City and to the south of U.S. 30, is a Nebraska historical marker commemorating the famous Lone Tree.

LONE TREE

Lone Tree, a giant, solitary cottonwood, was a noted Platte River landmark as early as 1833. Standing on the north side of the river some three miles southwest of present Central City, the tree was visible at great distances. Several travelers estimated they could see it twenty miles away. The tree was especially prominent since timber was rare on the Nebraska prairies except in stream valleys, where it received protection from prairie fires.

The Mormon Trail passed by Lone Tree, as did the Omaha–Fort Kearny stage route. The tree also gave its name to a stage station and a town, later renamed Central City. Ten to twelve feet in circumference, the tree's total height was about fifty feet; its lowest branches were about twenty feet above the ground.

Passing travelers often camped beneath Lone Tree and carved their initials on its trunk. This probably hastened its end, for the tree was dead by 1863. A severe storm in 1865 brought it to the earth. In 1911 residents of Merrick County erected a stone in the shape of a tree trunk on the site once occupied by Lone Tree.

This stone tree trunk still stands. To see it go due south 2 miles on a dirt road next to the historical marker just referred to. The monument is to the left, just beyond where the dirt road turns to the right. It is inscribed "On this spot stood the original Lone Tree on the old California Trail."

VIII

The Mormon Pioneer Trail of 1847 across Wyoming

(see maps 5 and 6)

Wyoming is the most scenic of all the states that the Mormon emigrants trekked through. It is also the most difficult state in which to follow the original trail. Many sites require county maps and may be reached only with off-road vehicles (ORVs). In Wyoming the Mormons crossed the Platte River and picked up the Oregon Trail, which they followed west some four hundred miles from Fort Laramie to Fort Bridger. There the Oregon Trail turned to the north and Mormons took the year-old Reed-Donner party track into the Valley of the Great Salt Lake. Mormon Pioneer National Historic Trail road signs have been located every 10 miles along all-weather roads that either follow or approximate the old trail across Wyoming (see trail I, 3).

The Pioneers of 1847 entered Wyoming just beyond the Prayer Circle Bluffs (see trail VI, 72) near Henry, Nebraska, and for the first time spotted the pyramidal bulk of Laramie Peak rising majestically above the Wyoming Black Hills (today's Laramie Mountains)—the first mountains seen by westering Americans. To the wise, this famous peak symbolized the rigors of what lay ahead.

En route to Fort Laramie you can see the Stuart Campsite marker. Robert Stuart first laid out and traveled eastward in 1812 on what later became the Oregon Trail. This marker is north of U.S. 26 and east of Torrington, about 3 miles beyond the Wyoming state line. There are also small trail markers on U.S. 26 in Lingle and Fort Laramie (city).

Fort Laramie Historic Site   82

Near Fort Laramie (city), Goshen County
Approximately 30 miles northwest of the present Wyoming state line traveling on U.S. 26 (which here follows the old trail quite closely) is the most famous historic site in all Wyoming—Fort Laramie, established

in 1834. Here the Mormons crossed the North Platte River and picked up the Oregon Trail.

The present Fort Laramie, now a national historic site, dates mainly from the Civil War period and little remains of the 1847 fort. At the moment there is no Mormon marker in the area, only a brief reference to them in the fort's museum. On the way to Fort Laramie be sure to notice the marker commemorating old Fort Platte, dating from 1841. During 1986–87, the National Park Service and the BLM cooperated in making some little-known trail ruts accessible to the public. To reach them, turn west on a gravel road from the fort's cemetery and drive a mile or so toward Guernsey. There are signs and a pull-out to the north of the road. If, however, for reasons of time or other considerations the traveler elects not to take the gravel road to Guernsey, it is possible to view the whole area between Fort Laramie and Guernsey from the Olinger Overlook. This site is located south of Highway 26, 2 miles east of Guernsey. Here descriptive panels and sighting posts explain and point out ten important sites in the immediate area.

83 Mexican Hill Historic Site (P)

Near Fort Laramie, Goshen County,
in sec. 8, T26N, R65W

About 7 miles west of the old fort, following the river road rather than the plateau, the Pioneers came to what later was called Mexican Hill. It is a steep and dramatic cut down through the river bluffs to the floodplain. The site is unmarked, difficult to find, on private ground, and ORVs and permission are required. Impressive trail ruts lead up to the hill from the east.

84 Register Cliff Historic Site / Marker

Guernsey State Park, Guernsey, Platte County

The famous Register Cliff site is 2 miles west of Mexican Hill and can be reached from there only by crossing private ground. Travelers are advised to approach it via Guernsey—it is 2.8 miles southeast of that community. Most Mormons seemed to have ignored this cliff, but later emigrants covered it with names, carving them into the soft sandstone.

There is a monument at the site and an interpretive panel 0.7 mile north of the cliff on U.S. 26.

Guernsey Ruts Historic Site / Marker 85

Guernsey State Park, Guernsey, Platte County

One and one-half miles beyond Register Cliff are some of the most dramatic ruts of any trail in the world—cut shoulder deep through solid rock. These ruts must be visited and are located a short walk from a marked parking area. The interpretive panel near them bears an almost poetic inscription.

OREGON TRAIL RUTS

Registered National Historic Landmark

Wagon wheels cut solid rock, carving a memorial to Empire Builders. What manner of men and beasts impelled conveyances weighing on those grinding wheels? Look! A line of shadows crossing boundless wilderness.

Foremost, nimble mules drawing their carts, come poised Mountain Men carrying trade goods to a fur fair—the Rendezvous. So, in 1830, Bill Sublette turns the first wheels from St. Louis to the Rocky Mountains! Following his faint trail, a decade later and on through the 1860's, appear straining, twisting teams of oxen, mules and heavy draft horses drawing Conestoga wagons for Oregon pioneers. Trailing the Oregon-bound *avant garde* but otherwise mingling with those emigrants, inspired by religious fervor, loom footsore and trail-worn companies—Mormons dragging or pushing handcarts as they follow Brigham Young to the Valley of the Salt Lake. And, after 1849, reacting to a different stimulus but sharing the same trail, urging draft animals to extremity, straining resources and often failing, hurry gold rushers California bound.

A different breed, no emigrants but enterprisers and adventurers, capture the 1860's scene. They appear, multi-teamed units in draft—heavy wagons in tandem, jerkline operators and bullwhackers delivering freight to Indian War outposts and agencies. Now the apparition fades in a changing environment. Dimly seen, this last commerce serves a new, pastoral society: the era of the cattle baron and the advent of settlement blot the Oregon Trail.

Once here visitors should do a little exploring on foot. Follow the ruts to your right for at least 100 yards. Also cross the ruts and poke around for traces of other emigrant attempts to cross this difficult terrain. From the Guernsey ruts it is very difficult without ORVs and county maps (Platte County, sheet 2; Converse County, sheets 1 and 4) to follow the old trail more than 80 miles west to near Glenrock. General travelers are advised to follow U.S. 26 and I-25 to Ayers Natural Bridge, skipping historic sites 86, 87, and 88.

86   Warm Springs Historic Site

Near Guernsey, Platte County, in sec. 4, T26N, R66W
The famous Warm Springs are located in a sandy draw a little over a mile west of the famous ruts near Guernsey. ORVs are required. These springs were also known as the Emigrants' Washtub because the water is warmer than the river, about 70° F.

87   Porter's Rock Historic Site / Ruts (P)

West of Guernsey, in Platte County,
in sec. 27, T27N, R67W
A natural formation, apparently named after Joseph Smith's one-time bodyguard, Orrin Porter Rockwell, is 7 miles west of Guernsey, on private ground. ORV is required. Ruts pass the rock on both sides.

88   Heber Springs (P)

West of Glendo, Platte County, in sec. 1, T28N, R70W
Heber Springs are located 11 miles southwest of Glendo on the Esterbrook Road, to the east of where this road crosses Horseshoe Creek. Locally known as Mormon Springs, the Mormons did not discover them. Heber C. Kimball was simply the first of the 1847 Pioneers to see them. Permission should be secured before visiting them.

There is no easy way to get from these springs to the next historic site. It is best to return to Glendo and take I-25 west to the Natural Bridge Road. The adventurous, however, can secure a Platte County map (sheet 2) and a Converse County map (sheets 1 and 4) and some beautiful country, several trail markers, the Red Earth country, and the site of the La Bonte stage station can be seen.

Ayers Natural Bridge Park   89

East of Glenrock, Converse County,
in sec. 21, T32N, R73W

A twenty-foot high, ninety-foot wide rock span, the only natural bridge with a running stream under it in the United States, is 12 miles west of Douglas on I-25 and then 5 miles south on the Natural Bridge Road. Although somewhat off the trail, Ayers Natural Bridge was visited by many emigrants. The area is now a small park.

Mormon Canyon Road   90

Glenrock, Converse County

Mormon Canyon Road is located at the east end of Glenrock and goes south, up Deer Creek. It is so named because some Mormons wintered here in the 1850s. The returning Pioneers found coal deposits here and several, including my ancestor Heber C. Kimball, were chased by a mother grizzly bear. The escarpment above Deer Creek, up which the Mormons scrambled to get away from the bear, is clearly visible about one-half mile up the road on the right bank of Deer Creek. (The grizzly is the only bear in the American West that cannot climb well.)

Between Glenrock and Casper, I-25 follows the old trail along the Platte for some 25 miles. U.S. 26 is closer to the old route, but modern construction has eliminated all traces of the trail and travelers should proceed directly to the Casper area.

Mormon Ferry (1849) Historic Site   91

Evansville, Natrona County

The Mormon Ferry site is about 3 miles east of Casper in the little community of Evansville, in a small riverside park. This is not the original 1847 ferry site (see this trail, 92), but a later one established in 1849.

Here may be seen the reconstruction of part of a toll bridge built in 1852 by John Reshaw (Richard).

92   Mormon Ferry (1847) Historic Site / Marker

Old Fort Caspar, Casper, Natrona County

The 1847 Mormon Ferry site is located at rebuilt old Fort Caspar west of the city of Casper, 0.4 mile west of the fairgrounds. Built in 1858, the old fort is worth visiting. There is an excellent Mormon exhibit in the fort museum, a full-size replica of the original Mormon ferry, and a 1932 Utah Pioneer Trails and Landmarks monument on the fort grounds.

THE MORMON FERRY

First Commercial Ferry on the Platte River was established ½ mile south of here [this marker has obviously been moved from its original site] in June 1847 by Mormon Pioneers on their way to the Valley of the Great Salt Lake.

Brigham Young directed nine men to remain to operate the ferry. They were Thomas Grover, Capt. John S. Higbee, Luke S. Johnson, Appleton M. Harmon, Edmond Ellsworth, Francis M. Pomeroy, William Empey, James Davenport, [and] Benj. E. Stewart.

The first passengers were Missourians bound for Oregon. The ferry was made of two large cottonwood canoes fastened with crosspieces and covered with slabs. It was operated by oars.

From here it is possible to follow the old trail closely for 60 miles to Independence Rock and then fairly closely for another 56 miles to Sweetwater Station in Fremont County.

93   Red Buttes Crossing Historic Site / Marker

12.5 miles southwest of Casper, Natrona County,
in sec 3, T32N, R81W

Some Mormons, for a variety of reasons, used the well-known Red Buttes crossing of the North Platte River, the uppermost fording of that river. To reach this site take Highway 220 southwest for 10 miles to a blacktop road leading west to Bessemer Bend. After 2.5 miles you reach the river and a Bureau of Land Management (BLM) pull-off is just on the other side. One of the information signs refers to the Mormons: "The Mormons sought freedom from religous, social and economic intolerance and aggression."

Emigrant Gap   94

West of Casper, Natrona County, in sec. 10, T33N, R81W
To reach the historic gap through the Emigrant Gap Ridge drive about 1 mile north of the old Fort Caspar to U.S. 26, turn northwest (or left), about another mile to the Poison Spider Road, which turns west at a right angle to U.S. 26. The shallow gap, 8 miles west on Poison Spider Road, is the real beginning of the ascent of the Rocky Mountains.

Avenue of Rocks Historic Site   95

6 miles west of Emigrant Gap, Natrona County,
in sec. 16, T32N, R82W
Drive 3 miles beyond Emigrant Gap to the Oregon Trail Road (now marked Natrona County 319), which turns due south off Poison Spider Road. Seven miles beyond this tee intersection is a rock ridge to the north. This is the famous Avenue of Rocks, also known as the Devil's Back Bone. Some of the formation and the ruts have been destroyed by road builders. Trail signatures can be found on the rocks near the present road.

Willow Springs Site   96

9 miles west of Avenue of Rocks, Natrona County,
in sec. 9, T31N, R83W
Willow Springs provided the only good campground for the emigrants between the Platte and Sweetwater rivers. The springs can be seen to the north of the road next to some abandoned ranch buildings.

97   Prospect (Ryan) Hill Site

1 mile beyond Willow Springs, Natrona County,
in sec. 8, T31N, R83W

Now known as Ryan Hill, this 400-foot climb was very hard on draft animals. It was originally called Prospect Hill because from its summit emigrants could see the gentle valley of the Sweetwater River, giving them hope or good prospects for better water and an easier road. An excellent set of original trail ruts may be seen going up the hill about one-quarter mile northwest of the present road. (I left some ruts here myself once when, with a BLM friend, our ORV got stuck in April mud.) In 1987 the BLM installed an interpretive site at the crest of this hill.

98   Independence Rock Historic Site / Markers

22 miles beyond Prospect Hill, Natrona County,
in sec. 9, T29N, R86W

Thirteen miles west of Prospect Hill, the Oregon Trail Road intersects Highway 220. Turn right (west) and follow Highway 220 about 9 miles to Independence Rock, one of the most famous landmarks on the old trail. Near this rock, emigrants picked up the gentle, beneficent Sweetwater River, which they followed for about 93 miles west to the continental divide at South Pass.

The rock derives its name from the story that some early trappers once celebrated July 4 here. Here you can see information signs, many names carved and painted on the rock, and several bronze plaques, one of which honors the Mormons.

> In honor of THE MORMON PIONEERS who passed Independence Rock June 21, 1847, under the leadership of BRIGHAM YOUNG, on their way to the Valley of the Great Salt Lake. And of more than 80,000 [50,000 is closer to the truth] "Mormon" emigrants who followed by ox teams, handcarts, and other means of travel, seeking religious liberty and economic independence. Erected June 21, 1931, by descendants of the Pioneers who have made the desert blossom as the rose.

The information sign reads:

INDEPENDENCE ROCK

Father De Smet, early missionary, on July 5, 1841 named this rock "Great Record of the Desert" on account of many names and dates carved into its surface. It was an important landmark and camp site for the emigrants of the Oregon and Utah trails. . . .

Devil's Gate Historic Site (P)   99

6 miles west of Independence Rock on Highway 220, Natrona County, in sec. 35, T29N, R87W

Devil's Gate landmark is a 370-foot high and 1,500-foot long cleft, or water gap, through the Sweetwater Rocks. Some Mormon Pioneers tried to walk or ride horses through it, but the current was too strong. Emigrant signatures may be found in the gap, as I discovered the hard way. Both entrances are on private ground, but it can be climbed from the road, which is also on private land. The climb is rough, but worth the effort. On top watch the winds; be careful!

Four miles west of Independence Rock, old road 220 turns sharply right off new 220. Follow old 220 if you wish to climb the gate. It is also necessary to follow old 220 to visit the Martin's Cove marker (see this trail, 101), but first travelers should visit the BLM pull-off (this trail, 100) to read the signs.

BLM Information Pull-Off   100

Near Devil's Gate on new Highway 220, Natrona County, in sec. 35, T29N, R87W

Before proceeding west on old 220, this Bureau of Land Management pull-off should be visited. Four signs tell the history of the Devil's Gate (this trail, 99) and Martin's Cove (see this trail, 101).

MARTIN'S COVE

Two miles to the northwest, nestled at the foot of the Sweetwater Rocks, is Martin's Cove. Here Captain Edward Martin's exhausted company of Mormon handcart emigrants sought shelter from an early winter storm in November of

1856. Of 576 men, women and children, 145 had died before rescue parties from Salt Lake City reached them. . . .

101   ## Martin's Cove Historic Site / Marker (P)

*2 miles west of Devil's Gate on old Highway 220,
Natrona County, in sec. 28, T29N, R87W*

The actual cove where many Mormons froze to death in 1856 is north of the road, across the Sweetwater River on the Sun Ranch, and permission must be secured to visit it. ORVs are required. In 1986 some Boy Scouts from Layton, Utah, erected a rock cairn on a rise in this cove honoring those who perished here. I found the real cove by accident. In 1979 a newspaper friend and I decided to push our four-wheel drive vehicle as far as possible into the area—suddenly the ground sloped steeply away and there was the cove about a hundred feet beneath us. The 1933 marker put up by the Utah Pioneer Trails and Landmarks Association is to the north of old Highway 220, 2 miles west of the Sun Ranch and nearly 2 miles from the cove; get permission to drive this road, which is now private. The general area of the cove is in the Rattlesnake Mountains, more than a mile north of the road.

MARTIN'S COVE

Survivors of Captain Edward Martin's handcart company of Mormon emigrants from England to Utah were rescued here in perishing condition about Nov. 12, 1856. Delayed in starting and hampered by inferior [hand]carts, it was overtaken by an early winter. Among the company of 576, including aged people and children, the fatalities numbered 145. Insufficient food and clothing and severe weather caused many deaths. Towards the end every campground became a graveyard. Some of the survivors found shelter in a stockade and mail station near Devil's Gate where their property was stored for the winter. Earlier companies reached Utah in safety.

These deep trail ruts at Mexican Hill, east of Guernsey, Wyoming, were made by the wheels of pioneer wagons traveling this route over many years. Today the site is on private land and difficult to find. *See trail VIII, 83.*

Cut through solid rock, these Oregon Trail ruts at Guernsey State Park are a registered national historic landmark. The author, shown standing in them, considers these to be among the most dramatic trail ruts still existing. They are easily accessible, with parking a short walk away. *See trail VIII, 85.*

Ayers Natural Bridge is somewhat off the trail, but many emigrants visited it. *See trail VIII, 89.*

Devil's Gate, a cleft through the Sweetwater Rocks, was a famous landmark known to westward emigrants. The climb to the top is worth the effort, as the view is spectacular. *See trail VIII, 99.*

More Oregon Trail ruts cut into the rock are visible on private land east of Jeffrey City, Wyoming. *See trail VIII, 102.*

above, This photograph records some Mormons in 1926 planting a shrub at the South Pass marker erected in 1906. Photo courtesy of the Church of Jesus Christ of Latter-day Saints. *See trail VIII, 106.* **right,** During the Utah War of 1857–58, the Mormons campaigned against army troops sent out to subdue them, as recorded on this marker at Simpson's Hollow, Wyoming. *See trail VIII, 110.*

SIMPSON'S HOLLOW

HERE ON OCT. 6, 1857, U.S. ARMY SUPPLY WAGONS LEAD BY A CAPT. SIMPSON WERE BURNED BY MAJOR LOT SMITH AND 43 UTAH MILITIAMEN. THEY WERE UNDER ORDERS FROM BRIGHAM YOUNG, UTAH TERRITORIAL GOVERNOR, TO DELAY THE ARMY'S ADVANCE ON UTAH. THIS DELAY OF THE ARMY HELPED EFFECT A PEACEFUL SETTLEMENT OF DIFFICULTIES.

THE DAY EARLIER A SIMILAR BURNING OF 52 ARMY SUPPLY WAGONS TOOK PLACE NEAR HERE AT SMITH'S BLUFF.

Church Butte was a famous landmark on the Mormon and Oregon-California trails. *See trail VIII, 113.*

One remnant of the cobblestone wall that was built by the Mormons following their purchase of Fort Bridger in 1853 is still standing. *See trail VIII, 116.*

The beehive is a typical symbol of Mormon industry. This marker is on the Mormon Trail near Bear River, Wyoming. *See trail VIII, 117.*

Split Rock Mountain Ruts (P)   102

*East of Jeffrey City, Fremont County,
in sec. 16, T29N, R90W*

Split Rock Mountain was an important landmark on the old trail. Follow old Highway 220 for 5 miles west to its intersection with new 220, then turn west 7 miles (through Muddy Gap) and take U.S. 287 / 789 north for 8 miles, where the mountain will be seen directly north of the road; 2 miles farther, to the north of the road, is a Split Rock marker.

> Split Rock. A famous natural landmark / used by Indians, Trappers, and / emigrants on the Oregon Trail. / Site of Split Rock Pony Express / 1860–1861, stage, and telegraph / station is on the south side on the Sweetwater. / Split Rock can be seen as a / cleft in the top of the Rattlesnake Range.

About 1.5 miles west of this marker are some famous Oregon Trail ruts in solid rock. They are on private ground and permission must be secured to visit them. There is also a BLM interpretive site near Split Rock.

The Three Crossings Area (P)   103

Near Jeffrey City, Fremont County

Along the Sweetwater River 2 miles north of Jeffrey City is the famous Three Crossings—where the river was crossed three times within a short distance. Going west the Mormons took the Deep Sand Route, which is near but not on the river. When they returned they took the river route. Both routes now require ORVs and permission. The Western Nuclear Company has all but blocked the Deep Sand Route with tailings. With permission and a four-wheel drive vehicle it can, however, be driven. I tried it once in a passenger car and it took two trucks in tandem to pull me out—considerably wiser for the experience.

Ice Springs Historic Site / Marker   104

*West of Jeffrey City, Fremont County,
in sec. 32, T30N, R93W*

Nine miles west of Jeffrey City on U.S. 287 / 789, north of the road, is an information sign about Ice Springs. Many emigrants, including the

Mormons in 1847, found ice in this marshy area by digging underneath the deep, insulating turf. The actual springs are 1.5 miles north of the sign, on a rough road.

Here the old trail crosses the modern highway following the Sweetwater River towards the continental divide at South Pass, 50 miles to the west. Only travelers with county maps (Fremont sheets 1 and 2) and ORVs, however, can follow this section of the trail. (And even then, one time I got lost while showing the area to a writer for *National Geographic*.) Other travelers have to drive a long detour and visit what they can by probing gravel roads off Highway 28.

From the Ice Springs continue north on U.S. 287/789, about 40 miles toward Lander. Eight miles before reaching Lander take Highway 28 west toward Atlantic City and Farson.

105   Willie's Handcart Company Grave Site/Marker

South of Atlantic City, Fremont County,
in sec. 35, T29N, R99W

South of Atlantic City is the general site of the second handcart disaster of 1856. On Highway 28, approximately 20 miles west of the intersection of 287/789 and 28, watch for directions to the old gold mining town of Atlantic City, 3 miles south of 28. Here ask directions to the Mormon Grave on Rock Creek, which is 7 miles south on a gravel road up and over a mountain. The area is totally desolate. (I had a flat tire on a rental car here once, only to find that the car had the wrong size spare; I discovered how desolate the area really is.) The site, marked in 1933 by the Utah Pioneer Trails and Landmarks Association, is about 200 feet south of the road near the bridge over Rock Creek.

WILLIE'S HANDCART COMPANY

Captain James G. Willie's handcart company of Mormon emigrants on the way to Utah, greatly exhausted by the deep snows of an early winter and suffering from lack of food and clothing, had assembled here for reorganization by relief parties from Utah, about the end of October, 1856. Thirteen persons were frozen to death during a single night and were buried here in one grave. Two others died the next day and were buried near by. Of the company of 404 persons 77 perished before help arrived. The survivors reached Salt Lake City November 9, 1856.

It is very difficult to follow the old trail west of here, via Burnt Ranch, to South Pass (see this trail, 106). A Fremont County map (sheet 2) and an ORV are necessary.

South Pass Historic Site / Markers 106

West of Atlantic City, Fremont County,
in sec. 4, T27N, R101W

Returning from Rock Creek to Highway 28, proceed west for 16 miles to the continental divide and South Pass (1 mile beyond the bridge across the Sweetwater River, which the old trail now leaves for good). About 0.8 mile beyond the bridge, the adventurous can take a dirt road to the left and, with luck, follow it for 3 miles to the point where the Oregon Trail crosses the South Pass. There are two markers. One, which Ezra Meeker placed in 1906, simply reads "Old Oregon Trail / 1843–57." Another, erected in 1916, notes "Narcissa Prentiss Whitman / Eliza Hart Spalding / First white women to cross this pass / July 4, 1836."

Pacific Springs Historic Site 107

4 miles west of South Pass, Fremont County,
in sec. 1, T27N, R102W

Pacific Springs, a famous campsite, are so named because these were the first waters that flowed to the Pacific seen by westering Americans. From the springs dirt roads lead back to Highway 28. A Fremont County map (sheet 1) and ORVs are advised.

Fortunately, you can see the entire area without leaving Highway 28 (see this trail, 108).

South Pass Exhibit Site 108

Highway 28, in Fremont County,
in sec. 2, T27N, R102W

Four miles beyond the last bridge over the Sweetwater, to the south of the road, is the South Pass exhibit overlooking South Pass (the Cumberland Gap of the Old West) and Pacific Springs.

From this exhibit site it is about 25 miles west to Farson on Highway 28, and the old trail is within 1 or 2 miles north of the road. Six miles beyond the exhibit, north of the road, is the "false" parting of the ways marker. The real parting of the ways (that is, where the Sublette Cutoff left the main Oregon Trail, bypassing Fort Bridger) is out of sight 9 miles farther on. In this same general area, along the Little Sandy Creek, Brigham Young met Jim Bridger in 1847 (see this trail, 109).

109 The Young-Bridger Marker

Farson, Sweetwater County

At the intersection of Highway 28 and U.S. 187 is a plaque set in a pyramid concrete base commemorating the famous meeting of Brigham Young with Jim Bridger in 1847. The actual site is about 8 miles northeast of Farson along the Little Sandy. The marker was erected in 1933 by the Utah Pioneer Trails and Landmark Association.

LITTLE SANDY CROSSING

On Monday evening, June 28, 1847, Brigham Young and the Mormon Pioneers met James Bridger and Party near this place. Both companies encamped here over night and conferred at length regarding the route and possibility of establishing and sustaining a large population in the Valley of the Great Salt Lake. Bridger tried to discourage the undertaking. In this conference he is reported to have said that he would give one thousand dollars for the first bushel of corn grown in the Salt Lake Valley.

From Farson, Highway 28 follows the old trail closely for about 28 miles. The entrance to this road is 1 mile north of Farson, to the left or west. A number of turnouts and short hiking segments over the Oregon Trail are located along this highway thanks to negotiations with the Wyoming State Highway Department and the Oregon-California Trails Association.

The sharp eye can spot some of the Bureau of Land Management four-foot high concrete posts marking the Oregon Trail. These posts scattered throughout Wyoming are placed only on BLM land, not on private property. Because of these gaps, one can get lost, as I have, trying to follow the old trail with only these posts as guides.

Simpson's Hollow Historic Site / Marker   110

West of Farson, Sweetwater County,
in sec. 36, T24N, R108W

A granite marker, 12 miles beyond Farson to the north of the road, probably placed by the Mormon church, commemorates an event in the Utah War of 1857–58. The hollow is to the south towards the Sandy Creek. (Although I have tried to find wagon iron here using a metal detector, I have only found bailing wire.)

SIMPSON'S HOLLOW

Here on Oct. 6, 1857, U.S. army supply wagons lead [*sic*] by a Capt. Simpson were burned by Major Lot Smith and 43 Utah Militiamen. They were under orders from Brigham Young, Utah Territorial Governor, to delay the army's advance on Utah. This delay of the army helped effect a peaceful settlement of difficulties.

The day earlier a similar burning of 52 army supply wagons took place near here at Smith's Bluff.

This marker, as in the case with many other markers in the western United States, is slowly being destroyed by hunters using it as a target. Not only is this happening, but also many bronze plaques and medallions have been stolen from historic sites all over the country. It has become necessary and wise to lessen the prominence of markers and to use anodized aluminum rather than bronze for plaques.

The Mormon Knolls   111

West of Farson, Sweetwater County,
in secs. 22, 23, 24, 27, 28, and 29, T23N, R108W

Five miles beyond the Simpson's Hollow marker and 3 miles east of the road, are five low knolls that have picked up the designation of Mormon Knolls. They are not worth a hike to visit them.

112   Green River Mormon Ferry Historic Site

On Green River, Sweetwater County,
in sec. 18, T22N, R109W

After passing the Mormon Knolls, the old trail keeps going for 13 miles southwest across the Little Colorado Desert to the Green River, where the Mormons established another ferry in 1847, often called the Lombard ferry site. The present Highway 28 bridge crosses the river adjacent to the site of the old ferry. The highway continues another 2 miles to an intersection with Highway 372.

From this intersection proceed some 38 miles to Granger via 372, I-80, and U.S. 30.

113   Church Butte Historic Site

10 miles southwest of Granger, Uinta County,
in sec. 25, T18N, R113W

From Granger proceed carefully southwest on what used to be U.S. 30, the famous Lincoln Highway; it is now an unmarked, decaying blacktop kept up by oil interests. Here the old trail is picked up and followed fairly closely for 32 miles to Fort Bridger.

Ten miles down this road is the magnificantly eroded landmark appropriately named Church Butte. At one time there was a 1930 cast iron marker here: "In honor of the Mormon Pioneers who passed this point early in July 1847 and in subsequent years." All that is left today is a concrete slab to the left of the road. Staying on this old road another 13 miles to its intersection with modern U.S. 30, continue on to Lyman. (If you have had enough of this tire-banger, it is possible to take a gravel road 5 miles straight south from Church Butte to the Church Butte interchange on I-80.)

114   Lyman Historic Marker

Lyman city park, Lyman, Uinta County

In the Lyman city park next to U.S. 30-S is a tall concrete marker topped by a beehive (a sure symbol of Mormon country) commemorating the traverse of the Pioneers 2 miles to the north in 1847. The marker was erected by the Woodruff Stake (Diocese) of the Mormon church.

THE MORMON PIONEERS

Who passed this point / Wednesday July 7, 1847 / and in subsequent years.

Fort Bridger Historic Site 115

Fort Bridger State Park, Uinta County

Six miles beyond Lyman is the second most important fort on the old Mormon Pioneer Trail, the first one being Fort Laramie (see this trail, 82). Here the main Oregon Trail (which the Pioneers of 1847 picked up nearly four hundred miles back at Fort Laramie) turns north and the Mormons continued west about a hundred miles on the year-old track of the Reed-Donner party into present-day Salt Lake City.

There is nothing left of the original fort of 1843–44, but there is an excellent fort museum with some references to the Mormon presence here.

The Mormon Wall at Fort Bridger 116
Historic Site / Marker

Fort Bridger State Park, Uinta County

In 1853 the Mormons bought Fort Bridger, enlarged it, and built a cobblestone wall around it. At the approach of the U.S. Army in 1857, they burned the fort. One small section of the wall is all that is left of the Mormon occupation. Rebuilt by the WPA during the Depression, it is located under a shelter at the far end of the fort, opposite the front entrance. In 1933 the Utah Pioneer Trails and Landmarks Association placed a bronze plaque on the wall.

THE MORMON WALL

On August 3, 1855 the Church of Jesus Christ of Latter-day Saints concluded arrangements for the purchase of Fort Bridger from Louis Vasquez, partner of James Bridger, for $18,000. Final payment was made October 18, 1858. A cobblestone wall was erected in the fall of 1855, replacing Bridger's stockade. A few additional log houses were built within the fort . The place was evacuated and burned on the approach of Johnston's Army September 27, 1857. A portion of the wall is here preserved. In 1855 Fort Supply was established by Brigham Young six miles west where crops were raised for the emigrants.

From Fort Bridger travelers have two options. The easy one is to pick up I-80, following it some 40 miles via Evanston, into Echo Canyon down along the route of old trail. The other, which follows the old trail rather well, requires a Uinta County map (sheets 1 and 2) and careful driving. Those who take the I-80 option should skip to Cache Cave, Utah (trail IX, 120).

117   **Bear Town Marker**

Near Bear River, Unita County, in sec. 29, T14N, R119W
To approximate the old Mormon Pioneer Trail west from Fort Bridger to the Bear Town marker, follow a dirt road about 35 miles west, past the Fort Bridger Cemetery, Bridger Butte, and abandoned Piedmont, to its intersection with Highway 150 near the Sulphur Creek Reservoir. It should be noted that Piedmont can be reached more easily by turning south at the Leroy exit of I-80. A more accurate route is via Altamont instead of Piedmont, but it is much harder to follow.

About one-half mile before reaching Bear River, east of Highway 150, is a cobblestone marker topped by another beehive.

Erected/ by members of/ the Woodruff Stake/ of the Church of/ Jesus Christ of/ Latter-day Saints/ in honor of the Pioneers who/ passed this spot/ July 12, 1847/ under the leadership/ of Brigham Young./ Dedicated/ September 28, 1924.

It is also possible to visit the Bear Town marker out of Evanston by simply driving south on Highway 150 for about 8 miles.

118   **Oil Spring Historic Site (P)**

12 miles south of Evanston, Uinta County,
in sec. 4, T13N, R119W
This oil spring, well known to many westerning Americans as a source of lubrication for their wagons, still flows. It is on private property and

permission must be secured to visit it. The entrance to the ranch is 3 miles south of the bridge over the Bear River on Highway 150 south of Evanston.

The Needles Historic Site (P)   119

Near the Wyoming-Utah state line, Uinta County, in sec. 26, T14N, R121W

Three miles north of the Bear Town marker is the entrance to Coyote Creek Canyon. Follow a ranch road 9 miles west to the landmark known as the Needles or Pudding Rocks, very close to the Utah state line. It was here, just east of the Needles, that Brigham Young was taken sick with Rocky Mountain tick fever, causing him to enter the Valley of the Great Salt Lake two days after the vanguard.

To drive this canyon requires not only permission, but also a Uinta County map (sheet 2), an ORV, and luck. (The last time I was there a bridge was out. The first time I was there a kindly rancher's wife cured my "G.I.'s" with a shot of plum brandy.) An alternate route to the Needles is via Evanston. Continuing north from the Bear Town marker 8 miles on road 150 to Evanston and then going west on the Yellow Creek Road 8.4 miles, the 7,600-foot high formation of conglomerate rock will be visible to the east.

From here to the first historic site in Utah, travelers can either take a dirt road 4 miles west from the Needles to I-80 in Echo Canyon or return to Evanston and pick up I-80.

IX

The Mormon Pioneer Trail
of 1847 in Utah
(see map 7)

The 70-mile long trail in Utah winds through a string of canyons in the Wasatch Range of the Rocky Mountains, the last barrier to the new Mormon Zion. It is the best-known section of any of the many emigrant trails used by the Mormons, and with the exception of the 4-mile hike up Little Emigration Canyon, also very easy to follow. Unfortunately, however, very few of the original ruts have been preserved (see this trail, sites 125 and 129). Because of Brigham Young's sickness at the Needles, the Pioneer Camp split into three groups. The vanguard reached the valley on July 22 and those with Young arrived two days later, giving rise to the celebration of Pioneer Day among Mormons worldwide every July 24. Recently improvements have been made in the marking and signing of the Pioneer Trail in Utah. Several vandalized markers have been restored, several new ones erected, and about twenty directional signs placed. Coming from the Needles (see trail VIII, 119) you reach I-80 by taking a dirt road 4 miles west to the tiny railroad community of Wahsatch or via Evanston, Wyoming. The 25-mile long Echo Canyon is itself a famous landmark down through which the old trail goes. With all the various widenings, however, the echo is long gone. Mormon Pioneer National Historic Trail road signs are located every 10 miles along all weather roads that either follow or approximate the old trail in Utah (see trail I, 3).

120   Cache Cave Historic Site (P)

Near Castle Rock, Summit County, in sec. 23, T5N, R7E
Cache Cave is a famous rendezvous place now on private land, and permission is seldom given to visit it. The general area of the cave, but not the cave itself (which is about the size of a large living room and covered with names), can be seen from I-80 in Echo Canyon. Actually

it is not a true cave; it appears to be a cavern hollowed out of limestone as a result of solution action. It lies to the south of I-80 4 miles down the canyon from Wahsatch.

About 4 miles farther down Echo Canyon from the Cache Cave Canyon is another tiny railroad community called Castle Rock. Near here, on old U.S. 30, a Mormon Trail marker was erected in 1927. Because of road work, especially the building of I-80, the monument was moved southwest of Henefer in 1967 (see this trail, 124).

Pioneer Defense Fortifications Historic Site / Marker   121

21 miles south of Wahsatch, Summit County,
in Echo Canyon, in sec. 10, T3N, R5E

There is a historical marker on old U.S. 30, which parallels part of I-80 in Echo Canyon. The exit to U.S. 30 is 12 miles down the canyon from Wahsatch and the wooden marker is 7 miles down U.S. 30 to the right of the road. Erected by the Utah State Road Commission, the sign is weathering badly.

PIONEER DEFENSE FORTIFICATIONS

In 1857, due to false official reports and other misrepresentations, troops under General Albert Sidney Johnston were sent to suppress a mythical rebellion among the Mormons. Brigham Young, then governor, exercising constitutional rights, forbade the army to enter Utah on the grounds that there was no rebellion and that he had not been officially informed of the government's action in sending the troops.

Strategic places between Fort Bridger and Salt Lake City were fortified. Remnants of these fortifications can be seen on the sides of the cliffs in this section of Echo Canyon. [here the text is unclear:] Settle . . . and all public buildings. Fort Bridger and Fort Supply, then in Utah and owned by the Church, were burned.

Following negotiations between Governor Young and Captain Stewart Van Vliet and mediation of Col. Thomas L. Kane, the army was held east of Fort Bridger during the winter of 1857–58 and entered Utah without opposition the following spring. It was recalled at the outbreak of the Civil War.

122   Weber Canyon Explorers Trail Marker

Near Henefer, Summit County, east of U.S. 30-S

A wooden sign, nearly ruined by neglect and vandals, was placed in Weber Canyon by the Utah State Road Comission, and it tells the story of the Weber River entrance into the Valley of the Great Salt Lake, which was used extensively before the Reed-Donner party in 1846 and the Mormons in 1847 forced a road through the mountains west of Henefer; the Weber River runs north and west.

WEBER CANYON EXPLORERS TRAIL

Weber Canyon has always been the most important gateway into the Valley of the Great Salt Lake. Through its portals passed many important persons of early Utah history, including John Weber, a trapper who is supposed to have been killed by Indians in the winter of 1828–29, Etienne Provot, who in 1824 reported one of the first explorations of the river, and Osborne Russell who reports expeditions in 1841.

In 1846 California emigrants took the first wagons down the Canyon [some words unclear here]. . . .

In this vicinity the Donner-Reed party of 1846, which later met a tragic fate on the east slope of the Sierras in California, turned southwest and blazed a trail through the mountains to the Salt Lake Valley. The trail was followed by the Mormon Pioneers (1847), the California "Gold Rush" Emigrants (1849–50), the Mormon Handcart Pioneers (1856), Overland Stage (1856), and the Pony Express (1860–61).

123   Mormon Pioneer Trail Historic Site / Marker

Main Street, Henefer, Summit County

At present-day Henefer the old trail crosses the Weber River and goes west up Main Canyon. On the west side of Main Street in Henefer is a 1931 marker put up by the Utah Pioneer Trails and Landmarks Association.

"MORMON" PIONEER TRAIL

Under the leadership of BRIGHAM YOUNG the "MORMON" PIONEERS exploring their way to the valley of THE GREAT SALT LAKE passed here JULY 15 to 20, 1847. Orson Pratt's advance company reached here July 15, others following at intervals. The rear company, including Brigham Young, who was ill with mountain fever, encamped near here July 20.

The trail turned to the left at this point to avoid Weber Canyon, then impassable to wagon trains, ascending Henefer Creek to its head and passing thence into East Canyon approximately along the route now traversed by the highway.

Old Pioneer Trail of 1847 Marker   124

1.6 miles southwest of Henefer, in Summit County, west of Highway 65

Near Henefer you can see a curious marker, topped by a beehive sitting on the Mormon Standard Works (the Bible, Book of Mormon, Doctrine and Covenants, and the Pearl of Great Price). It used to be in Echo Canyon, but was moved because of the widening of roads. It was erected in 1927 by the Summit Stake and relocated to its current location in 1967.

1847–1927

INTERSECTION OF OLD PIONEER TRAIL OF 1847

AND THE LINCOLN HIGHWAY

The Pioneers passed this spot July 13, 1847 under the leadership of Brigham Young. This monument erected by the members of the Church of Jesus Christ of Later Day Saints of Summit Stake to the memory of the Mormon Pioneers July 13, 1927.

About 2 miles beyond this marker is the vandalized marker to the Lone Tree Campsite.

Hogsback Summit Historic Site / Marker / Ruts   125

6 miles west of Henefer, in Summit County, in Main Canyon, in sec. 25, T3N, R3E

Six miles west of Henefer on Highway 65 the crest of Main Canyon is reached. Here emigrants got their first disheartening sight of the mountains they still had to pass through to reach their new Zion. Some

Mormon Explorer Scouts placed a marker to the right on the road. (The marker has since been vandalized and is now a pile of stone.) Also near the marker are the best of the very few remaining Mormon trail ruts in Utah. They can be seen just to the north of the crest of the summit and extend several hundred yards.

HOGSBACK SUMMIT

Here, on July 19, 1847, the main party of Mormon Pioneers caught their first, discouraging view of the rugged mountains ahead. On this summit a guidepost was erected which read ". . . 80 miles to Fort Bridger [,]" one hundred yards northwest are deep tracks worn by the passage of thousands of wagons.

126   Broad Hollow Historic Site / Marker

7 miles west of Henefer, in Morgan County,
in sec. 1, T2N, R3E

About 1 mile beyond the Hogsback is the historic site known as Broad Hollow. There are two plaques on this stone marker erected by the Boy Scouts of Syracuse, Utah.

> Unable to fight the brush and willows down Dixie Hollow [just beyond the Hogsback], the Donner Party turned right up Broad Hollow at this spot, climbed to a broad bench above, dropping down to East Canyon just above the present dam site. Mormon Pioneers followed, as did many others, until a road was cut through the hollow years later.

The second plaque reads:

> In memory of the sick detachment of the U.S. Mormon Battalion which traveled north from Pueblo, Colorado to Ft. Laramie, Wyoming and then followed the Pioneer Trail into the Salt Lake Valley, July, 1847.

127   Little Emigration Canyon Historic Site

17 miles southwest of Henefer, in Morgan County,
in sec. 14, T1N, R3E

Approximately 8 miles southwest of the Hogsback marker on Highway 65 (1 mile beyond a bridge over Canyon Creek), a dirt road goes left

A wagon train in Echo Canyon, Utah, in the 1860s. Photo courtesy of the Union Pacific Railroad. *See trail IX*.

A typical Mormon emigrant company in Echo Canyon circa 1867. Photo courtesy of the Church of Jesus Christ of Latter-day Saints. *See trail IX*.

Cache Cave was an important rendezvous site, with walls covered by emigrant names. It is on private land and rarely seen by visitors. *See trail IX, 120.*

The Mormons dedicated a trail monument on July 30, 1927, in Echo Canyon at a spot near Castle Rock. *See trail IX, 120.* Due to road construction, the monument was moved in 1967 to a spot west of Henefer, where it can still be seen. Photo courtesy of the Church of Jesus Christ of Latter-day Saints. *See trail IX, 124.*

(south) for 3 miles to Mormon Flat and the presently unmarked mouth of Little Emigration Canyon. (About 1 mile down this dirt road is the vandalized Camp Clayton marker.) On elevated ground at the canyon mouth, across unbridged Canyon Creek, can be seen some stone breastworks from the Mormon War of 1857–58 (see this trail, 121).

The old trail goes 4 miles up this gentle canyon, which makes a pleasant hike, to the crest of Big Mountain (see this trail, 128).

Big Mountain Historic Site/Marker   128

19 miles southwest of Henefer, Summit County

The crest of Big Mountain is one of the most important of all historic sites on Mormon trails. From here the Pioneers of 1847 and many thousands of subsequent emigrants caught their first view of their new home—the Valley of the Great Salt Lake. It was also here, and not where the This is the Place monument is today (see this trail, 131) that Brigham Young uttered his famous words "This is the Place, drive on."

BIG MOUNTAIN

On 19 July 1847, Scouts Orson Pratt and John Brown climbed the mountain and became the first Latter-day Saints to see the Salt Lake Valley. Due to illness, the pioneer camp had divided into three small companies. On 23 July, the last party, led by Brigham Young, reached the Big Mountain. By this time, most of the first companies were already in the valley and planting crops. Mormons were not the first immigrant group to use this route into the Salt Lake Valley. The ill-fated Donner Party blazed the original Mormon trail one year earlier. They spent thirteen days cutting the trail from present-day Henefer into the Valley.

That delay proved disastrous later on when the party was caught in a severe winter storm in the Sierra Nevada Mountains. The Mormons traveled the same distance in only six days. Until 1861, this trail was also the route of California gold seekers, Overland Stage, Pony Express, original telegraph line, and other Mormon immigrant companies, after which Parley's Canyon was used.

This monument, erected and dedicated 25 August 1984, by South Davis Chapter, Sons of Utah Pioneers, replaces the original [stolen] plaque erected 23 July 1933, by Utah Pioneer Trails and Landmarks Association and the Vanguard Association of the Salt Lake Council, Boy Scouts of America.

129   Last Camp Historic Site / Marker

*In Emigration Canyon, Salt Lake County,
in sec. 33, T1N, R2E*

About 6 miles beyond the summit of Big Mountain is a wye intersection. Turn right and follow Highway 65 up and over Little Mountain into Emigration Canyon. Approximately 2.5 miles from the intersection, to the north of the road is the Last Camp marker, erected by the Daughters of Utah Pioneers in 1936. Before turning off Highway 65, however, you might wish to continue down Highway 65 for 1.25 miles to the place where the Pioneers crossed Little Mountain. There appear to be some trail ruts looking up the mountain to your right. To continue, return to the wye and drive over Little Mountain.

LAST CAMP SITE

July 23, 1847.

This monument was erected July 23, 1933 [1936] and marks the last camp site of the first company of Mormon Pioneers, under the leadership of President Brigham Young, before entering the Salt Lake Valley, July 24, 1847.

130   Donner Hill Historic Site / Marker

*Near mouth of Emigration Canyon,
east of Salt Lake City*

A marker (about 3 miles from the Last Camp site) to the left of Highway 65 commemorates an unnecessary and tragic decision by the Donner party in 1846. Pulling this steep hill southwest of the marker jaded their draft animals and contributed to their later troubles across the Great Salt Lake Desert and in the Sierra Nevada—costing the lives of forty-four of their party of eighty-nine. The marker was erected by some Mormon Explorer Scouts.

DONNER HILL

After 4½ miles of fighting boulders and brush along stream-bed, Donner Party gave up here, and on August 22, 1846, climbed steep hill to south-west. A survivor wrote "we doubled teams, almost every yoke in the train (of 23 wagons) being required to pull up each wagon."

Mormon pioneers a year later built road through to mouth of canyon with four hours labor.

This Is The Place Monument 131

On Highway 65 in Pioneer Monument State Park, Salt Lake City

In 1922, during the Pioneer Diamond Jubilee, a small monument was placed here reading "THIS IS THE PLACE / BRIGHAM YOUNG / July 24, 1847." At that time sixty-six original Pioneers were present. In 1947, to better commemorate the centennial of the arrival of the Pioneers into the Valley of the Great Salt Lake, a more suitable monument was built here in the Pioneer Monument State Park, east of the Salt Lake City on Highway 65. This massive memorial, sixty-feet high and eighty-four-feet wide, designed by Mahroni M. Young, features fifteen plaques and many statues and bas-reliefs honoring not only the Mormon Pioneers but also others who explored the Great Basin, including the native Indians, Fathers Dominquez and Esclanate, and the Reed-Donner party. There is also a visitors' center and an outdoor museum in this 500-acre park, which constitutes the end of the famous Mormon Pioneer Trail from Nauvoo, Illinois, to Salt Lake City, Utah.

X

The 1850 Golden Road in Utah
(see map 7)

The Golden Road, perhaps so named because many gold seekers used it, was developed because one Pioneer of 1847, Parley P. Pratt, wanted to find an easier way into the Salt Lake Valley; he started looking in 1848 and had it worked out by 1850. This 42-mile long variant of the Pioneer Trail of 1847 runs from the mouth of Echo Canyon south along Weber River (the Pioneers turned north along this river), then west down what is known today as Parley's Canyon into the valley. By 1862 the Golden Road had become the preferred emigrant route into the valley until the coming of the railroad in 1869.

Except for one 6-mile section, this old trail is very easy to follow today simply by driving along I-80. Several markers commemorate this old route.

132   Old Fort and Hoyt Grist Mill Historic Site / Marker

Mormon Chapel grounds, Hoytsville, Summit County
From I-80 at the mouth of Echo Canyon turn south on road 333 towards Coalville, where the old trail crossed the Weber River. Modern travelers should go 3 miles farther south to Hoytsville. There, on the grounds of the Mormon Chapel, is the old fort and Hoyt grist mill marker erected by the Daughters of Utah Pioneers in 1938.

OLD FORT AND HOYT GRIST MILL

This monument is near the site of the old fort, 300 ft. so. west of here. It was on old Emigrant Trail. Route also used by Overland stage and part of Johnston's Army going east in 1861, to participate in the Civil War. The fort was built during the Black Hawk [Indian] War in 1866. On the advice of President Brigham Young to Bishop Winters, 25 families moved their log cabins there. Centrally located, it provided protection for families, livestock, and grist mill. The mill was the first in this county. Built in 1862 by Samuel P. Hoyt.

Continue south from Hoytsville 3 more miles, where the road (variously known as 333 and 188) crosses I-80 and the Weber River on the way to Wanship.

Wanship Station Historic Site / Marker   133

1 mile east of Wanship, Summit County

A short distance beyond the Weber River crossing, to the west of the road, is a 1951 marker erected by the Daughters of Utah Pioneers commemorating a stagecoach station on this old trail.

WANSHIP STATION

In 1861, Aaron Daniels built a stage coach station here to change horses and as an overnight stop for the Overland coach from the east to Salt Lake City. Gilmer and Salsbury operated the line until 1870. In 1869, Kimball Brothers stage between Echo and S.L.C. also used the station in 1870. It became the Moorehouse family home; and in 1877, the Andrew Peterson family made it into a rooming and boarding house. Later, it served as a grainary [*sic*] and in 1912, it was torn down.

From Wanship take U.S. 189 south 4 miles along the Rockport Reservoir to Three Mile Canyon. Here a gravel road leads up the canyon about 1 mile to an active mine. To follow the trail beyond the mine it is necessary to hike 6 miles up and over the canyon to the Silver Creek Juction on I-80.

Otherwise return to I-80 at Wanship and follow it 8 miles south to the Silver Creek Juction (of U.S. 40 and I-80). Intersect the Golden Road here and follow it to Salt Lake City.

About 2.2 miles beyond the Silver Creek Junction is the Kimball Junction of I-80 and Highway 60. Just to the north of this junction is a famous Overland Stage station.

134   Overland Stage Station Historic Site (P)

At Kimball Junction, Summit County

The Kimball Junction Overland Stage station is the best-preserved station of its kind. It was built originally as a hotel by William Kimball, son of Mormon apostle Heber C. Kimball, and it became a stage station in 1862. It is on private ground, but permission can be gained to visit the area. The building is not open to the public, and it should be but is not on the National Register of Historic Sites. To visit the site continue west on I-80 for 2 miles, exit north to an access road, and return 2 miles east.

Return to I-80 and continue west for 14 miles to the mouth of Parley's Canyon, where there is a splendid view of the Mormon Zion. From this canyon I-80 continues to follow the old trail closely for 4 miles down through Parley's Hollow, by the country club, and Sugar House Park to the original terminus near Twenty-first South and Eleventh East in Salt Lake City.

135   The Golden Pass Road Marker

On the grounds of the Sons of Utah Pioneers (SUP) Headquarters, 3301 East 2920 South, Salt Lake City

The SUP headquarters is located to view most of the route of the Golden Road from the mouth of Parley's Canyon to its original terminus near Twenty-first South and Eleventh East in Salt Lake City. This marker was erected by the SUP in 1984 and is placed on the headquarters balcony.

THE GOLDEN PASS ROAD—PARLEY'S CANYON

"Travel the Golden Pass, open July fourth. Immigrants coming into the valley may now avoid the difficult route over Big and Little Mountains by taking the new route. Several thousand dollars have been spent by the proprietor to make the new road possible." Parley P. Pratt Proprietor. So ran an advertisement in the third issue of the *Desert News* of June 29, 1850.

Parley P. Pratt cut the road through Parley's Canyon in 1849–50. The beginning (or end) of the road was about Twenty-First South and Eleventh East and thence east to what was called Dell Fork. To defray the cost of construction a toll or passage was charged—"$.75 for a two-horse outfit, ten cents for each additional pack or saddle animal, and sheep a mere cent per head." The road was described as poor with rocks and stumps. However it opened up the hollow and canyon to industry, farming and recreation.

From this vantage point, the toll gate was located on the north side of Parley's Creek directly below the SUP building. Portions of the old dirt road can still be seen going up the hollow around Suicide Rock to the awesome magnitude of Parley's Canyon.

At sunset one may get a spectacular view of the aureate colored face of the canyon walls from which was derived the original name, "Golden Pass Road."

Pratt sold the road to finance his mission to Chile. By 1862 the Golden Pass Road, an approximately forty-two mile long immigrant trail from Sugarhouse east to Silver Creek Junction, through Coalville to the mouth of Echo Canyon was the preferred route into the Valley. The Overland Stage began using it that year.

There are three other markers at SUP headquarters. One, shaped like the state of Utah, honors those pioneers who established industry in Parley's Canyon. This marker is outside on the grounds. There are two other markers on the headquarters' balcony, commemorating Early Pioneer Mills and the Big Canyon Tannery.

XI

The Oregon-California Trail
in Missouri and Kansas
(see maps 8 and 9)

The Oregon-California Trail is the most famous and the best marked of all historic trails in the United States. There are more than fifty markers in Jefferson County, Nebraska, alone, all marked on county maps for those who wish to find them. This trail is currently being marked with the brown-and-white National Park Service signs (see trail I, 3). They read OREGON TRAIL NATIONAL HISTORIC TRAIL and are placed every 10 miles on all-weather roads that either follow or approximate the old trail.

Between 1841 and the coming of the railroad in 1869, over 250,000 emigrants, including many Mormons beginning in 1846, followed all or parts of this 2,000-mile long Main Street of the Old West. This trail south of the Platte (the famous Mormon Trail was north of the Platte as far as Fort Laramie) had two advantages for Mormons and for other emigrants whose jumping-off places for the Far West were already south of the Platte: it was a little shorter, and it avoided the difficult crossings of the Elkhorn and Loup rivers as well as the crossing of the Platte River at Fort Laramie.

Following my coverage of the Oregon-California Trail proper, I also consider several feeder trails to and variants of the main trail. (Visualize the Oregon Trail between the Missouri River and Wyoming as a long rope frayed at both ends and in between.) These feeders and variants include the Mormon Grove Trail, also called the Fort Leavenworth–Military Road; the St. Joseph Trail; the Ox-Bow Trail and its two variants; the Republican River Trail; the Nebraska City Cutoff; and the Mitchell Pass variant; as well as what some call the Overland–Bridger Pass Trail.

Missouri

Independence, Court House Square Historic Site / Marker
136

Independence, Jackson County (see map 8)

Independence likes to consider itself the "Queen City of the Trails," meaning the Oregon, the California, and the Santa Fe. Two markers on Court House Square, of which one is repeated here (see the dedication to this book), deal with the trails.

Here / The Oregon Trail / Began
This monument honors / the pioneer spirit of / those coura-
geous men / and women, who by / their heroic trek across /
the continent established / homes and civilization / in the
Far Northwest. / Erected in 1948 / by order of the / Jackson
County Court.

Strictly speaking, however, the Oregon Trail did not start until near Gardner, Kansas, some forty-five miles southwest of Independence. This is because the Oregon Trail followed the older Santa Fe Trail that far. Since it has become traditional to present the Oregon Trail as commencing in Independence, so shall I. To make matters just a bit more confusing, there are several variants of the Oregon Trail (Santa Fe Trail) between Independence and Gardner. In this book I will present only the main route via present-day Minor Park (see trail XXVII).

The next important site along the Oregon-California and Sante Fe trails in the Independence area is Old Westport. To reach it from the Independence Court House, take Noland Road south to I-70 and go west about 8 miles to The Paseo, exit south to Thirty-ninth Street, turn west to Broadway, and turn south right into Old Westport.

Westport Landing / Westport Historic Sites
137

Near A.S.B. Bridge, Kansas City (see map 8)

Many Mormons disembarked from Missouri River boats at the Westport Landing, where they picked up the Oregon Trail. This was their principle jumping-off place in 1854. The site today is an industrial area on the north bank of the Missouri River between the Broadway and A.S.B.

bridges. From the landing emigrants went due south 4 miles to their staging ground at the town of Westport. Today Old Westport is a registered historic district and several buildings date from the nineteenth century; one from the 1850s is alleged to have been associated with Jim Bridger. The area is an interesting place to visit because of its historic value.

From Westport, emigrants followed some variant of the Oregon–Santa Fe Trail southwest via Overland to near Gardner, Kansas.

Kansas

138   Oregon Trail–Santa Fe Trail Junction Historic Site

Southwest of Gardner, Johnson County,
in sec. 27, T14S, R22E (see map 8)

The junction of the Oregon and Santa Fe trails, one could argue, is the real beginning of the Oregon Trail. An information sign is located 1.8 miles southwest of Gardner in a pull-off on the west side of U.S. 56. Near here the Oregon Trail turns due west and the Santa Fe Trail continues southwest (for the text of this marker, see trail XXIV, 233).

139   Blue Mound Historic Site

Near Lawrence, Douglas County,
in sec. 22, T13S, R20E (see map 8)

Little is left of the Oregon Trail between this junction and Topeka. Blue Mound, 18 miles west of Gardner, however, qualifies as an important landmark in eastern Kansas. It rises dramatically and offers a good view from the top. To reach it, go due west 6 miles from the center of Gardner on U.S. 56, keep going west even when U.S. 56 turns southwest, then turn north on a gravel road 6 miles to Hesper. From that defunct town proceed west 5.8 miles to Blue Mound, situated north of the road.

140   St. Mary's Mission Historic Area

St. Marys, Pottawattomie County (see map 9)

West of Blue Mound the sprawl of Lawrence and Topeka has long since destroyed all remnants of the trail. One may as well leave the area as

Wagon train on Main Street of Salt Lake City in 1867. Photo courtesy of the Union Pacific Railroad. *See trail X, 135.*

Old Salt Lake House (hotel), about 1870, was the end of the trail for many travelers to Salt Lake City. Photo courtesy of the Union Pacific Railroad. *See trail X, 135.*

The Oregon Trail began for many in Independence, Missouri, a popular jumping-off point for the westward migration. Photo by Violet Kimball. *See trail XI, 136.*

quickly as possible. Go west 4.2 miles to U.S. 59, then north to I-70, then west into Topeka and pick up Alt. U.S. 75 north to U.S. 24. Proceed 24 miles west to St. Marys where a Catholic mission to the Pottawattamie Indians was established in 1848.

Here the traveler can pick up the old trail by following a twisting, gravel road northwest. The gravel road parallels U.S. 24 north of the railroad tracks. In 9 miles you come to the Red Vermillion Creek crossing and the historic Vieux Cemetery with an information sign. This is also the site of a trail cemetery and the largest elm tree in the world. From there continue west 4 miles on a dirt road (which has four turns in it) to Highway 99 north of Louisville.

Scott Spring Historic Site / Ruts / Marker   141

Just south of Westmoreland, Pottawattomie County
(see map 9)

Take Highway 99 north from Louisville for 11 miles to Westmoreland. About 1 mile before reaching Westmoreland, watch for a Kansas historical marker commemorating this famous spring in a pullout west of the road. Turn around, go 0.3 of a mile back on Highway 99, turn around again and watch for hard-to-see, but impressive trail ruts east of the road.

THE CALIFORNIA-OREGON TRAIL

From the 1830's to the 1870's, the 2,000 mile road connecting Missouri river towns with California and Oregon was America's greatest transcontinental highway. Several routes led west from the river, converging into one trail by the time the Fort Kearny (Neb.) vicinity was reached. One of them began near present Kansas City and passed this point, crossing Rock Creek not far from the highway bridge.

Here a great campground was located because of the several fine springs in the vicinity. Scott Spring, 180 yards north, still offers the "delicious cold water" mentioned by one traveler in 1846. Local legend says that at times the whole of what is now the Westmoreland townsite was covered by the camps of travelers, their wagons and cattle. Nearby are the graves of several pioneers who died on the trail. One unidentified grave is located just north of the spring.

From a point about two miles south of this marker, Kansas highway 99 follows the trail to Westmoreland; in places ruts of the old trail may still be seen from the modern traveler's car window.

142   Alcove Springs Historic Site (P)

6 miles south of Marysville, Marshall County,
in sec. 32, T3S, R7E (see map 9)

Alcove Springs was one of the most romantic and frequently mentioned sites along the Oregon Trail in present-day Kansas. Unfortunately, because of littering and vandalism, the site (on private ground) is locked up and permission must be secured to visit it. A Marshall County map is helpful even to locate its general area. Most travelers are advised to take Highway 99 for 24 miles north of Westmoreland to Highway 9. Then turn west 13 miles to U.S. 77. In a roadside park south of this intersection is a Kansas historical marker.

ALCOVE SPRINGS & THE OREGON TRAIL

Six miles northwest is Alcove Springs, named in 1846 by appreciative travelers on the Oregon Trail who carved the name on the surrounding rocks and trees. One described the Springs as "a beautiful cascade of water . . . altogether one of the most romantic spots I ever saw."

This country was well-known to early-day traders and "mountain men" as well as to later travelers to the Far West. John C. Fremont and his 1842 exploring expedition bivouacked at the Springs, and Marcus Whitman, with a thousand emigrants to Oregon, stopped there in 1843. Utah-bound Mormons and California-bound goldseekers followed, for only a short distance above was Independence Crossing, the famous ford across the Big Blue river. The Donner party, most of whom later froze or starved in the Sierras, buried its first member, Sarah Keyes, near the Springs in 1846. . . .

Going 4 miles north on U.S. 77, you will be about 1 mile due east of Alcove Springs.

Next travel to Marysville, 6 miles north of Alcove Springs on U.S. 77. The main Oregon Trail did not pass this way, but two feeder trails did.

One was known as the Fort Leavenworth–Military Road; in Mormon history, it is known as the Mormon Grove Trail. The other feeder was known as the St. Joseph Road (see trail XVI, 164). For the location and text of this marker at Marysville, see trail XIV, 163. Those travelers wishing to follow only the main branch of the Oregon Trail should now skip to site 145. The curious, however, may wish to check out nearby Mormon Spring and some Mormon graves.

Mormon Spring Historic Site / Marker (P)   143

3 miles south of Washington, Washington County,
in sec. 23, T3S, R3E (see map 9)

There is a tradition that some Mormons passed this way and carved their names into a rock cliff on Ash Creek, hence its name Mormon Spring. Names can still be seen on the low cliff, but none are old. The site is on private ground, permission is required, and the spring is hard to find.

I have never found any Mormon reference to Mormons traveling through this part of Kansas, which is 15 miles west of the main Oregon Trail, and it is difficult to explain how this spring acquired its name. The name possibly comes from the fact that one little known variant of the Oregon Trail turns southwest at Topeka, toward Eskridge, Wabaunsee County, then northwest across the Kansas River near Junction City and Fort Riley, then follows the Big Blue River north to near Waterville, Marshall County; this trail runs northwest across Washington County via the Mormon Spring, finally rejoining the main Oregon Trail along the Little Blue River in Jefferson County, Nebraska (see map 3).

On U.S. 36 in a roadside park 1 mile east of Washington is a Kansas historical marker.

> Several historic trails crossed this area. Seven miles west the Fort Riley–Fort Kearny road ran diagonally south-to-north and four miles southwest, on Ash Creek, was a favorite Mormon campground. The Parallel Road from Atchison to the Colorado gold fields, much used about 1860, was three miles south. The main stem of the Oregon-California Trail, formed by the junction of roads from St. Joseph and Independence near the east border of Washington County, clipped the northeast corner as it ran toward the Platte River in Nebraska. . . .

144 Mormon Graves (P)

East of Scandia, Republic County (see map 9)

About 40 miles due west of the Mormon Spring on U.S. 36 is Scandia (short for Scandinavia), on the Republican River. Although I know of no Mormon reference to the Scandia area, there is a persistent rumor that Mormons are buried on a hill just east of Scandia. Locals have shown me the hill, but no one can point to any specific grave site.

For various reasons, some Mormon emigrants apparently left the main Oregon Trail at Topeka, proceeded west via Eskridge, Wabaunsee County, and the Kansas River, to pick up the Republican River Trail (also known as the Fort Riley to Fort Laramie Trail, which commenced use at Fort Riley, Kansas, in 1856 and follows the north bank of the Republican River via Clay Center, Clyde, and Scandia, eventually intersecting the Lodgepole Creek Trail in Wyoming, see trail XIX). At the point where the trail turns west near the Nebraska state line, the Mormons probably rejoined the main Oregon Trail some 20 miles to the north along the Little Blue River in Nuckolls County, Nebraska.

145 The Hollenberg Ranch Pony Express Station Historic Site / Marker

1 mile east of Hanover, Washington County (see map 9)

The Hollenberg Ranch Pony Express Station building is directly on the old trail and is unique in that it is the only extant example of an unmoved, unrestored Pony Express station. If you are lucky, the little museum here will be open. There is a Kansas historical marker here.

Beginning in 1860 the Pony Express operated like a giant relay race between the Missouri river and the Pacific coast. Along the Oregon trail, through Forts Laramie and Bridger, around the Great Salt Lake, riders carried the mail through a wilderness infested with hostile tribes. Their mounts were Indian ponies, nearly 500 altogether, kept in relay stations 15 miles apart. At each station two minutes was allowed for transferring saddlebags to a fresh pony. Every few stations a new rider took over. Day and night, summer and winter, over sunbaked plains and icy mountain trails, the schedule was maintained. When the transcontinental telegraph line replaced the express, ponies and riders had made the remarkable record of 18 months with only one mail lost. The Hollenberg or Cottonwood Ranch House four miles north, built in 1857, is said to be the only original and unaltered Pony Express station. It is now owned by the state.

Proceed 12 miles west of Marysville on U.S. 36 to Highway 15E. (To the south of this intersection is another Kansas historical marker concerning this station.) Turn north 3.5 miles to Hanover. The station is one-half mile north and 1 mile east. Seven miles north of here the Oregon Trail enters Nebraska.

XII

The Oregon-California Trail in Nebraska
(see maps 3 and 4)

The main Oregon trail enters Nebraska near present-day Steele City, Jefferson County, and follows the Little Blue River as closely as possible nearly to Fort Kearny. Then it turns west along the Platte and North Platte rivers for a total distance of about 400 miles to Wyoming. As in Kansas, many Mormons used all or parts of the Oregon Trail in Nebraska.

The state of Nebraska marks its historic trails better than any other state in the union. As already noted, there are more than fifty markers in Jefferson County alone. Most of these markers are scattered along section-line roads, and county maps are necessary to locate them.

146   Rock Creek Station Site Historical Park / Ruts / Markers

3 miles northeast of Endicott, Jefferson County
At the Rock Creek Station State Historical Park are some impressive trail ruts that many Mormon wagons helped deepen. To reach the area just follow the signs out of Endicott for 3 miles to the northeast. Near the entrance to the park are Oregon Trail and Pony Express markers. A new visitors' center is now open here and must be visited. Also noteworthy is a nature walk through the main historic area. Along this path are identified growing specimens of about thirty-five native prairie grasses, flowers, and other plants.

147   Susan Hail Grave Historic Site / Marker

West of Hastings, Adams County, in sec. 18, T8N, R12W
From Rock Creek Station to the Susan Hail grave, the Oregon Trail follows the north bank of the Little Blue River closely. Today this route can only be approximated by zigzagging around on section-line roads, using maps of Jefferson, Thayer, Nuckolls, Clay, and Adams counties.

Travelers are advised to take any combination of roads that suits their fancy to Hastings, in Adams County. From there take U.S. 6 for 14 miles west to county road S-1A, then go 3.5 miles north to Kenesaw. From the center of that town go 1.5 miles north, 0.5 mile east, then 1 mile north. Then turn west 3.5 miles to the grave of Susan Hail.

This grave is reminiscent of the Rebecca Winters grave on the Mormon Trail of 1847 (see trail VI, 70 and 71). Both women died in 1852, probably from cholera, and both graves were later discovered by surveyors. A Nebraska historical marker is on a section-line road one-half mile west and a little to the north.

SUSAN O. HAIL GRAVE

To overland emigrants the rigors of the trail began with the "Coast of Nebraska," the ridge of sandhills separating the Platte Valley from the open prairie behind it. Thousands of emigrants passed this way during the peak emigration years of the 1850s. Hundreds died of disease, principally of Asiatic cholera. It is believed that a grave near here is of one such victim. Of all those who died, only a few graves are known. On August 3, 1859, a surveyor noted the grave and its marker:

Memory of Susan O. Hail

of Lafayette County, Missouri

Who died June 2, 1852

Age 34 Yrs. 5 months, 12 days

That marker, since destroyed, was of polished workmanship, unlike most trail gravestones. It is said her husband returned to Missouri, had the stone made, and brought it to this spot on the prairie. The people of the area have cared for the grave and the land was purchased in 1958 and presented to Adams County by the Federated Woman's Club of Kenesaw and the Adams County Historical Society.

Fort Kearny State Historic Park 148

Near Kearney, Kearney County, in sec. 22, T8N, R15W

To reach Fort Kearny go 16 miles west from the Hail grave on a county road that makes three right-angle turns; be sure always to turn west and south.

This is the second Fort Kearny, honoring Stephen Watts Kearny; the first fort was on the Missouri River at Nebraska City (see trail XVII). This second fort was built in 1848 and lasted until 1871, providing protection for thousands on the Oregon-California Trail. It was also the site of a Pony Express and a telegraph station. Near here four famous western trails converge. On the south bank there are the Ox-Bow Trail (see trails XV and XVI), the Nebraska City Cutoff (see trail XVII), and the Oregon Trail. On the north bank is the Mormon Trail (see trails VI and VII). Near this fort is the Council Bluffs Road Crossing and for many years emigrants crossed here from the Oregon Trail to the Mormon Trail and vice versa.

Emigrants rested themselves and their draft animals here, bought supplies, received and sent mail and telegrams, and got medical attention. They also tried to avoid the temptations of nearby Dobytown and the Dirty Woman Ranch, both of which catered to the baser desires of soldiers, freighters, and emigrants. There is a Nebraska historical marker about Dobytown at a point 9 miles west of the fort site.

The old fort site is worth visiting, with its excellent visitors' center, historic markers, and information signs.

149   Historic Platte Valley Marker

West side of U.S. 183, Phelps County

To reach another Nebraska historical marker, drive about 20 miles west of Fort Kearny. (About 4 miles from the fort, the road turns 1 mile north before continuing west.) The marker is 0.3 mile south on the west side of U.S. 183.

HISTORIC PLATTE VALLEY

Through this valley passed the Oregon Trail, highway for early explorers, fur traders, California-bound gold seekers, freighters, and brave pioneers seeking new homes in the West. Traffic was especially heavy from 1843 to 1866. At times as many as 800 wagons passed this point daily, heading both directions.

The Pony Express passed through the valley, followed by the first telegraph lines. This was also the military road to western destinations. Beginning in 1847, the Mormons broke a new trail [not really] on the north side of the Platte.

Indian raids by the Sioux and Cheyenne were severe in the 1860's, and several attacks occurred near here. During the Plum Creek Massacre a few miles west, wagons were burned and several people killed or captured.

Huge herds of buffalo once roamed these prairies, often stopping traffic on the trail. In the 1870's hunters slaughtered them by the thousands.

Today the Platte Valley is one of the nation's rich agricultural areas, disproving the opinion of early explorers who saw the Great Plains only as the Great American Desert.

The Plum Creek Massacre referred to took place on August 7, 1864, as part of the general uprising of the Sioux, Cheyenne, and Arapahoe that extended from Julesburg, Colorado, along the Platte Valley to Plum Creek and the Little Blue River. A small cemetery and information sign concerning this massacre is located 13 miles west of U.S. 183 on the same county road you have been on since leaving Fort Kearny. (Seven miles west the blacktop jogs 1 mile to the north and then continues west.)

West of this marker the Oregon Trail is difficult even to approximate for some 85 miles, all the way to Fort McPherson. The best you can do is zigzag around on section-line roads using maps of Phelps, Dawson, and Lincoln counties. The easiest way to continue is to take U.S. 183 to I-80, then west to the Maxwell exit. En route, two information signs can be seen. For the text of these markers, see trail VI, 61 and 62.

Cottonwood Spring Historic Site   150

*Fort McPherson National Cemetery,
near Maxwell, Lincoln County*

Proceed south 2 miles from the Maxwell exit off I-80. In a rest area east of Fort McPherson, off I-80, is an information marker concerning the old fort. Fort McPherson, founded in 1863, would have been unknown to most Mormon emigrants, but they would have been aware of the spring located here. The fort site today is a national cemetery and resting place for hundred of soldiers from various western military posts. From here it is rather easy to visit another famous landmark on the old trail, the Sioux Lookout (see this trail, 151).

151   Sioux Lookout Historic Site / Marker (removed)

Near North Platte, Lincoln County,
in sec. 33, T13N, R29W

A few miles west of Fort McPherson is a famous landmark, known as the Sioux Lookout because it is assumed that the Sioux utilized this highest point in Lincoln County to scout the area, especially the Oregon Trail. Unfortunately, the road makes six changes of direction in these 7 miles. Stay on the blacktop and keep heading west. The lookout is about one-half mile to the southwest of the road. A climb by trail to its summit is worth the effort. The ascent up the front face is difficult; try the path around the back side. A larger-than-life concrete Sioux warrior is at the top. Unfortunately, it and its base have weathered badly.

On the road at the beginning of the trail up to the lookout is the site of a damaged Nebraska historical marker. After this marker was vandalized, it was removed to the grounds of the Lincoln County Historical Society at North Platte (see trail VII, 64). Some efforts have been made to have the sign restored to its original site.

SIOUX LOOKOUT

Sioux Lookout, the highest point in Lincoln County, was a prominent landmark on the overland trails. From its lofty summit, the development of the West unfolded before the eyes of the Sioux and other Indians. Trappers and traders came by here in 1813, the first wagon train in 1830, and the first missionary in 1834. In 1836 Narcissa Whitman and Eliza Spalding became the first white women to travel the trail. During the Indian War of 1864–1865, its prominence gave a clear view of troop and Indian movements below.

Gold seekers enroute to California, homesteaders seeking free land in the West and a religious people seeking a haven in Utah—all are part of the history of this valley. Here echoed the hooves of the Pony Express. From 1840 to 1866 some 2,500,000 [really 250,000] people traveled the valley, engraving into the sod a wide, deep trail. Indians called the route "The Great Medicine Road of the Whites."

In 1869 the transcontinental railroad was completed, ending much of the trail travel. Yet even today, the valley with its ribbons of concrete remains the Great Platte River Road to the West.

O'Fallons Bluffs Historic Site / Ruts / Markers   152

In the rest area on the eastbound lane of I-80,
5 miles west of the Hershey exit in Lincoln County

Some famous ruts can be seen about 30 miles west of the Sioux Lookout in an I-80 rest area; they are some of the most dramatic ruts in Nebraska, and some Mormons helped deepen them.

With the help of a a Lincoln County map you can zigzag to the area, more or less following the Oregon Trail, but most travelers are advised to follow the blacktop road from the lookout into North Platte and then take I-80 for 20 miles west to the Sutherland exit and return 2 miles east on I-80 to the rest area, where a Nebraska historical marker tells the story of the area.

Crossing the Overland Trail

Beneath this platform, evidence of the great westward migration still remains. These shallow depressions were once deep ruts created by thousands of hooves, shoes and wheels. The Overland Trail is often visualized as a single, well-defined roadway. However, except in narrow spots such as this, the actual route through the Platte Valley during any given year varied considerably, depending upon such factors as soil conditions and the availability of grass for the animals. Traveling an average of fifteen to twenty miles a day in various conveyances, the emigrants spent from four to six months on the trail during the long trek from the Missouri River to Oregon or California. At best, the journey was arduous, often marked only by the dusty monotony of daily routine. At other times, disease and Indian attacks were very real dangers, and the number of fresh graves along the road bore testimony to the sacrifices made by many pioneers. Some emigrants were better equipped than others, some were wiser, some were simply luckier; but all suffered weariness, hardship and danger. However, as the many overland diaries and letters testify, this was a great human experience, one which was vital to the settlement of the west.

The next important historic site on the Oregon Trail is 50 miles west near Brule, Keith County. Near there is the Lower California Crossing of the Platte and the impressive trail ruts at California Hill. En route travelers should visit the rest area in the westbound lane of I-80, 1 mile west of the Keystone exit (or exit 133). Here are three important Nebraska State Historical Society information signs—about Ash Hollow, the town of Ogallala, and the Platte Valley; Court House Rock and Chimney Rock; and Scotts Bluffs.

153   The Lower California Crossing and the California Hill Ruts (P)

West of Brule, Keith County, in secs. 13 and 14, T13N, R41W

At California Hill you can see some of the most dramatic trail ruts on this old trail. They are on private ground, and permission is required to visit them. Also watch out for a temperamental bull.

Until 1859 most emigrants, including all the Mormons who came this way, crossed the South Platte at what came to be known as the Lower California Crossing (to distinguish it from the Upper California Crossing, which came into use that year—see trail XVIII, 183). After crossing the South Platte the trail proceeds via California Hill and Ash Hollow to the south bank of the North Platte.

To reach these ruts take U.S. 30 for 4 miles west from Brule to a trail marker north of the road near a house. The ruts are 0.5 mile west and 0.8 mile north of this marker.

154   Ash Hollow State Historical Park / Museum / Ruts / Markers

On U.S. 26 near Lewellen, Garden County

From California Hill the Oregon Trail angles northwest some 17 miles to Ash Hollow. To reach Ash Hollow from California Hill return to U.S. 30, go west 5 miles, turn north 10 miles on a blacktop to U.S. 26, and turn left 4 miles to the hollow. In 1847 some Mormon Pioneers crossed the North Platte River to investigate Ash Hollow so they could better position themselves in relation to their maps (see trail VI, 65).

There are many things to see in this important park. The excellent visitors' center refers to the Mormon use of the area; the angry gash on the east side of Windlass Hill is made of eroded trail ruts; there are also some well-preserved ruts extending southwest from the brow of Windlass Hill. Walking these ruts you will pass a granite Oregon Trail marker.

In the park near the visitors' center is a Nebraska historical marker.

Ash Hollow

Ash Hollow was famous on the Oregon Trail. A branch of the trail ran northwestward from the Lower California Crossing of the South Platte River a few miles west of Brule, and descended here into the North Platte Valley. The hollow, named for a growth of ash trees, was entered by Windlass Hill to the south. Wagons had to be eased down its steep slope by ropes.

Ash Hollow with its water, wood and grass was a welcome relief after the arduous trip from the South Platte and the travelers usually stopped for a period of rest and refitting. An abandoned trappers cabin served as an unofficial post office where letters were deposited to be carried to the "States" by Eastbound travelers. The graves of Rachel Pattison and other emigrants are in the nearby cemetery.

In 1855 a significant fight, commonly called the Battle of Ash Hollow, occurred at Blue Water Creek northwest of here. General Harney's forces sent out to chastize the Indians after the Grattan Massacre of 1854 here attacked Little Thunder's band of Brule Sioux while the Indians were attempting to parley, killed a large number and captured the rest of the band.

From Ash Hollow the Oregon Trail proceeds northwest along the south bank of the North Platte, within sight of the Mormon Trail on the north bank, some 56 miles to present-day Bridgeport. Any attempt to do this today requires Garden and Morrill County maps. Travelers are advised to cross the river to Lewellen and take U.S. 26 to Bridgeport. In

Bridgeport there is a marker about the Oregon and Mormon Trails (see trail VI, 68 and 69).

155   Paul C. Henderson Memorial Marker

Cemetery, Bridgeport, Morrill County

In the Bridgeport Cemetery, located on the Oregon Trail, is the grave of Paul Henderson, the great Oregon Trail expert. In his honor the Oregon-California Trails Association erected a suitable monument in this cemetery.

In Memory of/ Paul C. Henderson/ of Bridgeport, Nebraska/ 1895–1979/ Honored historian and map maker/ of the Oregon-California Trail/ which passed this way/ with his wife, Helen, he explored/ and recorded trail remains and shared his knowledge/ with a legion of trail followers

Dedicated August 17, 1985/ Oregon-California/ Trails Association.

156   Chimney Rock State Historic Site / Markers

Near Bayard, Morrill County, in sec. 17, T20N, R52W

From Bridgeport west to the Wyoming state line travelers can stay pretty close to the old trail. Twelve miles west of Bridgeport on U.S. 26 and Highway 92 is located the most famous of all landmarks on the Oregon and Mormon trails—Chimney Rock. This tusk of soft brule clay has eroded considerably since trail days, but it is still an impressive sight. To the left of Highway 92 is a pull-off with a small museum and several markers, including a Nebraska historical marker. Chimney Rock itself is 1 mile due south on a county road.

Chimney Rock

No single sight along the Oregon and Mormon trails attracted more attention than Chimney Rock, 1½ miles south of here. Rising 475 feet above the Platte River, the natural tower served as a beacon to pioneers.

Tired travelers described it in many ways during the three to four days it was part of their horizon. For some it created mirage-like effects. Some judged it to be 50 feet high, others 700. Many tried to scale it, but none succeeded. Later it became the setting for pony express, telegraph, and stage stations.

Many pioneers speculated on the fragility of the tower. They feared the Brule clay with interlayers of volcanic ash and Arikaree sandstone would soon crumble to nothingness on the prairie.

Hundred of names were scratched on the soft base. The names have washed away, but the tower remains, as do references in faded diaries that attest Chimney Rock was one of the celebrated landmarks on the pioneer trunklines to the west.

Visitors can drive down the dirt road 1 mile to the south where there is a parking area and where a path leads to the rock itself. The ambitious can clamber partway up its base, but watch out for snakes. Near the southeast base of the rock is another, seldom seen, marker placed there in 1940 by the Nebraska State Historical Society.

> CHIMNEY ROCK / site of this historic landmark on the old / Oregon Trail, Mormon Trail, Deadwood Trail, / and Pony Express. Given to the public by / Roszel Frank Durnal / (1860–1939) / to whose memory / this monument is gratefully dedicated / with recognition of participation / of his wife, Mary B. Durnal, and cordial / cooperation of his family.

Scotts Bluff National Monument and Museum   157

Just south of Scottsbluff, Scotts Bluff County

From Chimney Rock Highway 92 follows the old trail fairly closely until you come to the famous formations known as Scotts Bluffs, located today in the Scotts Bluff National Monument. In this parklike area you can drive to the top of the bluffs, visit the Oregon Trail Museum, and hike the Mitchell Pass trail ruts (see trail XVIII, 186). The museum features a Mormon exhibit and a full-size handcart. Heber C. Kimball, who came this way in 1848, was probably the first Mormon to do so.

From here emigrants on the Oregon Trail first entered Wyoming via Robidoux Pass, later via Mitchell Pass.

158   ## Robidoux Pass Historic Area

Southwest of Scotts Bluff National Monument

The crest of the famous, rather shallow Robidoux Pass is about 11 miles west of the monument over a very pretty drive. Return to the entrance to the monument, to the intersection of Highway 92 and the main road to Scottsbluff, turn 1.5 miles south to a sign directing you west to the pass. Eight miles from this sign is the site of a famous trading post and several emigrant graves. (New landowners have removed signs and eliminated access to the ruts in this pass.) From the top of the pass emigrants got their first sight of Laramie Peak, their first view of the western mountains. By road the pass is about 17 miles from the Wyoming state line. From the crest drive west 5 miles, past Signal Butte to the south, to a blacktop road. Turn north 7.5 miles, then 5 miles west to Lyman, which is right on the state line. To continue following the Oregon Trail turn now to trail XIII.

XIII

The Oregon-California Trail in Wyoming to Fort Bridger

(see map 5)

Here I treat only the 30 miles of the Oregon Trail from the Wyoming state line to Fort Laramie. The Oregon Trail beyond Fort Laramie to Fort Bridger has already been presented (see trail VIII).

Grattan Massacre (Mormon Cow) Historic Site / Marker   159

Near Lingle, Goshen County, in sec. 15, T25N, R63W

In 1854 a stray cow belonging to some Danish Mormon emigrants was butchered by Sioux Indians. This led to military action in which a party of white soldiers was killed. Evidence suggests the attack was totally unnecessary. (It is called a "massacre" because the whites lost.) This engagement broke the peace of the Horse Creek Treaty of 1851 and led to the Sioux Wars, which lasted off and on until 1890.

With a Goshen County map (sheet 2) you can zigzag around to this site, more or less following the Oregon Trail, from Lyman, Nebraska (see trail XII, 158). The recommended way, however, is to drive by various roads from the Robidoux Pass area and Lyman to Lingle on U.S. 26, then take a blacktop county road (off U.S. 26) due west 3 miles to the Historical Landmark Commission marker on the north side of the road.

> SIOUX INDIANS MASSACRED / 29 SOLDIERS WITH THEIR / OFFICER, / BREVET 2ND LT. L. GRATTAN. / ON AUG. 19, 1854. SITE IS / ½ MILE NORTH-WEST
>
> An Indian killed a cow from a Mormon caravan. The detachment of soldiers was sent to receive the offender. In the ensuing fight all soldiers and the chief of the Brulés Sioux, Martoh-Ioway, were killed.

With a Goshen County map (sheet 2) you can reach the Fort Laramie historic site from the Grattan marker following the old trail. The recommended way is to return to Lingle and take U.S. 26 west 12 miles. For a description of Fort Laramie, see trail VIII, 82.

XIV

Oregon-California Trail Variant:
The Fort Leavenworth–Military Road
in Kansas

(see maps 8 and 9)

The main Oregon Trail has a system of feeder trails and variants, five of which are important to this study. After Fort Kearny was established in 1848 on the Oregon Trail, a military road between Fort Leavenworth and Fort Kearny was necessary. It passed 9 miles west of Atchison to a junction with the Oregon Trail near Marysville, Kansas, about 130 miles west of Fort Leavenworth (see this trail, 164).

160   Fort Leavenworth Historic Site/Marker

Fort Leavenworth, Leavenworth County (see map 8)
During the mid-1850s Mormons sometimes took off for the Far West from Fort Leavenworth. (In fact Mormons had been at Fort Leavenworth as early as 1846, see trail XXIV, 232.) Fort Leavenworth, founded in 1827, is the oldest fort west of the Mississippi River continually in service. (I was inducted here during World War II.) The fort is worth a visit. Especially interesting is the Post Museum built around the theme The Army's Role in Opening the West. A Kansas historical marker tells the story of the famous fort.

HISTORIC FORT LEAVENWORTH
Long before white men settled Kansas, traffic over the Santa Fe trail was so heavy that troops were detailed to protect it from the Indians. Fort Leavenworth, established in 1827 by Col. Henry Leavenworth, was for thirty years the chief base of operations on the Indian frontier. In 1839, Col. S. W. Kearny marched against the Cherokees with the largest U.S. mounted force yet assembled: ten companies of dragoons. In 1846, Col. A. W. Doniphan set out on his Mexican expedition,

throughout the war with Mexico the Fort was the outfitting post for the Army of the West. During the 1850's, wagon teams hauled supplies over the Santa Fe, Oregon and other trails to all forts, posts and military camps of the West, some as far as the Pacific.

When Kansas territory was organized in 1854, Gov. Andrew Reeder set up executive offices at Fort Leavenworth. In 1881, General William T. Sherman established the school which later became the Command and General Staff College, the highest tactical school in the Army educational system combining all arms and services. A 1926 graduate, with highest honors in his class, was Maj. Dwight D. Eisenhower.

Atchison Historic Site / Marker   161

1 mile west on U.S. 59, Atchison,
Atchison County (see map 9)

From Fort Leavenworth the old trail can be followed rather closely along U.S. 73, crossing Salt Creek, mentioned in many old trail journals. At the Leavenworth County line is a Kansas historical marker very much like the one at Fort Leavenworth.

Continue north to Atchison. One mile west of town center on U.S. 59 is another Kansas historical marker.

On July 4, 1804, Lewis and Clark exploring the new Louisiana Purchase, camped near this site. Fifty years later the town was founded by Proslavery men and named for Sen. D. R. Atchison. The Squatter Sovereign, Atchison's first newspaper, was an early advocate of violence again abolition. Here Pardee Butler, Free-State preacher, was set adrift on a river raft and on his return was tarred and feathered. Here Abraham Lincoln in 1859 "auditioned" his famous Cooper Union address— unmentioned by the local newspapers.

During the heyday of river steamboating in the '50's Atchison became an outfitting depot for emigrant and freighting trains to Utah and the Pacific Coast, a supply base for the Pikes Peak gold rush, and in the early 1860's a starting point for the Pony Express and the Overland Stage lines. In this pioneer center of transportation the Santa Fe railway was organized in 1860, modestly named the Atchison & Topeka.

Between 1847 and the completion of the transcontinental railroad of 1869, the Mormons developed several points of departure to the Far West. Most of the outfitting stations were located along the Missouri River, including Weston and St. Joseph, Missouri and Fort Leavenworth and Atchison, Kansas. During 1855–56 the preferred placed was Mormon Grove, Kansas, four miles west of Atchison, an important Missouri River port city.

Along the Missouri, the Mormons always established themselves several miles from the large port cities in order to be at a safe distance from the assorted evils found there and to have space to build tent cities and to utilize grazing lands for their animals. Some Mormons also sought work grading Second Street and helping build homes in Atchison.

In February 1865 Milo Andrus, a St. Louis-based Mormon emigration agent, selected Mormon Grove as a point of departure for the Saints. It was located on the prairie at the head of Deer Creek, an excellent camping place with water, wood, and range for stock, and also close enough to Atchison for supplies. It was used mainly by Danish, Scottish, and Welsh emigrants.

From Mormon Grove the Mormons traveled on the Fort Leavenworth–Military Road. (In Mormon history this trail is known as the Mormon Grove Trail.) Later the Pony Express Trail from St. Joseph followed much the same route during its short life from 1860 to 1861.

The first Mormons arrived at Mormon Grove from Europe via New Orleans and St. Louis in April 1855 and soon fenced 160 acres and planted twenty. Between June 7 and August 3, 1855, eight companies—totaling 2,041 people and 337 wagons—left for Zion. A group of fifteen members remained behind to await the next year's emigrants. During the 1856 season, however, only one company of ninety-seven Saints left from Mormon Grove. Most emigrants were then going directly by rail from the East Coast to Florence, Nebraska. After 1856 a few Mormons formed a congregation in Atchison, and non-Mormon squatters took over the grove campsite.

Mormon Grove Campsite   162
Historic Site / Marker / Cemetery (P)

Near Atchison, Atchison County,
in sec. 5, T6S, R20E (see map 9)

Mormons disembarked at the foot of Atchison Street and proceeded 4 miles due west to their campsite. To reach this campsite, start at the foot of Atchison Street, follow U.S. 73 approximately 4.5 miles west, and turn south on a section-line road. The first farmhouse on the west side is the home of Floyd Armstrong, on whose land the old cemetery, all that is left of Mormon Grove today, is located. Permission and directions must be secured. At least fifty Mormons were buried there, but no trace of the graves remains. Most died of the great river scourge of the day, cholera.

This historic cemetery, about 150 feet long (north to south) and 35 feet wide (east to west), is located near the southwest corner of the Armstrong farm, or at the southwest corner of the S½ of the NE¼ of sec. 5, T6S, R20E, just north of new U.S. 73 from Atchison. An easier way to view the general area is to drive along new U.S. 73 about 4.5 miles west of Atchison. Here, to the south and immediately east of a section-line road, is a pull-off with a 1986 Kansas historical marker. The old cemetery site is directly northwest about one-half mile. The campsite itself was probably south of U.S. 73.

MORMON GROVE THE CITY THAT DISAPPEARED

Near here, located in a grove of young hickory trees, was an important rallying point in 1855 and 1856 for members of The Church of Jesus Christ of Latter-day Saints (Mormon), then emigrating to the Rocky Mountains.

The campground, really a temporary village covering about 150 acres, consisted of the grove, a large pasture fenced by native sod and a ditch, and a burial ground located on the elevated ridge between the grove and the farm. Though one or two permanent structures were erected, most residents lived in tents, wagon boxes or make-shift dwellings.

During the peak year of emigration at Mormon Grove in 1855, nearly 2,000 Latter-day Saints with 337 wagons left here for the Salt Lake Valley. It was also a tragic year for the

U.S., British, and European Mormons at the little waystation, many dying in a cholera epidemic.

In 1856, Iowa City, Iowa, became the major jump-off point for Latter-day Saint westward travel, and Mormon Grove became a forgotten gathering place.

There is little to see along this old military road between Mormon Grove and its intersection with the main Oregon Trail near Marysville, 85 miles westward, except for stagecoach station sites at Lancaster, Kennekuk, Capinoma, and Richmond and Pony Express station sites at Kennekuk, Seneca, and Marysville. You may as well check them out; you have to go this way anyway.

From the Mormon Grove campsite return to U.S. 73, go west 6 miles to Lancaster (founded directly on the old trail in 1860), where there is nothing to see. Continue on U.S. 73 for 16 miles to Horton, Brown County; Kennekuk is near there. Go south on U.S. 159 about 0.3 mile to a gravel road going east, follow this 1.5 miles to a group of houses—this is all that is left of Kennekuk. Return to Horton and take Highway 20 west for 11 miles to U.S. 75, go north for 3 miles to a section-line road, go west for 1 mile, north for 0.5 mile, then west for 3 miles to some houses—all there is to present-day Granada, Nemaha County. Capinoma, the stage stop, was just to the north.

One mile west of Granada is a blacktop. Take it due north for 8.5 miles to U.S. 36, then go west for 13 miles to Seneca, Nemaha County, where there is a red granite Pony Express marker on Main Street. Richmond, an old stage stop, was 3 miles north of Seneca, but there is nothing left there.

163 Marysville Historic Site / Marker

Marysville, Marshall County (see map 9)

From Seneca go 30 miles west on U.S. 36 to Marysville, where the old trail crossed the Blue River approximately where U.S. 36 does today. On U.S. 36 east of Marysville and on the north of the road there is a Kansas State Historical Society information sign about two fords on the Big Blue River. The first ford mentioned is the one near Alcove Springs (see trail XI, 142). The second is this one, 1 mile west of Marysville, both of which were used by emigrant companies over the years. (There is also a Pony Express station to be seen in Marysville.)

MARYSVILLE

A few miles below Marysville was the famous ford on the Oregon Trail known as the Independence, Mormon or California crossing. There thousands of covered wagons with settlers bound for Oregon, Mormons for Utah and gold seekers for California crossed the Big Blue River. In 1849 a ferry and trading post was established at the ford by Frank J. Marshall, despite constant danger from Indians. Two years later the military road between Forts Leavenworth and Kearny crossed the river at the site of present Marysville, one mile west. Marshall built another ferry and for years handled an immense traffic. He gave the name of his wife, Mary, to the town that developed here and his own name to Marshall County of which it is the county seat. In 1860 Marysville became a station on the Pony Express. For most of the 1860's it was an important stopping place for coaches of the great Overland Stage Line.

Junction for Leavenworth Road and Oregon Trail Marker

164

West of Marysville, in Washington County, in sec. 24, T2S, R5E (see map 9)

To reach the approximate site of this junction go 9 miles west from Marysville on U.S. 36 to the Washington County line, turn north on a section-line road for 2 miles; at the southwest corner of that intersection, nearly hidden by cedar trees, is an old marker to this junction. The actual junction was 0.2 mile northwest. To follow this trail farther, see trail XI, 145 and trail XII.

Junction/ of/ Oregon Trail/ with/ Overland Trail/ 60 rods [990 feet] N W.

Note on the St. Joseph Trail (see map 9): During the 1850s an alternative route from the Missouri River to the Oregon Trail proper evolved. It extended due west from the important river port of St. Joseph, Missouri, and in Kansas became known as the St. Joseph Trail, extending some 100 miles from the river to its junction with the Fort Leavenworth–Military Road at Marysville, Kansas (see this trail, 163), and the Oregon Trail a few miles further west (this trail, 164).

This trail passed through Elwood, Wathena, Troy, and Highland in Doniphan County; Hiawatha and Fairview in Brown County; and Sabetha and Bern, in Nemaha County. Modern U.S. 36 approximates part of this trail between Elwood and Fairview. I have heard rumors of trail ruts north of Sabetha. According to documents in the Kansas State Historical Society, some Mormons took this trail in the 1850s.

165   Elwood Historic Site / Marker

Elwood, Doniphan County

There is a Kansas historical marker east of the city limits of Elwood (north of U.S. 36) telling its history.

Elwood

Elwood, first called Roseport, was established in 1856. In its heyday scores of river steamboats unloaded passengers and freight at its wharves and every 15 minutes ferryboats crossed to the Missouri rival, St. Joseph. During the 1850's thousands of emigrants outfitted here for Oregon and California. Late in 1859, Abraham Lincoln, seeking the Republican nomination, here first set foot in Kansas and spoke in the three story Great Western Hotel. Elwood was the first Kansas station on the Pony Express between Missouri and California. Construction of the first railroad west of the Missouri River began here in 1859. On April 23, 1860, the first locomotive, "The Albany," was ferried over and pulled up the bank by hand. Elwood's ambitions for greatness were thwarted, not by St. Joe, but by the river which underminded the banks and washed much of the town away.

166   Troy Historic Site / Marker

Troy, Doniphan County

There is a Kansas historical marker two miles east of Troy, south of U.S. 36, telling its history.

Troy

Two miles west is Troy. . . . In 1860–61 the city was a station on the alternate route of the Pony Express which began at St. Joseph. . . .

XV

Oregon-California Trail Variant:
The Ox-Bow Trail in Nebraska

(see map 3)

Of all the early emigrant trails, surely one of the least known is the Ox-Bow Trail variant of the Oregon-California Trail, which came into existence in 1849 to connect Fort Kearny on the Platte with the Missouri River. It starts at present Nebraska City and generally follows the Platte in a huge bow 210 miles to Fort Kearny. This trail lasted until 1859, at which time it was replaced by the shorter and more direct Nebraska City Cutoff (see trail XVII).

The Ox-Bow Trail also has two variants (see trail XVI). Along all variants of the Ox-Bow, I have located only a few markers: two refer to Utah and the Mormons, one in Nebraska City and one in Ashland (see 167 and 168 below).

This trail developed during of the building of Old Fort Kearny on the Missouri River in 1846. Even though this fort was abandoned when New Fort Kearny was built on the Platte in 1848, the site developed as the eastern terminus of a military and freight trail to New Fort Kearny and Nebraska City was founded at the old fort site in 1854.

Nebraska City Historic Site / Markers   167

Nebraska City, Otoe County

There are several historical markers that are of interest in Nebraska City. One is a plaque set in a boulder at the intersection of Central Avenue and Fifth Street, briefly telling the history of this branch of the Oregon Trail.

OFFICIAL OREGON TRAIL MARKER

On this road now Central Avenue / was the overland branch / of the Oregon Trail, 1849 / From the steamboat landing thousands started westward / to Pikes Peak, Salt Lake, / California and Oregon.

Just east of this marker is a partial replica of Old Fort Kearny built in 1838 and a Nebraska historical marker.

Old Fort Kearny

The increase in overland travel after 1843 resulted in the establishment of a chain of military posts across the West to protect the travelers.

Early in 1846 the first of these posts was built by the army in this location near the mouth of Table Creek, an area explored and selected by Colonel Stephen W. Kearny. A two-story blockhouse was erected about ½ block west of here. Subsequently, a number of log huts were built as temporary shelter for the troops.

The Table Creek site was not on the main route of overland traffic and relatively few emigrants passed the fort. The War Department, in 1847, selected a new site on the widely used main branch of the Oregon Trail. Fort Childs, later designated as Fort Kearny, was built near the Platte River in present day Kearney County.

The Old Fort Kearny area remained important as the beginning of a secondary route of the Oregon Trail, the Nebraska City–Fort Kearny Cut-off. Nebraska City was started at the site.

There is also a DAR trail marker on the Courthouse Square:

Site of/ The Overland Trail/ 1846–66/ Otoe Chapter/ D.A.R./ 1911 A.D.

You should not miss the Nebraska historical marker concerning Nebraska City that is one-half mile northwest of downtown Nebraska City on U.S. 73–75.

Nebraska City

Permanent settlement in this area dates from 1846, with the establishment of old Fort Kearny on Table Creek. Nebraska City, founded in 1854, became an important depot for military and commercial freighting. Pioneer businessmen, such as S. F. Nuckolls, sought to attract freighting interests.

In 1858, Alexander Majors, of Russell, Majors and Waddell, decided to use Nebraska City as the point of departure for shipping military supplies west.

Steamboats brought rapidly growing volumes of goods and numbers of people heading west. In 1865, it was reported that up to 40 million pounds of freight were shipped west from Nebraska City.

In 1860, a direct road to new Fort Kearny on the Platte was completed, shortening that journey by forty miles. Known as the Nebraska City–Fort Kearny Cut-off and also as the Great Central Route, the trail was originally marked by a furrow ploughed in the sod. Another name for this trail, the Steam Wagon Road, resulted from an 1862 experiment. That summer, a locomotive-like "Steam Wagon" attempted to haul cargo to Denver, but soon broke down and was abandoned.

With the building of the Union Pacific Railroad, overland freighting from Nebraska City soon gave way to railroad shipment.

For more information on the Steam Wagon Road, see trail XVII, 173.

Ashland Historical Site / Markers   168

Ashland, Saunders County

From Nebraska City, the Ox-Bow Trail goes northeast close to where the "Steam Wagon" marker is located off Highway 2 (see trail XVII, 173), crossing Weeping Water Creek near today's community of Weeping Water, Cass County, and running north through Murdock to the famous fording place on Salt Creek at Ashland.

To approximate this route take Highway 2 for 18 miles west from Nebraska City to Syracuse (see trail XVII, 175), then north on Highway 1, then 5.5 miles west to Murdock, where you will cross the old trail. Continue west 5.5 miles to a blacktop road going north. Follow that road north for 7 miles to its intersection with U.S. 6, which is 2.2 miles from Ashland.

The Nebraska historical marker is located on the grounds of the waterworks on U.S. 6.

THE OX-BOW TRAIL

This marker sits astride the Ox-Bow Trail, also known as the Old Fort Kearny or Nebraska City Road. Beginning in the 1840's, this route carried thousands of emigrants and millions of pounds of freight destined for the settlements, mining camps, or military posts of the West. Many travelers were Mormons bound for the Great Salt Lake Valley. The trail, looping north to the Platte from such Missouri River towns as Plattsmouth and Nebraska City, resembled an Ox-Bow, after which it was named. Just west of here was an important ford across Salt Creek, where limestone ledges form a natural low-water bridge. Travel over the trail declined in the mid-1860's with the development of more direct routes from the Missouri to the Central Platte Valley. . . .

Nearby, also on U.S. 6, there is a marker which reads:

This Native Stone / Marks the / Old Government Trail / Erected by the / Ashland Woman's Club / 1847–1927.

169   Bethlehem Ferry Historic Site

Plattsmouth, Cass County

Emigrants picked up the Ox-Bow Trail by going west to Ashland from the Bethlehem Ferry on the Missouri River. This ferry was very popular with Mormons because it was only about 25 miles south of Winter Quarters and Council Bluffs, and during high water, travel through this ferry enabled them to avoid the Elkhorn River and Loup River crossings. It was used between 1849 and 1867, especially during the high-water years of 1850–52.

The site of the old ferry at Plattsmouth can be reached conveniently by going straight west from Glenwood, Iowa (see trail XXIV, 227) or 25 miles north of Nebraska City on U.S. 75. I know of no historic markers in this area.

From the ferry, emigrants reached Ashland by one of two routes: one was straight west via present Louisville, which is 16 miles west on Highway 66. Because of the river and I-80, there is no easy way to get the remaining 14 miles to Ashland from Louisville. (It can be done, but you need a Cass County map or ask locally for directions. Otherwise, a long detour to the north is necessary. It is better to ask locally for directions.) The other route from Plattsmouth to Ashland was to the south via Murdock (see this trail, 168).

Ox-Bow Trail Marker 170

West of Osceola, Polk County, in sec. 18, T14N, R4W
From Ashland the main Ox-Bow Trail meanders northwest through Saunders and Butler counties to the Platte, then west along the Platte to Fort Kearny. There is nothing left of this trail other than some probable traces, and there is only one historical marker along it. This one is located 14 miles due west of Osceola on Highway 92, north of the road where in the 1860s there was a small settlement.

Overland Trail / Erected by / Elijah Cove Chapter / Daughters of the / American Revolution / Stromsburg, Neb. / 1916.

XVI

Oregon-California Trail Variant:
The Ox-Bow Trail Variants
in Nebraska
(see map 3)

In an effort to find a better way to New Fort Kearny, two variants of the Ox-Bow Trail eventually came into existence. One took travelers to the north of the main trail via present Wahoo, Saunders County (and therefore might properly be termed the Wahoo variant), to Linwood, Butler County. There is nothing left of the old trail, but there are two Nebraska historical markers along this route.

171   ### Ox-Bow Trail Marker

Courthouse Square, Wahoo, Saunders County
This marker, facing U.S. 77, briefly mentions the fact that "The Ox-Bow Trail, the Primary Route from Nebraska City to Fort Kearny in 1856–59, passed through this area." Just 5 miles south of Wahoo on Highway 77 is what is left of tiny Swedeburg, which sits right on the old trail, and 1.5 miles farther south is the Pioneer State Wayside Park apparently commemorating the old Ox-Bow Trail.

172   ### Shinn's Ferry Marker

6 miles north of David City, Butler County
The second historical marker is north of David City, at the junction of Highways 15 and 64. It commemorates the historic Shinn's Ferry across the Platte River from 1859 to 1872. The ferry itself, until displaced by a bridge, was 6 miles northeast, near where the Schuyler bridge is today. Most likely some Mormons used this ferry for a variety of reasons.

The second variant of the Ox-Bow Trail has come to be called the Mormon Variant, for reasons unknown to me. This variant left the main trail near Elmwood and rejoined the main trail near Brainard, Butler County, going via Waverly, Lancaster County. There is nothing left of this old trail, and there are no historical markers along it.

In the general area of the Shinn's Ferry marker, all variants of the Ox-Bow Trail join and follow the south bank of the Platte River, joining the main Oregon Trail 10 miles east of Fort Kearny, in sec. 18, T8N, R13W (see trail XII, 148).

XVII

Oregon-California Trail Variant: The Nebraska City Cutoff Trail in Nebraska

(see map 3)

Another early trail, one largely forgotten today, was the once famous Nebraska City Cutoff used by emigrants during the years 1864–66. Running 169 miles west from Nebraska City on the Missouri River to New Fort Kearny on the Platte River, it is the last of the great overland trails developed before the transcontinental railroad was finished in 1869.

Nebraska City became the great eastern terminus of the famous shipping firm of Russell, Majors, and Waddell. In 1865 alone more than 44 million pounds of freight left Nebraska City on this trail. In 1859 it replaced the older and longer Ox-Bow Trail (see trails XV and XVI), which stayed close to the Platte. The cutoff, largely a military supply route, went straight west, saving some 40 miles or about 20 percent of the old travel distance. It lasted until 1866, when it began to give way to the Union Pacific Railroad.

This shortcut is often referred to as the Great Central Route and also as the Steam Wagon Road, because of an 1862 experiment with a tractorlike steam wagon to haul freight. On its first trial, however, the machine broke down a few miles out of Nebraska City and the whole project was abandoned.

The Mormons used this area as a jumping-off place for the Far West for two reasons: because railroads from the East stopped at St. Joseph, Missouri, to the south and because there were Indian troubles during the mid-1860s along the main Oregon-Mormon Trail. Indian problems developed during the Civil War as many regular troops were withdrawn from military posts on the plains. The Sioux, Cheyenne, Arapahoe, and other tribes seized this opportunity to try to drive emigrants off their ancestral lands by attacking ranches and stage stations. The area was also favored by Mormons coming up the Missouri from the railhead at

St. Joseph. They preferred to stop at nearby Wyoming, founded in 1855 as a satellite river port to Nebraska City. Situated 45 miles below Florence and Council Bluffs and 6 miles north of Nebraska City, Wyoming provided the Mormons with more open area for their staging ground and was well removed from the rough elements of Nebraska City.

Wyoming and the cutoff were important to the Mormons not only for transporting emigrants to the West, but also for freighting. The church's economic policy was to make Utah as economically independent as possible, and to this end home manufacture was promoted and the importation of goods from the East was discouraged. But because the Mormons could not produce all that they needed, many items had to be imported. To control as much of this trade as possible, the same oxteam trains sent to pick up emigrants at Wyoming also carried freight back to Utah. The various agents tried to send 1,000 pounds of such goods with each wagon.

There are no specific markers commemorating the Mormon use of this trail. From the markers and information signs that are found along this trail, however, some understanding of the emigrant experience may be gained. The trail starts in Nebraska City, on the the Missouri River. Nebraska City was founded in 1854 on the site of Old Fort Kearny (see XV, 167 for a discussion of historical markers in Nebraska City.) West of Nebraska City near Arbor Lodge State Historical Park is a street named the Steam Wagon Road commemorating that failed experiment of 1862. Actually the scheme might have worked, but the Civil War prevented the inventor, Joseph R. Brown, from securing spare parts. The engine remained on the prairie, and by the time the war was over the machinery had rusted beyond repair.

Steam Wagon Road Marker   173

West of Nebraska City, Otoe County, in sec. 3, T8N, R13E
Four miles west of Nebraska City on Highway 2 take a section-line road north 1 mile to another section-line road. To the north of this intersection, near a farmhouse, is a marker commemorating the site where the famous steam wagon, a steam-powered tractor to haul freight wagons, broke down.

Mormon emigrants coming from Wyoming, Nebraska (see this trail, 174), would have passed near this marker.

The first self propelled / road vehicle used west of / the Missouri River was in- / vented by Joseph R. Brown of / Minnesota. It was made in New York and arrived in / Nebraska City by steamboat / July 2, 1862. It started on its / first trip from Nebr. City to / Denver July 12, 1862. Was dis- / abled and abandoned 1000 feet / northwest of this spot.

174   Wyoming Historic Site

Wyoming, Otoe County, in sec. 7, T9N, R14E

A defunct river port, Wyoming is 6 miles north of Nebraska City on Highway 75. The unmarked road leading east to the site is exactly 1.5 miles south of the Cass County line.

To reach the old site, take Highway 75 north from Nebraska City about 6.5 miles from the courthouse. There are no road signs, so watch for a county road going west to Otoe; 2.5 miles north of this is a dirt road leading 1.5 miles east to the river. The course of the river has changed since 1866, and the present shoreline is nearly one-half mile east of where it was when the Mormons were there. (The current hamlet of Wyoming, 2.5 miles southeast of old Wyoming, has nothing to do with the older community of the Mormons.) There is nothing at all to be seen here today.

The first Mormon emigrant agent in Wyoming, Joseph W. Young, arrived there on May 14, 1864. The first company of 973 Mormon emigrants arrived in Wyoming one month later, on June 15, 1864, and like almost all the others, traveled west to Salt Lake City in church mule and oxteam wagon trains dispatched from Utah for that purpose.

Twenty-two organized Mormon emigrant companies left Wyoming during its three-year service. It is estimated that these companies comprised a total of about sixty-five hundred Danish, Swiss, German, Dutch, French, Norwegian, Swedish, and English converts. In addition, probably some five hundred or more Mormons traveled as individuals with other, non-Mormon freight trains from nearby Nebraska City.

Although the Mormons built a few buildings in Wyoming, nothing is left of them today. Old Wyoming, which for a season was later renamed Dresden, was finally doomed when the Missouri, Chicago, Burlington, and Quincy Railroad bypassed it. In fact, nothing at all of the old city is left except a forgotten and unmarked graveyard located about 1 mile north of the old town center. Perhaps as many as a hundred individuals are buried there, including some Mormons. Most deaths resulted from measles, scarlet fever, cholera, and diarrhea. In 1926 some effort was made to erect a suitable marker near this old cemetery, but regrettably, nothing was accomplished.

Little Nemaha Crossing Historic Site / Marker   175

Syracuse, Otoe County

From Wyoming the Mormons passed near the Steam Wagon Road marker (see this trail, 173) and picked up the Nebraska City Cutoff proper somewhere west of Nebraska City along today's Highway 2, crossing the Little Nemaha River at Syracuse, then known as Nursery Hill. The area was considered the first day's stage stop out of Nebraska City.

At Syracuse, 17 miles west of Nebraska City on Highway 2, is a Nebraska historical marker near the hospital west of the city, south of Highway 2.

NEBRASKA CITY–FORT KEARNY CUTOFF

You are near the old freighting trail of the Nebraska City–Fort Kearny Cutoff. Prior to railroad construction, thousands of wagons transported supplies to Fort Kearny and other military posts throughout the West. The Mormon War and the discovery of gold in the Colorado and Montana territories brought Nebraska City to prominence as a freighting center between 1858–1865. Early freighters used the Ox-Bow Trail which looped north to the Platte Valley. It provided abundant grass and water but it was overly long and often plagued by muddy lowlands.

Because of the competition from other Missouri River towns, Nebraska City freighters sought a more direct route. The Nebraska City–Fort Kearny Cutoff, proposed in 1858 and first traveled in 1860, was first marked by a plowed furrow. Bridges and improvements were added when the famed Steam Wagon was brought to Nebraska Territory in 1862. This experiment failed, but the route continued to be called the "Steam Wagon Road."

Freighting from Nebraska City peaked in 1865 when over 44 million pounds of supplies were shipped. Construction of the Union Pacific soon marked the end of major freighting on this road.

176 Second Night's Stop Historic Site / Marker

South of Palmyra, Otoe County

Near the Little Nemaha River, 1 mile south of Palmyra to the east of Highway 802, is a 1933 Oregon Trail marker "commemorating the Second Night's Stop" on this trail out of Nebraska City and Wyoming.

There used to be a DAR trail marker 8 miles south of Lincoln, Nebraska, on Highway 77, but it no longer exists. Highway 2 intersects I-80 near Lincoln, and travelers are advised to take I-80 because most of the remaining historic sites are near it. Furthermore, from here to York County the old trail is hard to follow. Generally, it stays close to the West Fork of the Big Blue River and Beaver Creek.

177 Crossing of the Big Blue Historic Markers

Rest area in the eastbound lane of I-80,
0.7 mile west of the Milford, Seward County, exit

Here is a Nebraska historical marker commemorating the crossing of the Big Blue River. The actual crossing was about 9 miles downstream (to the south) in sec. 32, T9N, R4E (see this trail, 178).

THE BIG BLUE RIVER

Except for the occasional Indian or white hunting parties, the scenic valley of The Big Blue River was seldom visited prior to 1860. The establishment of the Nebraska City—Fort Kearny Cut-off in 1861 brought through the region thousands of overland freighting outfits which crossed the river several miles south of here. Road ranches were soon established along the trail and scattered settlements soon thereafter. The Big Blue River played an important role in the history of the area and provided the necessary power for numerous watermills used in grinding grain for pioneer farmers. . . .

Modern travelers can catch a glimpse of what overland travel must have been like at restored Fort Kearny, Nebraska, which was an important stop along the Oregon-California Trail. *See trail XII, 148*.

The author standing in the trail ruts at California Hill, in Keith County, Nebraska. *See trail XII, 153*.

Chimney Rock, west of Bridgeport, Nebraska, was the most famous landmark along the old trails. You can still climb it, as the emigrants did, as you explore the trails they traveled.
See trail XII, 156.

The Grattan Massacre of 1854 began when an Indian killed a cow belonging to some Mormon emigrants. Although the emigrants continued west unmolested, soldiers sent out to apprehend the Indians were killed, setting a new pattern of violence in relations between Indians and whites in the West. *See trail XIII, 159.*

Mitchell Pass was opened as a route through Scotts Bluffs in 1851. These ruts are accessible on a path from the museum at Scotts Bluff National Monument. *See trail XVIII, 186.*

This marker is situated atop cliffs near a crossing site of the Platte River. It is difficult to reach, but worth the trip for the view and a glimpse of emigrant names carved at the base of the cliff. *See trail XIX, 194.*

Old Fort Vasquez on the Trappers' Trail has been reconstructed. Built by Louis Vasquez in 1835 and abandoned in 1842, the fort was originally on the South Platte River, which is now over a mile west of it. *See trail XXII, 219.*

Crossing of the Big Blue Historic Site   **178**

South of I-80, Seward County

To visit the actual crossing of the Big Blue River, continue west on I-80 about 2 miles to the Seward exit, turn south on Highway 6 / 15 for 8.6 miles (there are two turns in the road). Then turn east 6 miles. Here what is left of the road angles sharply to the right. You will see a marker about 0.4 miles farther down the road, on the right. The river crossing is about 0.2 miles farther.

> OREGON TRAIL / NEBRASKA CITY / CUT OFF
> The monument / in memory of / Nebraska pioneers, marks the site and / establishment of the Oregon Trail Cut-off, / Nebraska City to Fort Kearny, 1861. / Aspiring town of Camden, 1864. First Seward County School District, 1866. / Thomas Graham, Teacher. Erected by / Patriotic Citizens, 1944.

Return to I-80 via any combination of county roads going due north.

Waco Exit Marker   **179**

South of Waco, York County, exit off I-80

There is a trail marker south of the Waco exit off I-80; go 0.3 mile south on road L-93B, and west of the road is a 1933 DAR marker.

> This boulder / marks the / Nebraska City Cut-off / of the / Oregon Trail / DAR 1933.

There are three trail markers in the York, York County, area—two in rest areas and one in the town of York.

Nebraska City–Fort Kearny Cutoff Markers   **180**

East-and westbound lanes of I-80,
rest areas at York, York County

In both the eastbound and westbound rest areas near the York exit off I-80 are Nebraska historical markers commemorating the Nebraska City Cutoff. The text is similar to that on the marker at Syracuse (see this trail, 175).

181   Beaver Creek Crossing/Marker

Beaver Creek Park, York, York County

This DAR marker is 3 miles north towards York on U.S. 81 at the York exit off I-80. The park is just north of the bridge across Beaver Creek, to the west of U.S. 81.

> This boulder marks/ the/ Nebraska City Cutoff/ of/ the Oregon Trail/ D.A.R. 1928.

182   The Deep Well Ranch Marker

South of Aurora, Hamilton County,
in sec. 27, T10N, R6W

To reach the final historical marker along the Nebraska City Cutoff Trail, follow I-80 for 22 miles west of York to the Aurora exit and go south for 1 mile. The well-shaped marker is east of the road and commemorates an important water source on the old trail. This marker is unique in that it is the only marker on old western trails I have ever found which was erected by the Grand Army of the Republic (GAR), an organization of Civil War Union soldiers.

> Nebraska City Fort Kearny/ Cut Off/ The Oregon Trail/ 1851–73
>
> Over this trail passed the great bulk of/ freighting and passenger travel between/ Missouri River and Rocky Mountains Deepwell Ranch/ 6½ miles west and ½ mile south, Government/ relay station, watering place for man and beast. . . .

From this marker the trail continues west generally through Giltner, Hamilton County, to its intersection with the older Ox-Bow Trail near Doniphan, Adams County, in sec. 22, T10N, R9W, and then farther west to its intersection with the main Oregon Trail 10 miles east of Fort Kearny, in sec. 13, T18N, R13W.

XVIII

Oregon-California Trail Variant: The Upper California Crossing and Mitchell Pass Variants of the Oregon Trail in Colorado and Nebraska

(see map 4)

As a result of the 1859 gold rush in Colorado Territory, the Oregon Trail was extended farther along the South Platte River from the Lower California Crossing to the area of Julesburg, Colorado, where a new crossing, called the Upper California Crossing, was developed. From this ford the gold rushers followed the South Platte River to Denver (see trails XX and XXI). Mormons and Oregonians, however, picked up Lodgepole Creek and followed it northwest to where Sidney, Nebraska, is located today, then went north via Mud Springs and Courthouse Rock, joining the older route of the Oregon Trail near present-day Bridgeport. Despite the seemingly infrequent Mormon use of this fording area, one crossing place south of the Lodgepole Creek did acquire the name Mormon Ford.

Colorado

Upper California Crossing Historic Site / Markers   183

East of Ovid, Sedgwick County, on the South Platte River

To reach the Upper California Crossing from the Lower California Crossing (see trail XII, 153), return to Brule, Keith County, and take I-80 and I-76 about 24 miles west to the Julesburg exit off I-76. The old railroad station here has been turned into a local museum and is worth a visit. Here you can also secure a very detailed map of this whole historic area.

With or without this map, go west on a county road immediately after exiting towards Julesburg from I-76. Follow this road 10 miles to a blacktop road that leads north 2 miles to Ovid. Along this 10-mile stretch are three historical markers; on the left is one simply reading "Old Trail," and on the right is one commemorating the site of old Julesburg (burned in 1865 by Indians) and another to old Fort Sedgwick, a military installation that between 1861 and 1874 protected emigrants on this part of the Oregon Trail.

The Upper California Crossing is about 1 mile east of the Ovid Bridge, east of Lodgepole Creek; the so-called Mormon Crossing was nearer the bridge south of Lodgepole Creek (which runs right through Ovid.)

From Ovid emigrants using both crossings followed Lodgepole Creek some 40 miles northwest to present-day Sidney, Nebraska. U.S. 30 follows this old trail rather closely. Travelers should go 4 miles north from Ovid on a county road to U.S. 385, which intersects U.S. 30 at Chappell, Deuel County, Nebraska, and go west on U.S. 30 to Sidney.

For those who would just like to get a general view of the Upper California Crossing area, do not follow I-76 to Julesburg. Instead stay on I-80; in the eastbound lane of I-80, 3 miles west of the I-80 and I-76 junction there is a rest area offering a panoramic view of the whole area and three historic markers commemorating these crossings. The most important one reads:

THE GREAT PLATTE RIVER ROAD

Since 1841, Nebraska's Platte River Valley has been the historic highway of westward migration. In this area, The Overland Trail divided into two branches, one which followed the north and the other the south forks of the river. Emigrants bound for Oregon or California crossed the South Platte near there and proceeded up the North Platte Valley past such milestones as Chimney Rock and Scott's Bluffs. After gold was discovered in the Rocky Mountains in 1859, an increasing number of travelers followed the south fork of the Platte to Denver and the mining camps.

Although the South Platte could be forded at several points, most frequently used the "Old California Crossing," several miles west of present Big Springs. No matter which crossing was chosen, the wide sandy river proved a formidable obstacle for the emigrants and their heavily laden wagons.

Today the Platte Valley remains an important thoroughfare across Nebraska and the nation. A few miles east of here I-

80 divides into two major routes, recalling the role of the South Platte region as junction for overland travel in the 19th century.

Nebraska

Mud Springs Historic Site / Marker   184

*24 miles north of Sidney, in Morrill County,
near U.S. 385, in sec. 31, T18N, R50W*

To reach Mud Springs, an important water source on the Oregon Trail, take U.S. 385 for 24 miles north from Sidney, Nebraska (or exactly 3 miles north of the Morrill County line). Then turn west 1.5 miles to a Pony Express marker commemorating the springs. Nearby is a ranch house—a good place to ask directions.

Courthouse Rock Historic Site   185

*West of Bridgeport, Morrill County,
off Highway 88, in sec. 29, T19N, R50W*

To reach Courthouse Rock, take a dirt road north and west from Mud Springs for 4 miles to an intersection, turn north for 5.5 miles, west for 1 mile, then north again for 0.8 mile to the Courthouse Rock turnoff to the west. It is a common belief that this natural formation was named after its fancied resemblance to the Old Courthouse in St. Louis, but Greg Franzwa has found accounts calling it by this name prior to the building of that structure. The ambitious may clamber up its sides. Irene Paden once found rattlesnakes here—I did not. From here it is 4.4 miles due north to the intersection of this trail with the main Oregon Trail near Bridgeport (see trail VI, 69). For an account of the Oregon Trail between Bridgeport and Scottsbluff see trail XII, 155–157.

Mitchell Pass Historic Site   186

*Scotts Bluff National Monument,
near Scottsbluff, Scotts Bluff County*

In 1851 Mitchell Pass was opened up. Proceeding northwest from Scotts Bluff, it was believed to be better and shorter than the older Robidoux

Pass (see trail XII, 158). Here are some dramatic trail ruts. To hike them simply follow a marked trail about 1 mile west, beginning at the museum. Many Mormon wagons helped deepen these ruts. The Mitchell Pass route joined the Robidoux Pass road about 15 miles west near Lyman, Nebraska. This pass can be surmounted in a car by driving west from the national monument on Highway 92. (To follow the Oregon Trail into Wyoming, see trail XII, and to continue the Oregon Trail across Wyoming, see trails VIII and XIII.)

XIX

The Overland–Bridger Pass Trail
in Nebraska and Wyoming
(see map 10)

This long-ignored trail, once used by thousands of emigrants—including Mormons—throughout much of their immigrant period, needs and deserves to be better known. It runs generally from present Sidney, Nebraska, for 600 miles west to Fort Bridger via Lodgepole Creek, Cheyenne Pass, Rattlesnake Pass, Bridger Pass, and Bitter Creek, but it has faded almost totally from general consciousness. In a generic sense all trails west of the Missouri River are sometimes referred to loosely as overland trails. It is quite proper, however, to refer to this particular trail as *the* Overland Trail, or better as the Overland–Bridger Pass Trail. Parts of this trail in Wyoming are also called the Cherokee Trail, from the fact that in 1849 a party of Cherokee Indians from present-day Oklahoma went to California this way (see trail XX, 201) or the Lodgepole Creek Trail, since part of this trail follows that creek.

The western part, between Cheyenne Pass (just east the city of Laramie) and Fort Bridger had been scouted eastwards in 1850 by Captain Howard Stansbury of the U.S. Topographical Engineers, guided by Jim Bridger. Stansbury, aided also by the Mormon engineer Albert Carrington, was looking for a route south of the Oregon-California-Mormon Trail in order to avoid the heavy snows of that more northern trail.

The Wyoming portion of this trail was not much used until after 1862, when the postmaster general ordered the Overland Mail to change from the Oregon-Mormon Trail as a result of the great increase in Indian, especially Sioux, troubles along the northern route. These uprisings were a direct result of whites illegally settling on (rather than passing through) Indian land, the subsequent mistreatment of the Indians, and the recall of U.S. Army troops from the West to fight the Civil War.

This trail is probably the most difficult to follow of all the great western trails discussed in this book. From Sidney to Rattlesnake Pass is fairly easy with a regular passenger car and good weather. Thereafter, county maps and ORVs are often required.

Nebraska

From Sidney to the Wyoming state line 60 miles west, the trail can be approximated by driving either I-80 or U.S. 30. There is little to see, however, except the valley of Lodgepole Creek. In the town of Lodgepole, there is a Nebraska historical marker commemorating the U.P.R.R., which reached there in 1867. Ten miles into Wyoming the Lodgepole turns north and cannot be followed. Travelers should proceed directly to Cheyenne.

Wyoming

187   Lodgepole Creek Ranch Grave Historic Site / Marker

North of Cheyenne, Laramie County,
off U.S. 85, in sec. 12, T15N, R66W

An 1867 grave of 10-year-old Emily Patrick is right on the Overland Trail and offers a beautiful and dramatic view of Lodgepole Creek and its valley. To drive there take I-25 some 7 miles north of Cheyenne to its intersection with U.S. 85, go east on U.S. 85 for 7 miles to a ranch road off to the right, just before reaching the bridge across the Lodgepole. (If you cross the bridge you have gone too far.) Follow this ranch road east along the high ground above the valley for about 1 mile. The well-marked grave is north of the road.

188   Camp Walbach and Cheyenne Pass
Historic Site / Marker

About 26 miles west of Cheyenne, Laramie County,
off Highway 211, in sec. 12, T15N, R70W

To reach the site of Camp Walbach, return from the Patrick grave to I-25, go 1 mile south and exit west on Highway 211 towards Federal; go west 14 miles and keep going west even when Highway 211 turns sharply north. Cross the railroad tracks at Federal (which is just a railroad service area). Three and one-half miles beyond the tracks, cross Lodgepole Creek. To the north of the bridge and a ranch house is a prominent hill; a pyramidal Camp Walbach marker is there commemorating "Camp Walbach, U.S. Military Post, 1858–59," erected for the protection of emigrants in the Cheyenne Pass area. This was placed here in 1914 by the Sons of the American Revolution. Such markers are rare. I have seen but three scattered along more than 10,000 miles of western trails (see trails XXII, 215 and XXIV, 234). The mouth of Cheyenne Pass is via a ranch road just south of the ranch house.

Cheyenne Pass Marker / Ruts   189

West of Camp Walbach marker (see 188 above)

Cheyenne Pass is a 14-mile long, gentle pass through the Laramie Mountains. The pass crosses the Medicine Bow National Forest and intersects with I-80 just north of the city of Laramie. An ORV and a Laramie County map (sheet 2) and an Albany County map (sheet 2) are suggested. About 1 mile into this beautiful pass, at the top of the first rise and to the north of the road, sitting in the middle of some trail ruts, is a small, hard-to-find 1965 Boy Scout marker commemorating this pass.

Continuing west for about 3 more miles, there are ruts north of the road; then, unfortunately, there is a locked ranch gate. Permission must be secured in advance to get past this gate, but the effort is worth it. Otherwise, the traveler must return to Cheyenne and take I-80 for 40 miles west to the Lincoln Monument at the entrance to the Medicine Bow National Forest. With an Albany County map (sheet 2), it is possible to backtrack the Cheyenne Pass from the west, but it is hardly worth the effort as the prettiest part of the pass is before one reaches the locked ranch gate from the east.

Rock Creek Stage Crossing Historic Site / Marker (P)   190

On I-80 at Arlington, Carbon County

From Cheyenne Pass the old trail angles northwest more than 50 miles past today's Laramie, across the Laramie Plains, crossing the Little Laramie River, to Rock Creek at Arlington. (Before leaving the Laramie area, however, consult trail XX, 207–210. You may wish to see these historic sites before proceeding to Rock Creek.) To reach Arlington take I-80 west from Laramie about 40 miles to the Arlington exit, turn south under the interstate to some close-by ranch buildings. The 1914 gray granite marker to the Old Rock Creek Stage Crossing is near a barn to the left of the road; it reads, "The site of/ Old Rock Creek/ Stage Crossing/ Overland Trail, 1862–68."

There is an abandoned graveyard here in which at least one Mormon is buried—Anson V. Call who died there in 1867. No gravestones can be found, but friends and I once carried a large triangular boulder to the center of this graveyard in honor of Anson and others buried there. The graveyard is at the foot of Rock Mountain and difficult to find. Ask locally for both permission and directions.

191   Old Cherokee Trail Marker

Off I-80, 6 miles northwest of Arlington,
Carbon County, in sec. 8, T19N, R79W

There are very few markers on the Overland Trail referring to the Cherokee Trail. This gray granite marker was placed here privately in 1914 and can be reached rather easily. Proceed on I-80 one exit west from Arlington to a rest area. From the rest area there is a dirt road going northwest paralleling I-80; follow this 1 mile; the marker is to the left. If you look sharply this marker may be seen from I-80.

> The site of/ Old Cherokee Trail/ This monument is/ erect-
> ed by/ Mrs. R.D. Meyer/ Hana, Wyoming/ June 1914.

From the marker the old trail can be followed for about 1.5 miles farther to a locked ranch gate. Were it not for this gate, the old trail could be followed to Elk Mountain.

192   Fort Halleck Historic Site/Marker (P)

Off I-80 near Elk Mountain, Carbon County,
in sec. 16, T20N, R81W

A 1914 DAR marker commemorates the site of Fort Halleck, which for the years 1862–66 protected travelers along the Overland Trail. To visit this site return from the Cherokee Trail marker to I-80, go west one more exit to the Elk Mountain exit, turn west and take the only road there is about 2 miles to the community of Elk Mountain. The Fort

Halleck marker is only 4 miles west, but a Carbon County map (sheet 4) is advisable; otherwise ask locally for directions. Look for the only ranch building west of Elk Mountain, drive there and ask directions and permission to visit the site. If the ground is wet you will have to walk about 0.5 mile from the ranch house. The marker reads "Fort Halleck / U.S. Military Post / July 1862 / July 1866." From Elk Mountain the rest of the Overland Trail to Fort Bridger gets increasingly difficult to follow. The general traveler will only be able to visit some historic markers, not to follow the trail itself.

Rattlesnake Pass / Ruts 193

8 miles west of Elk Mountain, Carbon County,
commencing in about sec. 7, T20N, R81W

From the Fort Halleck marker the dirt road through Rattlesnake Pass goes 18 miles to an intersection with Highway 130. A Carbon County map (sheet 4) is advisable, and dry roads and skillful driving are essential.

Some ruts and BLM trail markers can be found along this pretty road, known locally as Rattlesnake Pass Road.

North Platte River Crossing Historic Site / Markers 194

9 miles west of Highway 130 in Carbon County,
in sec. 33, T19N, R85W

On Highway 130 there is a Wyoming Historical Landmarks Commission marker to this crossing. To reach it drive south 5 miles on Highway 130 from its intersection with the Rattlesnake Pass Road (see 193 above). It is also possible to visit this marker by *not* exiting at Elk Mountain, but following I-80 some 25 miles farther west to the Walcott-Saratoga exit and driving 9 miles south on Highway 130. The marker is west of the road. It reads "This marker on the / Overland Trail / Platte River crossing / nine miles west / 1861–68."

This marker is 9 miles due east of the river crossing, but a Carbon County map (sheets 3 and 4) and an ORV are necessary to reach the river. This crossing site is one of the most impressive places on the entire Overland Trail. There are cliffs above the river affording a magnificent view. Atop these cliffs are some graves and a marker.

Overland Trail / Platte River Crossing / Erected in memory of / those brave pioneers / who passed this way / to win / and hold the west. . . .

Along the base of the cliffs are numerous emigrant names similar to, but better carved than those at Independence Rock. There is even one in Spencerian script reading "A. Nelson, SCL [Salt Lake City], Utah, 1890." A plaque set high up on the face of these cliffs reads "Platte River Crossing / on the Overland Stage Route." There is also a natural stairway back up the cliff to the top.

Determined travelers have one other option in viewing this historic site—from the west side of the North Platte. To do this, do not visit the trail marker on Highway 130, but rather stay on I-80 and go 45 miles west of Elk Mountain to Rawlins. Exit at Rawlins and at the center of town pick up Highway 71. Go south 13 miles from where 71 passes under I-80 to the Bolton Road (a rough ranch road), going due east about 18 miles to the river. There are three BLM trail markers along this road, but a Carbon County map (sheet 3) is necessary. (The very determined will want to drive the Bolton Road even if they visit the river crossing site off Highway 130.)

195   Bridger Pass Summit Historic Site / Ruts

Off Highway 71, 20 miles southwest of Rawlins,
Carbon County, in sec. 8, T18N, R89W

Fortunately the historic and beautiful Bridger Pass Summit is fairly easy to reach. The marked entrance to this pass is either about 1.4 miles north on the Bolton Road on Highway 71 or 11 miles south of Rawlins on Highway 71, measured from the point where 71 cuts under I-80. The crest of the pass is 10 miles west of Highway 71 on a dirt road. A Carbon County map (sheet 3) will help, but it is not necessary. Dry roads and careful driving, however, are. There are some great ruts at the western end of the crest. Three miles beyond the crest is another locked ranch gate, so return to Rawlins.

Under ideal conditions you could drive west of Bridger Pass for 20 miles on the old trail to the marker described below (196), passing several old stage stops, but during three seasons of field research I could never get there by this route.

Overland Trail Intersection   196
Historic Site / Marker / Ruts

20 miles south of Creston Junction with I-80,
on Baggs Road, Carbon County, in sec. 9, T17N, R92W

The Creston Junction is about 25 miles west of Rawlins on I-80; exit, then go south on Baggs Road about 20 miles. The fenced marker is west of the road. From here good trail ruts are visible both to the east and to the west.

> Overland Stage Station Route / Washakee Station 4 miles
> east / Barrel Springs Station 14 miles west / Historic Landmark
> Commission / 1951.

From here the old trail meanders about 70 miles west to Point of Rocks in Sweetwater County on I-80, and much of the original trail is still visible in this utterly desolate section. It is, however, very difficult to follow. A Carbon County map (sheet 3) and Sweetwater County map (sheets 5 and 6) are absolutely essential, as is an ORV and a lot of luck. En route you can see the ruins of the Duck Pond, Barrel Springs, Dug Springs, La Clede, Big Pond, and Black Buttes stage stations, the Haystacks, Bitter Creek, and Black Butte. It is a great experience, but you must be well prepared in advance. General travelers are advised to return to I-80 and drive to Point of Rocks.

Point of Rocks Stage Station Historic Site   197

On I-80, Point of Rocks, Sweetwater County

The fourth stage station west of Baggs Road has been partially restored. To reach it drive 56 miles west of the Creston Junction on I-80 and exit south at Point of Rocks. The station can be seen from this exit across the railroad tracks and is on the National Register of Historic Places.

From here I-80 follows the old trail closely to Fort Bridger 90 miles west, but roads and railroads have obliterated all traces. At Fort Bridger this trail merges with the Pioneer Trail of 1847 (see trail VIII).

XX

The Overland–Bridger Pass Trail Mountain Division Variant in Colorado and Wyoming

One variant of the Overland–Bridger Pass Trail commenced in 1859 when thousands of Colorado gold rushers followed the Oregon Trail to the Upper California Crossing near Julesburg, Colorado (see trail XVIII, 183). Instead of continuing west along Lodgepole Creek, they followed the South Platte River southwest to Fort Morgan (founded that year for their protection) and on to the site of present Denver, Colorado.

Later, during the early 1860s, many emigrants, for a variety of reasons including Indian troubles, also followed the South Platte River to Fort Morgan, where instead of continuing on to Denver (on the Denver cut-off), they continued west to the Cherokee Trail. They then followed the Cherokee Trail northwest into Wyoming to rejoin the main Overland–Bridger Pass Trail on the Little Laramie River northwest of the city of Laramie (see trail XIX, 190).

Colorado
(see map 11)

198   Valley Station Historic Marker

Sterling, Logan County, in front of the local museum in Overland Park just west of the junction of I-76 and U.S. 6.
Along U.S. 138 and U.S. 6 today there is little of interest between Julesburg and Sterling, 55 miles southeast. At Sterling, there is a 1933 State Historical Society of Colorado plaque that commemorates Valley Station, an 1862–67 stop on this branch of the Overland Trail.

> Valley Station / built in 1859 as a stage coach / station on the Leavenworth / and Pikes Peak Express / Station on the Overland Trail / to California 1862–67 / Indian War outpost 1864–65 / Once defended by a breastwork / of sacks of shelled corn.

Fort Wicked Historic Site / Marker   199

On U.S. 6 in Merino, Logan County

Thirteen miles beyond Sterling, at Merino is the site of an old ranch and station of the Overland Trail near a South Platte River ford. U.S. 6 crosses the river at this same place today. About 2.7 miles west of Merino on U.S. 6 is a 1929 State Historical Society of Colorado marker commemorating old Fort Wicked on the Overland Trail.

> Fort Wicked / Famous Overland Stage Station / one of the few forts withstanding / the Indian uprising of 1864 / on the road to Colorado / Named from the bitter defence / made by Holon Godfrey.

Fort Morgan Historic Site / Marker   200

Fort Morgan, Morgan County

Thirty miles beyond Merino is Fort Morgan. Originally founded during the Colorado gold rush of 1859 as a station and military post on the Overland Trail and known as Camp Tyler; it was renamed Fort Morgan in 1866. The old fort is commemorated by a monument at 229 Riverview Avenue, near Prospect Street.

> To mark the site of / old Fort Morgan / occupied from 1864 to 1868 / and the divergence of the / Denver Cutoff / from the Overland Trail.
>
> This monument is erected by / Fort Morgan Chapter / Daughters of the American Revolution / 1912.

For a description of the Denver cutoff from Fort Morgan, see trail XXI.

Fort Latham Historic Site / Marker (P)   201

4 miles west of Kersey, Weld County

From Fort Morgan take Highway 144 along the South Platte for some 24 miles until it curves around and intersects U.S. 34. Follow U.S. 34 west along the South Platte for about 25 miles to Kersey. At a place 4 miles west of Kersey, just where U.S. 34 turns sharply northwest, there is a marker commemorating the cemetery of old Fort Latham, established in 1862 as a station on the old Overland Stage Line near the confluence of the South Platte and Cache la Poudre rivers.

This marker, enclosed by an white iron fence, is about 200 feet west of a home north of the highway.

1861 FT. LATHAM CEMETERY 1874
The known / buried here are / 1808 / Magdelena Simon
1861 / Two Plowhead infant sons / Several others unknown.

From here the old trail follows the Cache la Poudre River northwest to its intersection with the older Cherokee Trail near Laporte, Laramie County. The Cherokee Trail (see trail XIX) acquired its name when some Cherokee Indians used it going from Oklahoma to California in 1849. In 1846 some Mormon "Mississippi Saints" used part of it between Fort Pueblo and Denver (see trail XXI). The Mormon Battalion Sick Detachments also used part of it in 1846 (see trail XXV, 321), and I have already noted one marker referring to it (see trail XIX, 191). Emigrants who for whatever reasons ended up in Denver and who wished to pick up the Overland Trail would have followed the Cherokee Trail north from Denver to the Cache la Poudre River near Laporte—roughly the route U.S. 287 follows today (see trail XXI).

202 Laporte Historic Site / Marker

Laporte, Larimer County, on U.S. 287

Since there is nothing of the Overland–Bridger Pass Trail variant to see between Kersey and Laporte, travelers should take any of several routes via Greeley to Fort Collins, the site of the old fort by that name on this branch of the trail. From Fort Collins take U.S. 287 about 5 miles west to tiny Laporte, founded in 1860 as headquarters of this Mountain Division of the Overland Stage Company. This fact is commemorated in Laporte by the Overland Trail Shoppes and the fact that the main road south is named the Overland Trail. (The name is French, *la porte*, meaning the gateway through these mountains to Wyoming.) Also, just south on this road is a log cabin allegedly dating from 1852 and just beyond this cabin, west of the road, is a marker commemorating this cabin as an Overland Stage station.

In 1862 / this log house / was used as a / station house / for the / Overland Stage Company.

Virginia Dale Historical Marker   203

On U.S. 287 near Virginia Dale, Larimer County

From Laporte continue north on U.S. 287 for about 30 miles through beautiful country to the little community of Virginia Dale. En route a quick visit to Owl Canyon is convenient and interesting. The mouth of this canyon is 12 miles north of Laporte on U.S. 287. Turn northeast into the canyon and drive some 2.5 miles through beautiful country. Where the road starts to turn eastwards, there is a rocky formation close to the road on which emigrant signatures are supposed to be found, although I did not see any. One variant of the old trail came this way. From here you can go back to U.S. 287 and proceed about 17 miles farther north to Virginia Dale. One-half mile beyond that wide spot in the road is a marker east of the road commemorating the Virginia Dale Station on the Overland Stage route, established here in 1862. The site of the station proper is in sec. 33, T12N, R71W, about 0.8 mile northwest.

> ¾ mile northwest form this point is the original VIRGINIA DALE/ famous Stage Station on the Overland Route/ to California, 1862–67/ Established by Joseph A. (Jack) Slade/ and named for his wife, Virginia/ Located on Cherokee Trail of 1849/ Famous camp ground for emigrants. . . ./ State Historical Society of Colorado/ 1935.

Virginia Dale Historic Site (P)   204

On U.S. 287 near Virginia Dale, Larimer County

About one-quarter of a mile beyond the Virgina Dale marker a ranch road leads off to the right; follow it for approximately 1 mile to the considerably modified log remains of the old stage station referred to above. It is on private property; be courteous.

Virginia Dale Information Sign   205

At a rest area off U.S. 287 near Virginia Dale, Larimer County

In a rest area 2 miles north is a state highway department wooden sign also telling the story of Virginia Dale.

206   **Overland Stage Marker**

On the Colorado-Wyoming state line,
5 miles north of Virginia Dale on U.S. 287

Continue north from Virginia Dale 5 miles to the state line, where there is a DAR marker.

This stone marks the / place where / the Overland Stage Line / on way to the West / June 1862–1868 / Crossed the Colorado-Wyoming Boundary Line . . . / DAR 1917.

Wyoming
(see map 10)

It is 24 miles north from the state line to Laramie. U.S. 287 approximates the old trail fairly closely, the old trail being generally west of the highway.

207   **Fort Sanders Historic Site / Marker**

On Fort Sanders Drive 3 miles south of Laramie,
Albany County

Three miles south of downtown Laramie, Fort Sanders Drive intersects U.S. 287 from the west. Near this intersection on the east side of Fort Sanders Drive is the Fort Sanders monument. The fort was not built on the trail, which was 5 miles southwest, but apparently it was considered close enough for protection.

This monument marks the site of Ft. Sanders / established September 5, 1856 / abandoned May 18, 1882 / Erected by State of Wyoming and DAR / 1914.

208   **Laramie River Historic Crossing Site**

6 miles southwest of Laramie, Albany County,
off Highway 230 in sec. 28, T15N, R74W

To reach the historic crossing of the Laramie River take Highway 130 / 230 west from Laramie. In 2 miles Highway 230 turns southwest; follow it 4 miles to a tee intersection with a dirt road from the south. At this intersection is a large wooden sign informing you that "The Big Laramie Stage Station and river crossing of Overland Trail 1862–68" is 1 mile south. Turn south on this road to the Laramie River. The station was south of the river. There is nothing left to see, so return to Highway 230.

Overland Trail Marker   209

8 miles southwest of Laramie, Albany County, on Highway 230

After returning from the Laramie River crossing to Highway 230, continue southwest for 2 more miles. On the left, or south, of the road is a marker to the Overland Trail.

> The first stone / erected in Albany County / to mark the / Old Overland Trail / 1862–68 / Erected by . . . DAR, 1911.

Overland Trail Marker / Ruts   210

12 miles west of Laramie, Albany County, on Highway 130

From the DAR marker (site 207) take Highway 230 back towards Laramie 6 miles to the wye intersection with Highway 130; take 130 for 9 miles to the west; the marker, of pink concrete, is north of the road and was apparently erected by the Kiwanis Club.

> Overland / Trail / 1862–1868.

Near this marker, beyond a fence in a field, is a broken concrete post marked Overland Trail. It appears that a four-legged vandal damaged this one. Cattle find these concrete posts just right for scratching.

Looking to the south of the pink concrete marker you can see the great depression know as the Big Hollow. The old trail passes the DAR marker on Highway 230, crosses Big Hollow, passes by this pink marker, and heads northwest. Faint ruts may be seen in both directions (southeast and northwest) from this marker.

Eight miles north of this pink concrete marker the Overland Trail crosses the Little Laramie River and 6 miles beyond that joins the main

Overland Trail near Seven Mile Creek. With an Albany county map (sheet 1) this part of the old trail can be approximated, but it is hardly worth the effort. One may as well return to Laramie and take I-80 northward (see trail XIX, 190).

The site of the junction of the Overland variant and the main trail can be seen easily from I-80. Seven Mile Creek is crossed by I-80 1.5 miles beyond the fourth interchange beyond the I-80 / U.S. 30 interchange in central Laramie. This trail may be continued by turning to trail XIX, 190.

XXI

The Overland–Bridger Pass Trail
Fort Morgan-Denver-Laporte
Variant in Colorado
(see map 11)

Travelers can approximate the old variant of the Overland Trail between Fort Morgan and Laporte via Denver two ways. The easy way is simply to take I-76 towards Denver, bypassing greater Denver traffic by turning north at the intersection of I-76 and I-25 to U.S. 36, picking up U.S. 287 north at Broomfield.

The more historic route is some 30 miles east of I-76. To approximate this route take various county roads from Fort Morgan (trail XX, 200), more or less following Bijou Creek, to Hoyt, Morgan County, and then to Bennett, Adams County. Pick up Highway 36 at Bennett and go west towards Denver via Watkins. At Watkins the traveler is advised to pick up I-70 and, to avoid Denver traffic, follow I-70 to its intersection with I-25, exit north to U.S. 36, picking up U.S. 287 north at Broomfield. U.S. 287 is a pretty drive, but offers little of historical interest to see.

Old Stage Station Site / Marker   211

*One-half mile south of the town center of Longmont,
Boulder County, on U.S. 287 just south of the bridge
across the St. Vrain Creek*

1860–1928
The site of the first log cabin in the St. Vrain Valley lies 200 feet west of this marker. The cabin was built by Alonzo N. Allen and used as a stage station on the Overland Trail. Placed by the Long's Peak Chapter, DAR.

Continue north on U.S. 287 about 18 miles to Loveland.

212   ## Overland Stage Station / Marker

Namaqua Park, Loveland, Larimer County

At the intersection of U.S. 34 and U.S. 287 in Loveland turn west for about 2.3 miles, then turn south about 0.5 mile to Namaqua Park on the Big Thompson River. The 1931 State Historical Society of Colorado and the DAR marker is in this small park.

NAMAQUA

Home trading post and fort of / Mariano Modeno, early trapper, / scout and pioneer. / First settlement in the / Big Thompson Valley, / Station on the Overland Stage / route to California 1862.

Return to U.S. 287 and continue north to Laporte via Fort Collins (see trail XX, 202).

XXII

The Trappers'-Cherokee Trail in Colorado and Wyoming
(see maps 11 and 12)

This Trappers' Trail connected a string of forts from Bent's Fort and Fort Pueblo on the Arkansas River, to Forts Vasquez, Lupton, Johnson, and St. Vrain on the South Platte, and Fort Laramie on the North Platte. These seven forts were the economic and military centers for a vast western region and served the needs of trappers, traders, and Indians.

This old trail had been known since at least 1820, when Major Stephen H. Long followed it; subsequently Colonel Henry Dodge and his Dragoons used it in 1835; Lieutenant John C. Frémont in 1842 and 1843; General Stephen W. Kearny and Dragoons in 1845; and it was used extensively during the Colorado gold rush of 1859.

From near Colorado Springs for 75 miles north to the South Platte near present Denver there are three variants of this Trappers' Trail. One, the oldest, runs closest to the mountains along Fountain, Monument, and East Plum creeks; the middle variant, frequently called the Cherry Creek Trail, generally follows West Cherry Creek; the third, also known as the Jimmy Camp Trail, lies to the east of Jimmy Camp Creek, rejoining the middle trail near present-day Franktown.

From Pueblo the oldest variant of the Trappers' Trail can be followed easily for 80 miles, as far as present Castle Rock, by driving I-25 along Fountain, Monument, and Plum creeks. For directions regarding the other two variants, see trail XXIII.

Of all the many groups of Mormons to follow Brigham Young west, one of the most unusual was the Mississippi Saints. In April 1846 a group of forty-three Mormon converts from Monroe County, Mississippi, under the leadership of William Crosby, started north with the intention of joining Brigham Young and the main body of the Pioneers on the North Platte River somewhere near Fort Laramie and going west with them. These Mormons followed the Mississippi River north to the Iron Banks, near present-day Columbus, Kentucky, and then cut across Missouri, following various roads from one county seat to another as far as Independence, where they picked up the Oregon Trail and followed it to within a few miles of Fort Laramie (see trails XI and XII).

There they discovered that the Pioneers had not been able to start for the Rocky Mountain that year and were back in Winter Quarters on the Missouri River. Facing winter themselves, the Mississippi Saints accepted the welcome offer of French mountainman John Reshaw (Richard) to guide them along the Trappers' Trail (between Fort Laramie and Taos, New Mexico) south to Fort Pueblo on the Arkansas River in present-day Colorado; Reshaw was headed that way himself with his furs. The party reached Fort Pueblo, which had been established in 1842, on August 7. Later they were joined by three Sick Detachments of the Mormon Battalion (see trail XXIV, 250, 271, 278 and trail XXV, 321). A total of 287 men, women, and children wintered together in a little eighteen-room cottonwood log cabin settlement on the south side of the river, about one-half mile from the fort. While there, the reknowed American historian Francis Parkman met the Mormons and later mentioned them in his famous book *The Oregon Trail*.

Nothing remains of Mormon Pueblo; even the graves of those who died there have been obliterated by the floodwaters of the Arkansas River. The old fort was located at the junction of Fountain Creek and the Arkansas, but because the river has changed its course three times since 1846, we have no idea exactly where Fort Pueblo was located. It is possible, however, to drive to the present confluence of these two streams on Highway 227 (near the public stockyards) and imagine what it was like in 1846–47.

In the spring of 1847 the Mormons started north again for Fort Laramie, following the same Trappers' Trail they had previously used. Until recently it was not known which of the variants of this trail between Colorado Springs and Denver the Mormons used, but a marker that used to be on the Jimmy Camp Trail states they used that route (see trail XXIII, 224). This was confirmed in 1987 when I read the journals of John Steele and Joseph Skeen. By 1847, however, the South Platte forts had all been abandoned.

There are very few markers or monuments commemorating this trail. Two, however, are located in Pueblo.

Colorado
(see map 11)

Mormon Battalion Marker 213

*Intersection of Moffatt and Lansing Streets,
Pueblo, Pueblo County*

The first marker is located in Pueblo at the intersection of Moffatt and Lansing Streets, just south of the bridge over the Arkansas River on U.S. Business 50 (which is also marked as Santa Fe Drive). This State Historical Society of Colorado marker, about 1 mile west of the modern confluence of Fountain Creek and the Arkansas River, was erected in 1946.

> A detachment of United States soldiers of the MORMON BATTALION in the Mexican War spent the winter of 1846–47 near this site. With their families and Mormon immigrants from Mississippi they formed a settlement of 275 persons. They erected a church and rows of dwellings of cottonwood logs. Here were born the first white children in Colorado.

Also on U.S. Business 50, about 1 mile east, is a marker honoring Colonel Zebulon Pike, discoverer of Pikes Peak, who camped here on November 23, 1806.

Castle Rock Historic Site 214

Castle Rock, Douglas County

A dramatic outcrop of salmon-colored stone, Castle Rock served as a landmark for Indians, trappers, explorers, and Mormons. This formation, thought to resemble a medieval castle, was discovered and named by Major Stephen H. Long in 1820.

From Castle Rock take U.S. 85 north along Plum Creek to its confluence with the South Platte River just at the southern line of Arapahoe County, near Littleton. Continue north on U.S. 85 about 6 miles to an intersection with Dartmouth Avenue.

215   Little Dry Creek Historic Site / Marker

Englewood City Park at Darmouth Avenue and Galapago Street, Englewood, Arapahoe County

Turn east on Dartmouth Avenue for about 2 blocks to the city park entrance. The marker, placed here in 1975, is one of the only three markers I have ever seen by the Sons of the American Revolution (see trails XIX, 188 and XXIV, 234). It is located in the center of the park, beyond a footbridge crossing Little Dry Creek by a basketball standard. In 1927 this plaque was originally placed at the intersection of Dartmouth Avenue and U.S. 85, near where Little Dry Creek empties into the South Platte River.

> Placer Camp / Little Dry Creek. / In this stream / paying quantities of / gold / first discovered / in Colorado / 1858 / by the Russell / Party. . . .

Return to U.S. 85 (which becomes I-25) and continue north to I-70, go east to the Brighton Boulevard Highway 265-north exit, and turn north less than 1 mile to York Street.

216   Platte River Trail Marker

At the intersection of Brighton Boulevard and York Street, Denver

This 1932 Platte marker is gray granite and reads:

> Commemorating the route of the Platte River Trail. Principal route of the Colorado Pioneers. Trail of Major Long 1820. Trappers Trail of 1830–1840. The 1858–9 route of Gold-seekers with pack and pan, bull whackers with ox teams, stage coaches with treasure and mail. The path that became an empire. Erected by the State Historical Society of Colorado. 1932.

217   Brighton Trail Marker

Brighton, Adams County

Continue north of Brighton Boulevard to U.S. 85 and go some 17 miles to the community of Brighton. In a well-maintained median at the intersection of Main and Bush Streets, near town center, is this marker:

Dedicated to the / pioneer spirit / of the early settlers. /
Erected by Fort Vasquez Chapter DAR / 1940.

Old Fort Lupton Historic Site / Marker   218

On U.S. 85, 1.5 miles north of Fort Lupton (city),
Weld County

To the west of U.S. 85, 1.5 miles north of the community of Fort Lupton
is a 1939 State Historical Society of Colorado marker commemorating
an Overland Stage station on the South Platte River.

Due west 1 / 2 miles is the site of / FORT LUPTON / established
in 1836 by / Lieut. Lancaster D. Lupton / A rendevous of the
early fur traders / . . . Overland Stage Station and refuge / from
Indians in the sixties.

Old Fort Vasquez Historic Site / Markers   219

On U.S. 85 near Ione, Weld County

In the median of U.S. 85, 3.5 miles north of Ione, is the restored old Fort
Vasquez, built in 1835. At one time the Platte River ran by the fort, but
the river has changed its course and is now 1.2 miles to the west. The
restored fort and visitors' center are worth a visit; you should at least
read the information sign.

FORT VASQUEZ

In this area along the South Platte River, competing fur
companies in the late 1830s established a string of four adobe
trading posts—Fort Vasquez, Fort St. Vrain, Fort Jackson, and
Fort Lupton. Traversed by the old Trappers' Trail which connected Fort Bent on the Arkansas with Fort Laramie on the
North Platte, this country of wide horizons was the commercial center of a vast region. Here trappers, traders, and
Indians bartered calico, knives, and beads for buffalo robes
and beaver skins.

Built in 1835 by Louis Vasquez (later partner of Jim
Bridger) and Andrew W. Sublette, this fort once was flanked
by the South Platte River. In the spring of 1840 a Mackinaw
boat was launched here loaded with 700 buffalo robes and
400 buffalo tongues. It reached St. Louis in 69 days.

Abandoned in 1842, the fort was ransacked by Indians. Later partly restored, it sheltered gold rush emigrants and troops during Indian troubles.

Fort Vasquez was reconstructed on the original site from adobe bricks made from remains of its crumbling walls.

Here there is also a 1932 State Historical Society of Colorado marker with a plaque telling the story of the old fort.

220   Fort St. Vrain Historic Site / Marker

West of Gilcrest, Weld County

About 5 miles north of restored old Fort Vasquez on U.S. 85, just one-half mile south of the center of Gilcrest, is a dirt road going straight west for 4 miles to the site of old Fort St. Vrain. Built about 1837 by Ceran St. Vrain of the American Fur Company, it was the first and largest of the South Platte River trading posts, exceeded in size only by Fort Laramie and Bent's Fort. It was abandoned in 1844 and has totally disappeared; the site is marked by a gray granite marker.

FORT ST. VRAIN

Built about 1837 / by Col. Ceran St. Vrain / Gen. [Lieut.] Fremont reorganized his / historic exploring expedition here / July 23, 1843 / The fort was also visited by / Francis Parkman and Kit Carson / DAR, 1911.

Wyoming
(see map 12)

221   Lodgepole Creek Historic Site

On Lodgepole Creek 2 miles north of Burns,
Laramie County, in secs. 31 / 32, T15N, R62W

To approximate the old Trappers' Trail to this historic Mormon meeting site, continue driving north on U.S. 85 from Gilcrest for about 9 miles to Greeley (for a trail marker between Greeley and Kersey on U.S. 34, see trail XX, 201). Turn east on U.S. 34 and go 6 miles to Kersey, then 7 miles north on Highway 37 (which makes two turns), then 3.5 miles east on road 392 to Barnsville, Weld County, on Crow Creek—the creek the trail follows north into Wyoming. Here the Rockies fade into the west and the high plains commence.

From Barnsville take road 392 north for some 39 very sparsely populated miles to Hereford, Weld County, 2 miles from the Wyoming state line. Crow Creek will be east of the road and the modern Pawnee National Grasslands will be to the west. From Hereford proceed 6 miles farther north to Carpenter, Laramie County, Wyoming on a county road, crossing under I-80 to Burns.

A historic meeting took place on Lodgepole Creek about 2 miles north of Burns. On June 1, 1847, when Brigham Young and the Pioneers finally reached Fort Laramie (see trail VIII, 82), he found the first detachment of Mississippi Saints waiting for him and learned that other Mormons were still on the way north from Fort Pueblo. Accordingly, Young sent Apostle Amasa M. Lyman and three companions south from Fort Laramie to meet these Mormons and guide them west in the tracks of the Pioneer company. The two groups met on the Lodgepole Creek about 15 miles north of today's Wyoming-Colorado state line, and they were all back at Fort Laramie by June 16.

From the Lodgepole Creek crossing the trail continues north for some 80 miles to Fort Laramie. Travelers usually camped on Horse Creek and Lone Tree Creek. A few miles north of Lone Tree Creek they entered into the Goshen Hole, a large basin some 30 miles across, a very hot and dry plain noted by Frémont in 1842. Inside this basin the old trail divides; the Mormons could have taken the shorter, northwest route via Cherry Creek to Fort Laramie, or turned to the northeast, picking up the Oregon Trail near Lingle, Goshen County, Wyoming (see trail XIII, 159) and followed it along the Platte River to Fort Laramie. It appears they did the latter. The vanguard of the Mississippi Saints reached the fort on May 17, 1847, where they waited for the Pioneers to arrive on June 1. Both groups then traveled west together.

To follow this old trail today, continue north on road 214 from the Lodgepole Creek site for 12 miles to its intersection with U.S. 85 (coming north out of Cheyenne). Horse Creek is crossed near Meriden. Nineteen miles north of Horse Creek is road 313 going west to Chugwater. Seven miles west on this Chugwater Road is Bear Mountain, through a canyon of which Lone Tree Creek flows.

Return to U.S. 85. The easy way to approximate the old trail is to stay on U.S. 85 all the way to Torrington and take U.S. 26 for 21 miles north to Fort Laramie. The more adventurous will prefer to turn west off U.S. 85 for 1.5 miles to Yoder and follow Highway 154 west and north 22 miles to Lingle. From Lingle it is possible to follow either the Mormon Trail (trail VIII, 82) or the Oregon Trail (trail XIII, 159 and 160) 10 miles west to Fort Laramie.

XXIII

The Cherry Creek and Jimmy Camp
Variants of the Trappers' Trail
in Colorado

(see map 11)

The Cherry Creek Variant

As already noted in trail XXII, there are three variants of the Trappers' Trail along the 80 miles between Fountain and Denver. The easy way to approximate the middle or Cherry Creek variant is simply to pick up Highway 83 off I-25 just north of Colorado Springs and follow it all the way to Denver via Franktown and Parker.

The Franktown Marker   222

*Just south of the intersection of Highways 86 and 83,
Franktown, Douglas County*

This site on the old Trappers' Trail was marked in 1946 by the State Historical Society of Colorado.

Named for J. Frank Gardner, a pioneer who settled here in 1859.

First known as "California Ranch." It was a way station on the stage line between Denver and Santa Fe. In a stockade built here, neighbors found refuge from Indians in 1846.

Twenty Mile House Marker   223

*At intersection of Parker Road and U.S. 83,
Parker, Douglas County*

Eight miles north of Franktown is the small community of Parker. Here the State Historical Society of Colorado erected a marker in 1945.

Due west ¼ mile stood the Twenty Mile House (Twenty miles from Denver). First house built in Parker, 1864. On the Smoky Hill Trail, an emigrant route that was dotted with unmarked graves of pioneers. Junction of the Smoky Hill Trail and Santa Fe stage lines. A refuge of early settlers against Indian attacks. . . .

The Smoky Hill Trail referred to here was an emigrant, mining, and stage road that ran from Kansas City (Westport), Missouri, to Denver via Forts Riley, Hayes, and Wallace, all in Kansas, along the Smoky Hill River into Colorado, where it passed north of Cheyenne Wells, Cheyenne County; then to Parker via Hugo, Limon, and Kiowa, a route approximated today by U.S. 40 and Highway 86. This old trail was also the route of the Butterfield Overland Dispatch and the Wells-Fargo Express. At least one Mormon, Brigham Young, Jr., used it in 1866. It was much traveled until replaced by the Union Pacific Railroad in 1870.

From Parker continue north of U.S. 83 through Denver to I-76 and U.S. 85, there picking up the main route of the Trappers' Trail (see trail XXII, 216).

The Jimmy Camp Variant

The most difficult to follow of the three variants of the old Trappers' Trail is the Jimmy Camp route. El Paso and Elbert counties' maps are helpful.

224   The Jimmy Camp Site (P)
(this marker no longer exists)

*Off U.S. 24 approximately 9 miles east of Colorado Springs,
El Paso County, in sec. 9, T14S, R65W*

To visit the Jimmy Camp site, drive 7 miles east of I-25 at Colorado Springs on U.S. 24 to a wye intersection with Highway 94; bear left and remain on U.S. 24 for about 1.5 miles. Watch for a sign to the right of the road reading "Jimmy Camp Ranch." Here, from the road, you can see the location of a 1949 State Historical Society of Colorado marker that has long since disappeared, as well as the general area of the Jimmy

Camp site. The actual campsite and famous spring are out of sight to the east. It takes special permission and the ranch foreman as guide to see the campsite, spring, and dim trail ruts—but they are there. Look sharp. Some 2 miles straight ahead on the horizon is a prominent bluff. Trail signatures are supposed to be found there.

> One mile southeast are the spring and site of Jimmy's Camp, named for Jimmy (last named undetermined), an early trader who was murdered there. A famous camp site on the trail connecting the Arkansas and Platte Rivers, and variously known as "Trappers' Trail," "Cherokee Trail," and "Jimmy's Camp Trail." Site visited by Rufus Sage (1842), Francis Parkman (1846), Mormons (1847) and by many gold seekers of 1858–59.

To continue approximating the Jimmy Camp Trail, drive northeast on U.S. 24 about 7 miles to Falcon and take the Meridian Road due north. In about 4 miles you will notice that the treeless grasslands suddenly give way to the Black Forest—referred to in old trail journals as The Pinery. The sudden change from grass to forest is unmistakeable and very unusual.

The Charles Fagan Grave (P)   225

Approximately 12.5 miles due north of Falcon off a county road in El Paso County, in NE 1/4, sec. 7, T11S, R64W

From the onset of the Black Forest, go about 1 mile or less to the first bridge (over Black Squirrel Creek). Then continue about 6.1 miles to a section-line road going due east across West Kiowa Creek. There is a grave about one-half mile due north on the west bank of the creek. To walk there, permission and directions must be secured at the Steel Ranch. The grave is right along the trail and dim ruts can be seen nearby. Fagan was a soldier under the command of a Captain R. B. Marcy who was delivering supplies from New Mexico to A. S. Johnston's army at Fort Bridger. (This is the same army President Buchanan sent to quell a supposed rebellion in Utah, see trail IX).

You can continue to approximate the old trail from here, but an Elbert County map is advised. The trick is to reach Elizabeth on Highway

86 via section-line roads. Except for some beautiful, desolate scenery, however, it is hardly worth it. I recommend that travelers continue east for 2.2 miles beyond the bridge over West Kiowa Creek to a blacktop and drive due north about 17.5 miles to Kiowa, which is also on Highway 86. From either Elizabeth or Kiowa drive west for 9 or 16 miles along the Smoky Hill Trail to Franktown, Douglas County, and pick up the trail at site 222.

XXIV

The Santa Fe Trail–Mormon Battalion March in Iowa, Missouri, Kansas, Oklahoma, New Mexico, Arizona, and California

Before describing the military route of the Santa Fe Trail from Fort Leavenworth, Kansas, it is convenient to follow the famous Mormon Battalion (of General Kearny's Army of the West during the Mexican War of 1846) from Council Bluffs, Iowa, south through Missouri to Fort Leavenworth.

What has been called the longest infantry march in history commenced on July 20, 1846, in Council Bluffs. This march of more than 1,850 miles to San Diego, California, was the result of the Mexican War of 1846, during which James K. Polk, president of the United States, asked the Mormons to furnish 500 men to help in the war effort. Mormon leaders agreed to provide the men because it would help demonstrate their loyalty to their country and they would benefit materially from the military pay, from the arms that the men could keep, from the uniform money allotments (since the Mormons were allowed to wear their own clothes), and from the fact that many men would be transported west at government expense. One of these men was John W. Hess, my great-grandfather.

The battalion of 549 men, 60 women, and several children formed in the Council Bluffs area (see trail I, 20) and commenced the first leg of its epic march, a 180-mile stretch down the left bank of the Missouri toward Fort Leavenworth. The battalion was divided into five companies and did not always travel together. This accounts for different dates of activities at the same places found in the sources. Although no Mormons were killed during the venture, four men died en route. The first, Samuel Boley, expired only 28 miles from Council Bluffs, just inside Mills County, Iowa.

The first part of the trail hugs the river bluffs, following what became the stagecoach route from Council Bluffs to St. Joseph (Missouri). The old bluff roads still exist in Iowa and Missouri and are shown on county maps, but one can get a more convenient view of the area by taking I-29 as far south as Mound City, Holt County, Missouri.

Iowa
(see map 2)

---

226   Mustering and Departure Historic Site

Near Iowa School for the Deaf, Council Bluffs,
Pottawattamie County, in sec. 8, T74N, R43W

This site is located near the Iowa School for the Deaf south of Council Bluffs, just north of where Highway 375 crosses Mosquito Creek. Although there is nothing to see here today, it was from here that the Mormon Battalion commenced the 180-mile first leg of its march down the east bank of the Missouri River to Fort Leavenworth, Kansas. (A marker is scheduled to be placed here.) Between Council Bluffs and Glenwood, 15 miles south, there is little to see except the Missouri River floodplain. Glenwood may be reached via I-29 or U.S 275.

227   Glenwood Historic Trail Marker

Glenwood, Mills County, on Highway 275,
in sec. 18, T72N, R42W

The only marker in Iowa that refers even indirectly to the Mormon Battalion (hereafter MB) is located just east of Glenwood on the west side of the junction of County Road 26 and Highway 275. The marker is a bronze plaque set in a piece of red granite.

> This marker commemorates / the early trails across Mills
> Co. / Dragoon 1835 / Mormon 1846 / Stagecoach 1850 / and
> honors the valiant pioneers / who travelled them. / Glenwood
> Chapter / Daughters of American Revolution / 1952.

Return to I-29 and continue south (towards Missouri) to Pacific Junction. Just west of this junction on Highway 34 is Plattsmouth, Nebraska, where the famous Bethlehem Ferry across the Missouri River was located (see trail XV, 169). Continue south on I-29 (or county road L-44, which hugs the bluffs) to the Missouri state line near Hamburg, Iowa.

Missouri
(see map 13)

Just beyond Hamburg, the battalion crossed the Nishnabotna River and entered Missouri, from which they had been driven by mobs during the winter of 1838–39. They remained on guard, but suffered no difficulties along their 120-mile march through that state. Their first camp in Missouri was near Linden, a community of which little exists today save a graveyard.

Linden Campsite   228

Near the Linden Cemetery, Atchison County,
in sec. 34, T66N, R41W

This cemetery, all that is left of the defunct community, is not shown on ordinary road maps, but the proper exit and county road are shown. Take the Watson exit off I-29, turn east on road B and follow its twists and turns for 5 miles to the cemetery, which is marked with a fancy wrought iron gate. No other marker is in this area.

Between Linden and the next historic site, travelers can approximate the old trail by taking U.S. 275 for 5 miles south to Rock Port, Atchison County (where the battalion also camped), to Mound City, Holt County, on U.S. 59 (which in 1846 was a stage stop named Jackson's Point), and to Oregon, Holt County, also on U.S. 59.

Oregon Campsite / Marker   229

Courthouse Square, Oregon, Holt County

The Mormons camped in the Holt County seat in July and on the courthouse square is a state historical society information sign.

HOLT COUNTY

Holt County's first settlers were Peter and Blank Stephenson, 1838. Pioneers were from Va., Ky., Tenn., Ind., and a large number of Germans located near Craig and Corning in 1839–41. In the 1840's, Whig Valley, near Maitland, was settled and Jackson's Point (for A. P. Jackson), near Mound City, was a stage stop on St. Joseph to Council Bluffs route. Mormons, emigrants, gold seekers of '49 trekked through the county. . . .

About 9 miles east of Oregon City on Highway 59, the Mormons crossed another large river, the Nodaway, and proceeded 19 more miles to Savannah (originally named Union), the county seat of Andrew County, and then turned south for about 10 miles to St. Joseph, a route approximated today by U.S. 71. (There is some evidence that part of the Battalion did not go via Savannah, but continued along the Missouri River to St. Joseph.)

230 St. Joseph Historic Site

St. Joseph, Buchanan County

While St. Joseph is rich in Pony Express lore and history, I found no marker commemorating the passage of the Mormon Battalion in 1846. Old journals, however, note that while passing through St. Joseph "to show the Missourians a thing or two they marched double-file with music, astonishing many who had not believed that the Mormons would answer their country's call during the Mexican War." While here you should visit the Pony Express Station / Museum.

From St. Joseph take U.S. 59 south. For 25 miles there is little of interest. Travelers might wish to visit the Lewis and Clark Lake and State Park, 1 mile south of where U.S. 59 turns due west into Kansas. Here is a view of what the Missouri River probably looked like in 1846. Continue south on Highway 45 some 12 miles to Weston.

231 Weston Historic Site

Weston, Platte County

At one time Weston, founded in 1837, was a famous river port city—home of Ben Holladay, the "Stage Coach King," and jumping-off place for the Far West. Not only did the Mormon Battalion pass through this community, but also many other Mormons subsequently started to the Far West from here—until the Missouri River changed course and Weston fell into somnolence.

Perhaps the most interesting thing about Weston for the modern trail follower is that here it is possible to pick up a river road 3 miles south to Beverley. This gravel road is not marked, one must ask for directions, and it can be difficult in wet weather, but it is well worth the effort as it is the only part of the Mormon Battalion route from Council Bluffs to Fort Leavenworth I have found which looks like the road probably did in 1846.

From Beverley take Highway 92 south for 4 miles to a bridge across the Missouri to Fort Leavenworth, which the Mormons reached by ferry on August 1, 1846. The old ferry site is about 2 miles north of the bridge and can be seen from the bridge.

Kansas
(see maps 8 and 14)

Almost all of the Mormon Battalion Trail in Kansas is identical to the Santa Fe Trail (hereafter SFT) for about 500 miles—from Fort Leavenworth to the Oklahoma Panhandle. The main difference in the routing is that the Mormons did not follow the main SFT from Independence, Missouri (see trail XXVII, 47–48) via present-day Olathe, Gardner, and Baldwin, Kansas, but the Fort Leavenworth military branch which intersected the main SFT near present-day Worden, Douglas County, 50 miles southwest of Fort Leavenworth or some 60 miles west of Independence. (Part of the SFT in Kansas is also marked as the Ozark Frontier Trail.) Since the SFT actually began in Missouri, users of this guide may wish to read trail XXVII before following the SFT.

Fort Leavenworth Historic Site / Marker / Ruts   232

Fort Leavenworth, Leavenworth County
Founded in 1827 to protect the SFT, this fort played an important role in Mormon immigration from the time the MB camped here on into the 1850s, when many other Mormons passed through or by this fort on their way to Utah. (One of the ways of picking up the Oregon Trail was via Fort Leavenworth, see trail XIV). The MB arrived here on August 1, 1846, and camped in the public square.

In the excellent Post Museum, "emphasizing the drama of westward expansion," is a small exhibit pertaining to the Utah Expedition of 1857.

(A detailed map of the fort area is available in this museum.) Of more interest are the impressive trail ruts leading up from the Missouri River to the fort grounds—ruts the MB probably helped to make. The ruts are located by going east from the General Grant statue (at the intersection of Kearny and Grant Avenues), down a hill towards the river.

Also of interest is a MB marker located on Kearny Avenue just west of the Grant statue. It is one of five similar markers erected in 1981 and 1983 by the Mormon church, the Kansas State Historical Society, and the Oklahoma State Historical Society.

THE MORMON BATTALION AT FORT LEAVENWORTH

The Mormon Battalion garrisoned here from 1 to 13 August 1846. The battalion received arms, training, supplies, and equipment here before departing on a 2,000 mile march to California via Santa Fe, New Mexico, and Tucson, Arizona.

The Mormon Battalion was a supportive arm of General Stephen Watts Kearny's "Army of the West," a part of the United States Army that President James K. Polk used against Mexican forces in the Mexican War (1846–1848). The battalion of five companies consisted of about 500 Mormon soldiers (plus 49 others) and was officially mustered into service at Council Bluffs, Iowa Territory, on 16 July 1846.

Although they had had no government protection when they were driven by lawless mobs from their homes in Illinois only months before, these members of The Church of Jesus Christ of Latter-day Saints (Mormon) volunteered for military service to their government in a time of great hardship for their families and loved ones. Brigham Young, their church leader, encouraged them to volunteer because he saw their participation in the war as a demonstration of loyalty to the United States and their wages as help for the Mormon migration then underway to the Great Basin in the Rocky Mountains.

The Mormon Battalion's final commander, Lt. Col. Philip St. George Cooke, declared "History will be searched in vain for an equal march of infantry."

Today little remains of the 50-mile long Fort Leavenworth military branch of the Santa Fe Trail, and it has become the least-known section of the more than 800 miles of the SFT and the 2,000-mile march of the Mormon Battalion. It deserves to be restored to memory. The following partial reconstruction is based on a study of twenty-eight Mormon Battalion journals, six other contemporary military accounts, appropriate maps, and several guides.

Although Kearny went this way in 1845, in 1846 there appears to have been no clearly defined link between Fort Leavenworth and the SFT. In 1829, for example, one military escort proceeded down the *east* bank of the Missouri to intersect the SFT near its beginning. By 1842 there was the Fort Scott Military Road, which ran directly south, intersecting the SFT probably near present Olathe, Kansas. (Later, in 1853, there evolved the Fort Riley Road, which ran westward.)

The Army of the West, including the Mormon Battalion, appears to have started out on the Fort Scott Road, passing Pilot Knob and crossing Five, Seven, and Nine Mile creeks. The army then turned off the Fort Scott Road and went southwest to cross Stranger Creek several miles northeast of present Tonganoxie. The army probably passed near Tonganoxie, following a ridge for some 7 miles southwest before turning southeast toward an Indian ferry at the confluence of the Wakarusa River and the Kansas River, about 1 mile northeast of present Eudora.

After crossing the river, the army proceeded along the south bank of the Wakarusa, crossing the Little Wakarusa Creek and Spring Creek, passing Blue Mound, and intersecting the Oregon Trail at or near Coal Creek just west of Blue Mound. The army was heading for the SFT at Willow Springs at The Narrows, a long, low ridge between the Kansas River and the Marais des Cygnes River (Mara du Seen in these parts), which ran at least 12 miles between present Black Jack (3 miles east of Baldwin City, see 233 below) and Willow Springs. SFT traders kept to this ridge because it offered drier ground.

To approximate the route today, proceed south from the main entrance to Fort Leavenworth (on U.S. 73), taking Highway 7 about 2 miles to Thornton Street, and turning west 1 mile to the Pilot Knob High School on Tenth Avenue. Pilot Knob rises about 200 feet just west of the high school and is clearly marked by radio towers on its summit.

Turn south on Tenth Avenue and go about 2 miles, crossing unmarked Five Mile Creek, to Eisenhower Road, and turn west 2 miles to County Road 5. (Along this 2-mile section, Pilot Knob can be seen to the north. Look for the radio towers.) Bear left on County Road 5 and follow its twists and turns (not always well marked) some 14 miles to Tonganoxie, crossing Stranger Creek en route.

At the south end of town, north of U.S. 40, is a monument to Chief Tonganoxie whose tribe was located near here. The army may have met these Indians, but I have read of no such encounter. From this marker there are two ways to approximate the old trail. The easy way is to take U.S. 40 just over 1 mile south (where U.S. 40 turns southwest) and pick up County Road 1 and follow it south for 9 miles to the bridge over the Kansas River at Eudora. The army crossed about 1 mile to the east. The other, more historic route requires the traveler to stay on U.S. 40 for 10 miles to Highway 32, turn east for 5 miles to County Road 1, and then travel south to Eudora.

From Eudora take County Road 1061 straight south for 3 miles. (To pick up this road from the center of Eudora, turn east 0.1 mile.) At the 3-mile point, take a section-line road west for 5 miles, crossing the Little Wakarusa and Spring creeks. At 5 miles the famous landmark of Blue Mound will be just to the north. (In trail days it would not have been wooded and would thus have been more prominent, see trail XI, 139.) Here one is about 1 mile east of where the army crossed the Oregon Trail. Some students of the SFT have mistaken this intersection of the Fort Leavenworth military branch of the SFT and the Oregon Trail with the more famous junction near Gardner, Kansas (see trail XI, 138 and this trail, 233 below) and thus hopelessly confused the route of the Army of the West in this area.

Just west of Blue Mound take the first section-line road south for 1 mile and turn west for 4 miles to U.S. 59 and then turn south for 2 miles to Pleasant Grove. (Here take a mileage reading for future reference.) About 1.5 miles south of Pleasant Grove you will intersect The Narrows where the army picked up the SFT. Whatever The Narrows looked like in 1846 (some soldiers say they saw it from miles away), it is almost impossible to perceive it today. By noting the direction of streams on a Douglas County map, The Narrows can be plotted quite accurately between Black Jack and Willow Springs, but I never saw anything on the ground that looked like a ridge.

To reach Willow Springs, the specific water stop on The Narrows to which the army was marching, go exactly 2.5 miles south of Pleasant Grove or about 1 mile south of where The Narrows is supposed to be. (Check your mileage reading made at Pleasant Grove.) At this point take a section-line road for 1.5 miles west to an intersection with another section-line road. West of this intersection is a DAR marker to Willow Springs (see this trail, 234).

If you do not wish to follow the Fort Leavenworth branch on the Santa Fe Trail, you have three other options. One is to drive as conveniently as possible straight to Worden, picking up the main SFT there (see 234). Another option is to drive to Kansas City, Missouri, to intersect the main SFT at old Westport near the intersection of Westport Road and Southwest Trafficway, and then follow U.S. 56 west via Overland, Olathe, and Gardner to a famous trail junction (compare trail XI). The third option is to pick up the SFT at the Independence, Courthouse (see trail XXVII, 47).

The Junction of the Oregon and Sante Fe Trails Marker

233

2 miles southwest of Gardner, Johnson County, on U.S. 56
Here in a highway pull-off is a Kansas historical marker telling the story of the famous junction where the Oregon Trail splits off the older SFT and heads northwest some 2,000 miles to Oregon, and where the SFT continues southwest for 750 miles. This marker indirectly refers to the MB by stating "Down the Santa Fe Trail went troops bound for the Mexican War of 1846–47." U.S. 56 follows the old SFT quite closely for 500 miles all the way across Kansas. (We have mentioned this marker before in reference to the Oregon Trail, see trail XI, 138).

OREGON AND SANTA FE TRAILS

At this point U.S.-50 is identical with these famous trails which from the Missouri river followed the same general route. Near here they branched, the word "Road to Oregon" on a rough board pointing out the northern fork. So simple a sign, one writer observed, never before announced so long a journey.

Here a second sign pointed southwest along the Santa Fe trail. Of its 750 miles, two-thirds lay in Kansas. As early as 1821 pack trains hazarded this route between the Missouri and Spanish frontiers. By 1825 it had become a commercial wagon road.

From 1840 to 1870 thousands of travelers plodded the 2,000 tortuous miles of the Oregon trail, recording with fearful monotony the new graves along the way. Down the Santa Fe trail went troops bound for the Mexican War of 1846–1847. Over these two roads, branching here into the wilderness, traveled explorers, traders, missionaries, soldiers, forty-niners and emigrants, the pioneers who brought civilization to the western half of the United States.

Wherever travelers pick up the SFT in Kansas, either at Gardner or farther west at Worden, they should be alert for information signs and markers of all sorts scattered liberally along the trail in Kansas. Between 1906 and 1908, for example, the DAR placed ninety-six red granite SFT markers in Kansas, all bearing the inscription: "Santa Fe Trail / marked by the / Daughters of the / American Revolution / and the / State of Kansas / 1906."

This guide does not attempt to list or locate all these DAR, Sons of American Revolution, Boy Scout, Mormon, American Pioneer Trails Association, Old Settlers Association, state, and local markers, only the most important.

Those who visit the trail junction near Gardner should take U.S. 56 for 21 miles west to Worden. En route visit the SFT ruts in the Black Jack Park 3 miles north of Baldwin City, Douglas County, and the SFT Park 0.7 mile north of Baldwin City on Douglas County Road 1055.

234   Junction of Main and Military Branches of the Santa Fe Trail Marker

Off U.S. 56, 2 miles east of Worden, Douglas County,
in sec. 21, T14S, R19E

This junction, where the military branch from Fort Leavenworth joined the main SFT, is approximately 2 miles east and 2.5 miles north of Worden on a county road.

Santa Fe Trail / marked by the / Daughters of the / American Revolution / and the / State of Kansas / 1906.

A new marker erected in 1985 reads:

Willow Springs. Water stop on the Santa Fe Trail. One of the

earliest post offices in Kansas Territory. Called Davies from
1855 to 1880. . . .

From Worden follow U.S. 50 for about 28 miles west to Burlingame.
One of the ninety-six DAR markers is in front of the post office at
Overbrook, and 5 miles beyond Overbrook, south of the road, is the
Santa Fe Trail High School. Here, close to the road right in front of a
sign giving the name of the school, may be seen a small 1978 Sons of
the American Revolution marker commemorating the SFT. This is only
the third SAR marker I have ever seen; they are rare (see trails XIX, 188
and XXII, 215).

> The Santa Fe Trail / 1822–72 / This marker placed by /
> Thomas Jefferson Chapter / Kansas Society of Sons of the /
> American Revolution / 1978.

Burlingame is interesting for several reasons: its main street was once
part of the SFT, here in 1869 the Santa Fe Railroad first intersected
the SFT, and the community is also the eastern terminus of a 40-mile
long Boy Scout hiking trail following the SFT west to Council Grove.
This hiking route, generally following section-line roads, is marked with
seventeen wagon-wheel markers, and several sets of trail ruts may be
seen along it. (Detailed maps of the trail can be obtained from the
Jayhawk Area Council, BSA, Topeka, KS. 66612, or from the Chamber of
Commerce in Burlingame, KS. 66413.)

An easier and quicker way to Council Grove is to stay on U.S. 56 for
43 more miles to the west.

Council Grove Historic Site / Marker   235

Kaw Mission grounds, Council Grove, Morris County
Council Grove is one of the most historic spots on the SFT. Its name
derives from the fact that in 1825 a treaty was signed here with the Osage Indians guaranteeing safe passage for wagon trains. Council Grove
(founded 1847) is full of history, and there are at least six historic sites
right on U.S. 56, including the famed Council Oak Shrine. Of special
interest is a MB marker at the Old Kaw Mission.

To reach this mission, turn north off U.S. 56 on Mission Drive for 5
blocks to Huffaker Street; the mission is to the right. Built in 1850–51,

it is now a state museum. The MB marker is south of the main building in a grassy area. It was erected by the Mormon church and the Kansas State Historical Society in 1981.

THE MORMON BATTALION AT COUNCIL GROVE, KANSAS.

The Mormon Battalion camped here for five days beginning 27 August 1846. The battalion's more than 500 volunteers and officers had been recruited from the Mormon pioneers (members of The Church of Jesus Christ of Latter-day Saints) at Council Bluffs, Iowa, to fight in the war with Mexico. The commanding officer, Colonel James Allen, had died at Ft. Leavenworth because of a lingering illness, and was replaced by Lieutenant Andrew Jackson Smith, who took command here on 30 August. Smith then led the Mormon Battalion to Santa Fe, about half of the 2,000 mile march to San Diego.

Council Grove was a government way-station used by soldiers and traders preparing for travel along the Santa Fe trail. While awaiting the change in command, the Mormon soldiers repaired their wagons and equipment, gathered supplies, and held religious services here. The battalion acquired two cannon drawn by six horses each, a portable blacksmith shop, forty provision wagons, twelve family wagons, and a few private baggage wagons. Merchants in twelve wagons also joined the battalion here for the march to Santa Fe, selling the soldiers clothing, water, and other goods.

Also worthy of note in Council Grove is the Madonna of the Trails Statue north of U.S. 56 just east of the bridge over the Neosho River. In 1928 the DAR erected thirteen of these impressive statues, featuring a pioneer mother with children, on what was then the Ocean to Ocean Highway. Four of the twelve are on Great Western Trails here in Garden Grove, Kansas; in Lexington, Missouri; in Lamar, Colorado; and in Albuquerque, New Mexico.

West of Council Grove the land changes from rolling hills to the more flat and arid plains. The next historic site is 15 miles southwest, at Diamond Springs.

These trail ruts on the Santa Fe Trail in Kansas lead from the Missouri River to Fort Leavenworth. *See trail XXIV, 232*.

At the top of Pawnee Rock, along the Santa Fe Trail in Kansas, there is a stone shelter and a DAR marker memorializing the pioneers who passed this way. *See trail XXIV, 243*.

The names of emigrants on the Santa Fe Trail are carved into the soft clay at Name Cliff in Oklahoma. Photo by Violet Kimball. *See trail XXIV, 256.*

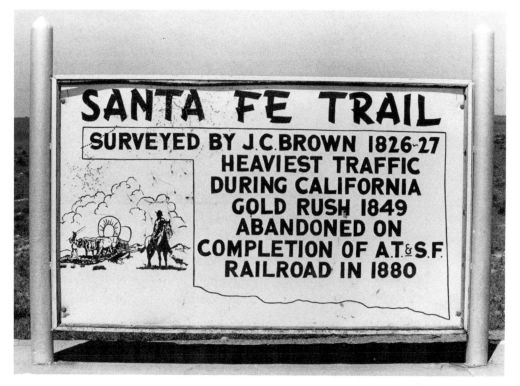

This sign commemorates the Santa Fe Trail through Cimarron County, Oklahoma. *See trail XXIV, 257.*

Rabbit Ears Mountain, New Mexico, is the most famous landmark on the Santa Fe Trail. *See trail XXIV, 258.*

Wagon Mound is a landmark along the Santa Fe Trail in New Mexico. Photo by Violet Kimball. *See trail XXIV, 262.*

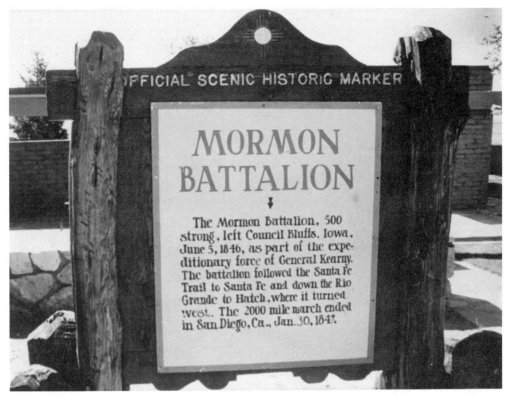

The Mormon Battalion March along the Santa Fe Trail covered many states between Iowa and California. This marker, south of Wagon Mound, New Mexico, is one of many to record the route of the march. *See trail XXIV, 263.*

Just beyond Cookes Spring, the Mormon Battalion encountered native American petroglyphs. *See trail XXIV, 281.*

The Butterfield Stage Trail followed parts of the same route blazed by the Mormon Battalion in 1846. This stage station is typical of those still standing in Arizona. *See trail XXIV, 288.* The only fully restored station is located along the Mormon Battalion Trail in California. *See trail XXIV, 300.*

Picacho Peak is one of the few landmarks along the Santa Fe Trail in Arizona. The Mormon Battalion camped near the base on December 17, 1846. *See trail XXIV, 291.*

There are several signs erected at this intersection of a dirt road with the Mormon Battalion Trail and the Butterfield Stage Trail. Part of the old trail is open to hikers. *See trail XXIV, 293.*

This unusual marker is located at Painted Rock Historic Park, Arizona. *See trail XXIV, 294.*

The Mormon Battalion Trail ran through Box Canyon, where cuts were made to widen the canyon so that the wagons could pass through. *See trail XXIV, 301.*

Located near the end of the trail followed by the Mormon Battalion, the San Luis Rey Mission has been restored and is open to visitors. *See trail XXIV, 303.*

CAPTAIN FREMONT TOOK
POSSESSION OF MISSION
SAN LUIS REY IN AUGUST
OF 1846. THE MORMON
BATTALION UNDER LT.
COOKE CAMPED AT MISSION
SAN LUIS REY IN FEB. 1847

Diamond Springs Historic Marker (P)   236

South of U.S. 56, 11 miles west of Council Grove,
Morris County, in sec. 34, T16S, R6E

Beyond Council Grove, water sources, especially springs, became of vital importance in the increasingly arid terrain. Diamond Springs were so named because they sparkled like diamonds in their dry surroundings.

To reach them go 11 miles west of Council Grove on U.S. 56, or exactly 4 miles west of the exit to Wilsey. Go south on this section-line road for 2.3 miles to the entrance (to the west) of the Diamond Springs Ranch, where permission to visit the springs must be obtained.

There is a DAR marker here. (The railroad hamlet of Diamond Springs, about 5 miles east, has nothing to do with the springs.) Return to U.S. 56 and proceed west 18 miles to Herrington. Turn south at Herrington and exactly 3 miles south of the Marion County line, a county road goes 1 mile west to the community of Lost Springs.

Lost Springs Historic Site / Marker   237

On a county road 2.3 miles west of the community
of Lost Springs, Marion County

Two and three-tenths miles west of the community of Lost Springs on the south side of the road is a large DAR marker commemorating these once-important springs. The springs themselves are identified by a sign north of the highway, where the MB camped on September 1, 1846.

The next historic site is 19 miles west, near Durham, Marion County. Continue west from Lost Springs through a crossroads community named Tampa to an intersection with Highway 15. About 1.7 miles to the south of this intersection watch for some trail ruts west of the road marked by an "Original Santa Fe Trail crossed here" sign. Durham is 3.3 miles farther south.

The Cottonwood River Crossing Historic Site / Markers   238

Just west of Durham, Marion County, on a county road

Go west 1 mile on the only road west of Durham, then 0.5 mile north to an intersection and the Cottonwood River. Markers may be found north and west of this intersection.

Returning to Durham, go south 8 miles to rejoin U.S. 56 and turn west 22 miles towards McPherson, McPherson County.

239   The Mormon Battalion at McPherson Marker

8 miles north of McPherson, McPherson County,
in a dual rest area off I-135.

Go north on I-135 for 8 miles to a dual rest area, turn west through the northbound area into the southbound rest area, where the marker is in front of the rest area building. It was erected by the Mormon church and the Kansas State Historical Society in 1981. The SFT actually passes 12 miles to the south.

THE MORMON BATTALION AT McPHERSON, KANSAS

On 3 September 1846, the Mormon Battalion camped near here on its way to fight in the war with Mexico. This small army of more than 500 men and officers had been recruited at Council Bluffs, Iowa, from among the Mormon pioneers (members of The Church of Jesus Christ of Latter-day Saints) who were en route to the Rocky Mountains. About one-tenth of the battalion suffered from "ague, billious, and congestive fever" during the march from Council Bluffs, but only the standard army medicines of "calomel, arsenic, and bitters of bayberry bark" were on hand to treat them with.

Here battalion members saw for the first time the prickly pear cactus and other semi-arid plants typical of the American Southwest. Their difficult 1700-mile journey through the dry and barren landscape between this campsite and the final destination at San Diego, California, evoked poems, songs, and art work, some of which have been preserved in the diaries kept by the battalion members.

240   The Little Arkansas River Crossing Historic Site Area

18 miles west of McPherson, south of U.S. 56,
in sec. 24, T20S, R6W in Rice County

The approximate site of the Little Arkansas River crossing is 18 miles west of McPherson on U.S. 56. For a closer inspection of this site, turn south off U.S. 56 about 14 miles west of McPherson on a section-line road that forms the boundary between McPherson and Rice counties. Drive 5 miles south, where there is a DAR marker on the southeast corner of an intersection. The crossing is 0.8 mile to the west. About 1 mile farther west, south of the road, is a sign commemorating a "Stone Corral" dating from the Civil War. Return to U.S. 56 and go 20 miles west to the next historic site.

Cow Creek Historic Site 241

On U.S. 56, 4 miles west of Lyons, Rice County,
The MB camped on Cow Creek September 5. To reach this site drive 4 miles west of Lyons on U.S. 56. At that intersection is an information sign and 30-foot tall cross honoring Father Juan de Padilla, a Franciscian missionary who accompanied Coronado in 1540 in the search for the fabeled Seven Cities of Gold. Padilla was martyred in 1542; the cross was erected in 1950. Turn south 1 mile on a section-line road to an information sign near Cow Creek. Return to U.S. 56.

Trail Ruts 242

8 miles west of the Father Padilla Cross,
in secs. 34 and 35, T19S, R10W, Rice County
Some of the most impressive SFT ruts in this part of Kansas are exactly 8 miles west of the Padilla Cross; then turn north 0.7 miles to a sign "Santa Fe Trail Crossed Here." Ruts in the form of a deep swale may be seen to the east. Return to U.S. 56, continue west 34 miles to the next historic site, passing through Great Bend, Barton County, where the SFT reaches the main Arkansas River (at its "great bend"), which the trail then follows for 120 miles.

Pawnee Rock Historic Site / Markers 243

At Pawnee Rock, Barton County
Pawnee Rock, although a most modest land feature, is nevertheless one of the most famous landmarks on the entire SFT, the first significant landmark on the trail at all. It is smaller today than originally, although

it was never much more than sixty feet high, because it was used as a quarry for the Santa Fe Railroad.

There is a DAR plaque on the rock and a tall marker near the stone shelter on top.

> In honor of the brave men and women who passing over the Santa Fe Trail endured the hardships of frontier life and blazed the path of civilization for posterity.

I know of no MB reference to this landmark, but surely it was noted in passing. In the center of the small town of Pawnee Rock, off U.S. 56, a sign points along Center Avenue to the rock. From the top an excellent view of the surrounding countryside is obtained.

At the immediate west end of the community of Pawnee Rock to the south of U.S. 56 is a Kansas Historical Marker giving a brief history of the area.

PAWNEE ROCK

> One-half mile northeast of Pawnee Rock, a famous landmark on the Santa Fe Trail. As a lookout and ambush, rising from the prairies where millions of buffalo provided an easy living for hostile Indians, the rock was one of the most dangerous points on the central plains. Pike, Webb, Gregg, Doniphan and other travelers mentioned it in their journals. Here 17-year-old Kit Carson, standing guard one night in 1826, shot his own mule, mistaking it for an Indian. Trappers, soldiers, gold-seekers, freighters and emigrants carved their names in the stone. In later years railroad builders and pioneers stripped the top of the rock and greatly reduced its elevation. It is now a state park. A road leads to a shelter house and monument on the summit.

244–246   The Fort Larned Area Historic Site / Markers / Ruts

Larned, Pawnee County

8 miles southwest of Pawnee Rock on U.S. 56 is Larned, in the area of which are several signs, markers, the Santa Fe Trail Center, reconstructed old Fort Larned (established in 1859), some splendid ruts, and a MB marker.

The first set of ruts is easily found at the southeast corner of the Larned Cemetery, which is 2 miles west of Larned on Highway 156, then 0.5 mile south. The ruts look like shallow ripples in the grass along the fence line.

Return to Highway 156 and drive 0.5 mile west to the Santa Fe Trail Center. It is the best SFT museum along the trail and must be visited. In front of this center is another MB marker placed there by the Mormon church and the Kansas State Historical Society in 1981.

THE MORMON BATTALION AT LARNED, KANSAS

The Mormon Battalion camped here on 8 September 1846. The more than 500 volunteers in this little army were enlisted to fight in the war with Mexico. They had been recruited from among the Mormon pioneers (members of The Church of Jesus Christ of the Latter-day Saints) who were camping for the winter near Council Bluffs, Iowa, during their famous trek to the Rocky Mountains.

At this campsite the soldiers found plenty of wood for their fires, but it was useless in the midst of the downpour that day, which drenched the army "like so many drowned rats." The foul weather also hampered the next day's crossing of the rain-swollen Pawnee River, making it necessary for wagons and gear to be pulled by ropes to the opposite bank. This was only one of many fatiguing experiences the Mormon Battalion endured during its 2,000-mile march across the American Southwest to San Diego, California.

From the center proceed 4 miles west on Highway 156 to a road sign directing you to turn south into the restored old Fort Larned National Historic Site. The fort dates from 1859 and is worth a visit. Much literature on the SFT is available here and a very informative film can be seen.

There is a second set of SFT ruts in the Larned area. Return to Highway 156, go west about 0.3 mile, turn south on a section-line road 4 miles, then west 1 mile, then south again 0.8 mile to a well-marked parking lot. In this 40-acre pasture the trail ruts are visible. Visitors should walk to the elevated observation stand in the pasture for the best view.

From these ruts there is little of interest to see for 54 miles to Dodge City. Go south from the ruts 2 miles and pick up U.S. 56 at Garfield.

Look for trail markers in the Garfield city park, at the western end of Kinsley in a roadside park, in the Offerle town park, and in Wright, just to the north on U.S. 283.

247   Dodge City Historic Area

Dodge City, Ford County

Dodge City is proud to be "The Cowboy Capitol" and there is plenty there for the tourist and traveler to do. Watch for some interesting signs approaching the city from the east: some huge sundials are at the railroad station, there is a trail marker in River Park, and restored Disney-esque Old Front Street is fun to visit, if on the expensive side. Just west of town, to the south of U.S. 50, is a DAR marker. Four miles from the town center is a white marker to the north of U.S. 50 (travelers will be off U.S. 56 for a while) commemorating the Caches, an old campsite of exceptional unimportance, but every trail study mentions it, so I feel I must too.

248   Santa Fe Trail Ruts / Marker

On U.S. 50, 10 miles west of Dodge City, Ford County

Here, north of the road, in a well-marked pull-off, travelers can see the most impressive SFT ruts in Kansas. Park your car near the DAR marker and walk about 150 yards to a National Park Service monument near the ruts. Sometimes longhorn cattle can be seen in the area. The next point of interest is 8 miles west.

249   Cimarron Cutoff Markers

Cimarron, Gray County

There are three trail markers in Cimarron. The first, one of the most handsome along the trail, is in the pleasant little Cimarron Crossing Park just west of town on Highway 23. This large red granite marker was placed here by the Cimarron Business and Professional Woman's Club to commemorate the Cimarron Cutoff. The marker is noteworthy for its incised map showing clearly the relation of the Cimarron Cutoff to the Mountain Route—with one mistake. This map shows the Mountain Route from the Cimarron Crossing as a separate trail all the way to Santa

Fe. Actually the Mountain Route intersected the Cimarron Route at La Junta (Watrous), New Mexico (see site 265 below and compare with a more accurate map incised on a DAR marker in Santa Fe, site 270 below).

In the same little park is a Kansas historical marker regarding the SFT and the Cimarron Cutoff.

THE SANTA FE TRAIL

Cimarron, settled in 1878, got its name as the starting point at one time of the shorter Cimarron or dry route to Santa Fe. Here the Santa Fe Trail divided, one branch heading directly southwest, the other (present U.S. 50) following the Arkansas River to Bent's Fort (near La Junta, Colo.), then south over Raton Pass.

William Becknell first traveled the dry route with a pack train via the Cimarron River in 1822, carrying trade goods for Mexico, newly freed from Spain. By 1824, wagons croked along with loads of calico, guns, tools, and shoes to exchange for silver, furs, wood, and mules. Trade became of such importance that in 1851 the government surveyed the route in U.S. territory north of the river, and the Upper Crossing, near Chouteau Island in Kearny County, was recommended because of the shorter distance between rivers. But despite the danger, the Middle Crossing—various points in the Cimarron-Ingalls area—was used the most.

Usually waterless and subject to Indian attacks, the 60 miles of trackless prairie between the Arkansas and Cimarron rivers was called by the Mexicans, Jornada del Muerte, or Journey of Death.

There is also a small SFT museum in the city hall. A DAR marker is at the western end of town on U.S. 50 in front of a gun club.

In the general area of Cimarron was the famous crossing of the Arkansas River, known as the Cimarron Crossing or the Cimarron Cutoff. Here the SFT split. Many crossed the river at various places in this area, others continued west along the river to Bent's Fort in present-day Colorado. This was called the Mountain Route to Santa Fe (see trail XXV). It appears that the MB crossed the Arkansas River 6 miles west of Cimarron, near present-day Ingalls.

250 The Cimarron Cutoff of the Sante Fe Trail Historic Site

Ingalls, Gray County

The original marching orders of the MB had been to proceed to San Diego via Bent's Fort in present-day Colorado. Mexican War developments, however, changed those orders. The new orders were for the MB to take the Cimarron Cutoff and hurry to San Diego. Since the Cimarron Cutoff necessitated a 50-mile march across a waterless desert (or *Jornada*) to Wagon Bed Springs, it was decided to trim the MB of any sick. Ten men and several families were sent up the Arkansas to Bent's Fort—the first of three Sick Detachments that eventually spent the winter of 1846–47 at Fort Pueblo, Colorado (see trail XXII). Here near Ingalls on September 16 another member of the MB died; Alva Phelps of Company E was buried south of the river.

One observation from the journal of Henry Standage for September 17, 1846, suggests how hard the cutoff was: "We traveled 25 miles this day across one of the most dreary deserts that ever man saw, suffering much from the intense heat of the sun and for want of water." Modern-day travelers can assess for themselves the accuracy of this statement (although irrigation has changed the area somewhat) by driving along various roads from Ingalls to Ulysses, Grant County, some 50 miles to the west. This is rough, desolate country so anyone straying from the main roads should have Gray, Haskell, and Grant counties' maps.

With such maps it is possible to approximate the dreaded *Jornada* of trail days, but it is not recommended. The best way to Wagon Bed Springs is to cross the Arkansas River as the MB did and then go 19 miles due south to pick up U.S. 56 at Montezuma. (Between Ingalls and U.S. 56 the road makes two right-angle turns.) Turn west 6 miles on U.S. 56 to Highway 144 (which soon becomes U.S. 160) and follow it straight west 44 miles to Ulysses.

251 Wagon Bed Springs Historic Site / Markers

On U.S. 70, 12 miles south of Ulysses, Grant County

At Ulysses take U.S. 270 due south 13 miles to a pull-off west of the road. (The springs themselves are about 2 miles west of this pull-off.) There are three historical markers: a Kansas historical marker referring to the spring, one commemorating the killing of Jedediah Smith by Comanches in 1831 near here, and the third honors the MB, which camped at these springs on September 19, 1846; this last was placed here by the Mormon church and the Kansas Historical Society in 1981.

THE MORMON BATTALION AT CIMARRON SPRINGS
(WAGON BED SPRINGS)

On 19 September 1846, the more than 500 men and officers of the Mormon Battalion arrived here. These Mormons (members of The Church of Jesus Christ of Latter-day Saints) had volunteered to fight in the war with Mexico, enlisting at Council Bluffs, Iowa, while en route to the Rocky Mountains. The battalion's arrival at this site marked the completion of the first third of its 2,000-mile trek to San Diego, California.

Thirsty and weary from a forced march of 50 miles across "one of the most dreary deserts that ever man saw," where no moisture but contaminated and dirty rainwater could be found, the little army finally located sufficient water to quench its thirst under the sand of this dry creek bed. With water to drink, plenty of grass for livestock, and buffalo chips to fuel fires, man and beast refreshed themselves before continuing the long march.

At these springs the MB finally picked up the Cimarron River, the generally dry bed of which they followed for more than 100 miles. Some 40 miles up this river is the next point of interest along the SFT, the Point of Rocks. With Stevens and Morton counties' maps it is possible to zigzag around approximating the old trail to the Point of Rocks. General travelers, however, are advised to go south of Wagon Bed Springs for 17 miles on U.S. 270 to Hugoton, Stevens County, once again picking up the by now old friend U.S. 56 and follow it 34 miles west to Elkhart.

Middle Springs and Point of Rocks Historic Sites   252, 253

Off Highway 27, 8 miles north of Elkhart,
Morton County, in sec. 12, T34S, R43W

Elkhart is proud of its location as the last community in Kansas on the old trail, as a sign to the south of U.S. 56 at the east end of town indicates. Another Kansas historical information marker is located at the western end of town on U.S. 56. The extensive text is all about Point of Rocks and La Jornada.

A well-known landmark of the Cimarron cutoff of the old Santa Fe trail is a rugged bluff known as Point of Rocks which rises near the Cimarron river nine miles north on Highway 27. Called the westernmost landmark of signficance on the trail in Kansas. It marked a campground much used by travelers because good water was always available from the nearby Middle Spring of Cimarron. William Becknell, who pioneered commercial use of the trail in 1821, and Santa Fe trader Josiah Gregg, author of the classic "Commerce of the Prairies," were among those who stopped there.

Point of Rocks was on the "dry" fork of the trail, which headed southwest from the several Arkansas river crossings. Part of this route, between the Arkansas and Cimarron rivers, was a perilous stretch of arid plains known to travelers as "La Jornada." Besides lack of water, caravans had to contend with marauding bands of Plains Indians who took the lives of several traders in this once empty land.

Elkhart, one of the youngest towns in Kansas, was established here in 1915.

Return to the center of town and turn north about 8 miles on Highway 27 to a bridge across the Cimarron River, where east of the road is a pleasant rest area. Proceed north 1 mile to a pull-off on the west where there is a DAR marker and a Cimarron National Grassland information sign. From here you get a good view of the Cimarron River valley, and Point of Rocks can be seen in the distance to the southwest. One-half mile north of here, northwest of an intersection, is a badly weathered DAR marker.

From this second DAR marker turn around and go south 1 mile to a dirt road, marked by a yellow cattle guard, leading due west off Highway 27. Follow this dirt road about 2 miles, turn north on another dirt road and you should quickly see another yellow cattle guard and just past it the Middle Spring information sign. Beyond this sign are the springs and some picnic tables. This spring was the first good water since Wagon Bed Springs and was very important in trail days. These springs are "Point of interest no. 16" on the Cimarron National Grassland Auto Tour, a map of which may be obtained at the office of the U.S.D.A. Forest Service in Elkhart.

From the picnic area return to the main dirt road and go west towards the Point of Rocks, which can be seen a little over 1 mile away. In 1 mile take the left-hand fork in the dirt road to the top of Point of Rocks. In the parking area is an information sign. Coronado passed this way in 1540 and this may be the "rocky bluffs" mentioned by the MB on September 22, 1846. This site provides the best view of the SFT (which here follows the Cimarron River) in all Kansas, if not along the entire extent of the trail. Point of Rocks itself is not very dramatic, but in the flatness of western Kansas it stands out prominently. Six miles to the southwest the trail passes out of modern Kansas.

To follow the trail into Oklahoma return to Elkhart.

Oklahoma
(see map 14)

The SFT passes through only one county in Oklahoma, the extreme western panhandle county of Cimarron; there are two trail crossings, some ruts, a "name cliff," and a MB marker. A Cimarron County map (sheets 1 and 2) is recommended, but not essential. From Elkhart, Kansas, follow U.S. 56 for 38 miles west to Boise City, Oklahoma, pronounced Boyce (one syllable) City by the natives.

The Mormon Battalion   254
in the Oklahoma Panhandle Marker

North side Court House Square,
Boise City, Cimarron County

This marker was erected by the Mormon church and the Oklahoma State Historical Society in 1983.

THE MORMON BATTALION IN THE OKLAHOMA PANHANDLE

From September 23 through 27, 1846, the Mormon Battalion crossed the northwestern portion of the Oklahoma panhandle. The little army's 500-plus volunteers, recruited for the Mexican War, were enlisted near Council Bluffs, Iowa, from among the first company of Mormon pioneers who were then en route to the Rocky Mountains.

The Battalion's 2,000-mile journey from Ft. Leavenworth, Kansas, to San Diego, California, then the longest march by infantry in U.S. military history, traversed for a lengthy distance the Santa Fe Trail. Sixty miles of that famous route passed through the panhandle. It followed the Cimarron River southwesterly into Oklahoma to the Cimarron Crossing, then west-southwest past Cold Springs into New Mexico at McNees Crossing.

Battalion members viewed the Oklahoma Panhandle as part of the "Great American Desert." The challenges of this portion of the march helped forge the Battalion into a disciplined force.

255   Oklahoma Trail Crossing / Ruts (Site 1)

On U.S. 287, 9 miles north of Boise City,
Cimarron County

From the MB marker at the courthouse go 9 miles north on U.S. 287 to a pull-off west of the road. This SFT crossing was authenticated as early as 1827 by a U.S. Survey that began at Fort Osage, Missouri (see trail XXVII, 44). Here ruts can be seen on both sides of the road. To the northeast is Wolf Mountain, past which the trail meanders. The historical marker that used to be here has disappeared. Some 12 miles to the northeast is the Cimarron Crossing where the SFT leaves that river, which it has followed for more than 100 miles from Wagon Bed Springs (see 251 above).

256   Upper Springs Historic Site / Name Cliff (P)

10 miles northeast of Boise City,
Cimarron County, in sec. 8, T4N, R4E

Upper Springs and the soft clay cliff called Name Cliff are on private ground and permission must be secured to visit the area. The cliff is covered with names, some from the time the MB passed this way; it is fragil and should not be marked. I have found non-Mormon names dating from 1846, probably left by Mexican War soldiers.

Take Highway 325 for 5 miles west from Boise City to a blacktop road and go 4 miles north, 2 miles west, then 3 miles north to the ranch of Mr. Dan Sharp and ask permission to view the area. Then return to Highway 325.

Oklahoma Trail Crossing/Ruts (Site 2) 257

16 miles west and 3.7 miles north of Boise City,
Cimarron County, in sec. 26, T4N, R2E

Sixteen miles west of Boise City (11 miles west of the Name Cliff turnoff) Highway 325 turns north. Oklahoma Trail Crossing is 3.7 miles north of this turn. In a pull-off there are two historic markers: one, an Oklahoma highway marker, refers to the site of Fort Nichols, 7 miles to the southwest, founded in 1865. The other refers to the U.S. Survey of the SFT in 1826–27. Here is one of the most unspoiled areas along the whole SFT. To the west the ruts appear as a discoloration on the landscape. The next historic site is in New Mexico, 11 miles straight west. To reach New Mexico, return 3.7 miles south to the curve, go 1 more mile south on a gravel road to a blacktop road, turn west 11 miles to the New Mexico state line.

New Mexico
(see map 15 and 16)

From the New Mexico state line the scenery along the SFT begins to get much more dramatic—there are famous landmarks and the Sangre de Cristo Mountains, in the arms of which nestles Santa Fe. Of the approximately 225-mile length of the Cimarron Cutoff of the SFT in New Mexico, more than 100 are easy to follow by simply driving along I-25. The section just beyond Oklahoma, however, is quite difficult to follow and is in very desolate country. Travelers who get off the main roads must be careful and have county maps. The DAR has placed twelve gray granite markers along the Cimarron Cutoff in New Mexico, most of which are easy to find, and all are inscribed the same: "Santa Fe Trail / 1822–72 / Erected by the / Daughters of the / American Revolution / and the / State of New Mexico / 1909."

258   Rabbit Ears Mountain Historic Landmark

6 miles northwest of Clayton, Union County

Just inside New Mexico the Rabbit Ears Mountain landmark can be seen 25 miles to the southwest. Although only 6,000 feet high, it is the most famous landmark on the whole SFT, the great symbol of the Cimarron Cutoff. The name comes from two closely related peaks that from certain angles and with much imagination faintly (very faintly) resemble rabbit ears. (Marc Simmons, the authority on the SFT, says the name may derive from Chief Rabbit Ears of the Cheyennes who was killed in the vicinity by the Spaniards.) On September 24, 1846, Standage of the MB recorded: "We came in sight of the Rabbit Ears, two very large mountains, known by that name, and which serves as a landmark for travelers."

The best view of the landmark comes from following the SFT to the north, but this requires a 45-mile drive, via Grenville, Union County, along desolate county roads, with the aid of a Union County map. It can be done and is certainly worth the effort. A much easier and safer way, however, is to pass the formation to the south, via Clayton. One less-used variant of the SFT came this way, so you are still on the old trail.

259   Clayton Area

Clayton, Union County

To reach Clayton from the Oklahoma state line, continue west and south on New Mexico Highway 18 for 26 miles. Highway 18 makes three turns before intersecting with U.S. 56 just 3 miles east of Clayton. One-tenth of a mile west on U.S. 56 is a pull-off with a Rabbit Ears Mountain information sign. Go west another 0.1 mile to a roadside park where there is a SFT sign near the entrance to the restrooms.

In Clayton the traveler gets an excellent view of Rabbit Ears Mountain. From Clayton it is a long 60-mile drive west on U.S. 56 to the famous landmark, the New Mexican Point of Rocks.

There is a second, more interesting, way to follow the old SFT out of Clayton—via U.S. 64/87. Along this route you get the closest and best view of Rabbit Ears Mountain. Also, about 21 miles northwest of Clayton to the right of the road is a white marker enclosed by a rail fence commemorating the "First wagon used on the Santa Fe Trail crossed here in 1822. Erected in 1930 by the Colorado and Southern Railway."

Seven miles beyond this marker is a crossroad community called Grenville. From here it is 21 miles south to get back to U.S. 56. Turn south at the crossroads on a rough dirt road. In 7 miles you will be directly west of Mt. Clayton (called Round Mountain in trail days), a historic landmark on the old SFT. Continue south another 14 utterly desolate miles to U.S. 56 and go west toward Point of Rocks.

Point of Rocks Historic Site/Markers   260

On U.S. 56, 60 miles west of Clayton, Union County
Here in a roadside park north of the road are two markers. One commemorates the Point of Rocks, which can be seen to the northeast and the other the Sangre de Cristo (Blood of Christ) Mountains, for just beyond here to the west travelers get their first view of those mountains, the first seen on the Cimarron Cutoff. These mountains are part of the Southern Rockies, rising above 13,000 feet.

Canadian River Historic Crossing   261

On U.S. 56, 6 miles east of Springer, Colfax County
A famous river crossing is located about 1 mile south of where U.S. 56 crosses the Canadian River today. Drive 6 miles farther west to Springer. Here U.S. 56 finally ends. It is also at Springer where you either begin or end the Mountain Route of the SFT (see trail XXV). Turn south on I-25 for 26 miles to Wagon Mound.

Wagon Mound Historic Landmark/Marker   262

Off I-25, Wagon Mound, Mora County
Wagon Mound, which from the north really does look like a wagon, is the last of the great landmarks on the SFT. It is east of the road near the little town of Wagon Mound. The first of the DAR's gray granite markers is located here at the Municipal Building. Standage recorded the following: "Traveled 18 miles to the Wagon Mound, arrived here at 11 o'clock, some Mexicans and Indians here selling whiskey." These is

a better and easier-to-find marker just in front of the first service station reached off I-25 in Wagon Mound.

263 Mormon Battalion Sign

Eastbound rest area off I-25,
14 miles south of Wagon Mound, Mora County

MORMON BATTALION

The Mormon Battalion, 500 strong, left Council Bluffs, Iowa, June 5, 1846, as part of the expeditionary force of General Kearny. The battalion followed the Santa Fe Trail to Santa Fe and down the Rio Grande to Hatch, where it turned west. The 2000 mile march ended in San Diego, Ca., Jan. 30, 1847.

Recently this Official Scenic Historic Marker was replaced and now reads:

The Mormon Battalion, composed of 500 volunteers, left Council Bluffs, Iowa, June 5, 1846, as part of the expeditionary force of Brigadier General Kearny. The battalion followed the Santa Fe and down the Rio Grande near here, where it turned west. The 2,000 mile march ended in San Diego, California, January 30, 1847.

This new sign is not well worded. For example, the MB had to march more than 125 miles to reach the Rio Grande and then it followed that river more than 200 miles before turning west. This sign suggests these soldiers both reached the river and turned west "near here."

At this same rest stop and also in the southbound lane rest stop are DAR markers to the SFT.

264 Santa Fe Trails Ruts

Off I-25, 15 miles south of Wagon Mound, Mora County
About 1 mile south of the Mormon Battalion marker (see 263 above) to the west of I-25 is an 8-mile stretch of SFT ruts that should not be missed. They can be seen best when in shadow.

Nearby, Fort Union is on the Mountain Route branch of the SFT (see trail XXV, 307). You can reach it easily from I-25 by taking Highway 477 north.

La Junta (Watrous) Historic Site / Ruts / Marker   265

Watrous, Mora County

La Junta was the first Mexican village reached by the MB and from here to Santa Fe there is a string of small communities, the uninhabited portion of the SFT being over.

This community at the junction (*La Junta*) of the Mora and Sapello rivers was (unfortunately) renamed Watrous, after a prominent local rancher, because there was already a La Junta, Colorado (see trail XXV, 320). This name change was spurious and obviously politically motivated, for the two communities are in different states.

Although the whole community is registered as a National Historic Landmark, there is little in Watrous today of interest, except the marker in a small park near the school, which officially states "Watrous, western junction of the Santa Fe Trail, has been designated a Registered National Historic Landmark, 1964."

There are also some very dramatic trail ruts nearby. To reach them continue south through Watrous on U.S. 85, take Highway 161 to the right (west), cross I-25 and the Sapello River, and at the first road go a short distance to the left (south). The ruts are west of this road, opposite the restored Sapello Stage Station to the left.

For those who would like to get off I-25 and see some of the old Mexican villages scattered along the SFT south of Watrous, I recommend Tecolate, Bernal, San Miguel, San Jose, Pecos, and Glorieta. DAR markers may be found in Tecolate, Bernal, and San Jose.

Las Vegas Historic Site   266

Las Vegas, San Miguel County

Las Vegas is a city of much history, but with little Mexican atmosphere. National Avenue, for example, is the exact route of the old SFT and there is a DAR marker at the plaza.

Other things to see include the Casa Musica at No. 210–218 on the old plaza, where from the roof General Kearny most likely made his first proclamation of occupation on August 15, 1846, and Theodore Roosevelt's Rough Riders Museum on Grand Avenue.

267   Kearny Gap Historic Site

*On Highway 283, 4 miles south out of Las Vegas,
San Miguel County*

Going south out of Las Vegas follow the signs to Mineral Hill, which will lead you west on Highway 283. About 1 mile on 283 west of I-25 is a very noticable gap through the low mountains. It was through this gap (named after General Kearny) that his army, including the MB, passed in 1846. (For those who do not wish to exit here the gap can be seen plainly from I-25.) Return to I-25 and proceed south.

268   Glorieta Mesa Pass and Historic Site

Between San Jose, San Miguel County, and Santa Fe

The 40-mile long Glorieta Mesa Pass through the Sangre de Cristo Mountains leads you straight to Santa Fe. It is a very beautiful drive with dramatic escarpments.

269   Pecos National Monument Historic Site

Off I-25 near Pecos, San Miguel County

Take the Pecos National Monument exit off I-25 and follow signs for several miles to an impressive ruin. There was a settlement at Pecos when Coronado passed in 1540, and the huge Spanish colonial mission church dates from 1620. The ruins of this mission, abandoned in 1782, are maintained by the National Park Service and should not be missed. Neither should the most beautiful visitors' center in the whole National Park Service (built with private money.) In this center there is an excellent film narrated by the actress Greer Garson, who has a ranch in the area.

Of Pecos, Standage noted on October 8: "Marched up the valley to Bagos [Pecos] until we came to the abbey of Bagos which was built 250 years ago. The walls are in a ruined state, still some of the walls are in good repair."

From here you are only about 20 miles from Santa Fe. Return to I-25 the way you came or go west via the old town of Pecos. Either way the traveler will soon reach the summit of the Glorieta Pass, "the gateway to Santa Fe," 14 miles farther on. (On March 28, 1862, the decisive battle of the Civil War in New Mexico was fought at the summit of this pass—destroying southern hopes of taking over New Mexico.) Take the first of the three Santa Fe exits (the Old Pecos Trail / U.S. 84 / 85) to the Old Santa Fe Trail, which leads right into the old Plaza area.

Santa Fe Historic City   270

Santa Fe, Santa Fe County

This famous city, La Villa Real de Santa Fe de San Francisco de Assisi or Royal City of the Holy Faith of St. Francis of Assisi, founded in 1610 is the oldest state capital in the United States. Santa Fe is full of many historic and cultural things to do and see and all kinds of maps and guides may be purchased or picked up free. A walking tour is a must.

Any visit should commence at the Plaza. Here on the southeast corner a DAR marker certifies the official end of the SFT, and another small marker on the north side of the Plaza commemorates the arrival of General Kearny and his army, of which the MB was a part. It is a very simple marker reading: "In this plaza GEN. S. W. KEARNY U.S.A. proclaimed the peaceable annexation of New Mexico, Aug. 19, 1846."

When the MB reached here on October 9, nearly 1,000 miles from Council Bluffs, it was greeted with a 100-gun salute and then camped in a wheatfield in back of the old cathedral, watering their animals in the nearby Santa Fe River.

From Santa Fe the MB still had about 1,000 miles more to march before reaching San Diego, California. Beyond Santa Fe the MB followed the famous *El Camino Real* or Royal Road, the oldest historical road in the United States, dating from the 1580s. It extended more than 1,500 miles from Mexico City via El Paso and Albuquerque to Taos Pueblo (70 miles north of Santa Fe) and later became known as the Chihuahua Trail. (One very early branch of the SFT passes through Taos.) If time permits, travelers should make a side trip to Taos, colonized by the Spanish in 1615. Be sure to note the Rio Grande Canyon, gorge, and several markers en route.

The MB followed this Royal Road toward and then along the Rio Grande del Norte over 200 miles south before turning west near Hatch (see 279 below). All along the Rio Grande the MB passed Mexican villages.

271   Aqua Fria Historic Site

A suburb of Santa Fe to the southwest on Aqua Fria Street
On October 19 the MB marched a few miles to Aqua Fria because of the good grazing ground here. There is nothing here of interest today, but from here the second Sick Detachment of eighty-six men (including my own great-grandfather John W. Hess) and twenty women and children were sent back to join the first Sick Detachment at Fort Pueblo, Colorado (see 250 above). From Aqua Fria it is about 2 miles via Siler Road to I-25 going south towards Albuquerque.

272   Mormon Battalion Monument

25 miles southwest of Santa Fe, southwest corner of intersection of U.S. 85 with Highway 22. [Note: This is the original location, but when U.S. 85 became I-25, the twenty-foot tall monument was removed and has not yet been replaced.]
This monument topped by a wagon wheel was erected by the Sons of Utah Pioneers in 1944. Affixed to the pylon is a large plaque showing an excellent map of the MBT with extensive text.

THE MORMON BATTALION

Council Bluffs, July 16, 1846, Fort Leavenworth, August 12, 1846; Santa Fe. October 9, 1846; San Diego, January 29, 1847.

The Mormon Battalion, composed of 500 men mustered into the service of the United States in the war with Mexico and was called to the colors as the Mormon pioneers were beginning their historic trek to the Rocky Mountains. At the conclusion of the 2,000 miles march from Council Bluffs, Iowa, to San Diego, California, the leader who took command at Santa Fe paid tribute to his men in part as follows: "History may be searched in vain for an equal march of infantry. Half of it has been through a wilderness, where nothing but savages and wild beasts are found, or deserts where, for want of water there is no living creature. There with almost hopeless labor, we have dug wells, which the future traveler will enjoy. Without a guide who had traversed them, we have ventured into trackless tablelands where water was not found for several marches. With crow bar and pick and axe in hand, we have worked our way over mountains which seemed to defy aught save the wild goat, and hewed a pass through a chasm of living rock more narrow than our wagons. To bring these first wagons to the Pacific, we have preserved the strength of our mules by herding them over large tracts, which you have laboriously guarded without loss.

"Thus, marching half naked and fed, and living upon wild animals, we have discovered and made a road of great value to our country."

Lieutenant Colonel P. St. George Cooke

Official order issued January 30, 1847, upon the safe arrival of the battalion in San Diego, California.

Sponsored by the Committee for the erection of the Mormon Battalion Monument in New Mexico and the Utah Pioneer Trails and Landmarks Association. Built through the donations of many friends.

San Felipi Pueblo Historic Site   273

San Felipi Pueblo, Sandoval County

The exit off I-25 to this pueblo founded in 1581 is about 12 miles south of the just mentioned Mormon Battalion Monument. Here the MB reached and commenced following the Rio Grande. About 17 miles beyond San Felipi is Bernalillo, where the MB camped on October 22.

Albuquerque Historic Site   274

Albuquerque, Bernalillo County

Part of historic Albuquerque has been restored as Old Town, located west of the modern business district off Lomas Boulevard, and is worth a visit. It is not known, however, whether the MB entered Old Town or simply passed by it. About 3 miles from town center the battalion waded across the Rio Grande to its west bank.

Of the various Spanish villages the MB passed along *El Camino Real* and the Rio Grande, perhaps the most representative today is old Isleta Pueblo, old when Coronado was there in 1540, 12 miles from downtown Albuquerque. Take the Isleta exit off I-25 and at least visit the main plaza, which gives you a feeling of what it might have been like in 1846. Return to I-25.

The MB continued south through Los Lunas, Los Chaves, Belen, and Sabinal.

275   Loma Blanca Sand Hills Historic Site

East of I-25, 13 miles south of Sabinal, Socorro County
In this general area are the Loma Blanca (White Hills) sand dunes, which gave the MB such trouble pulling and pushing their wagons through the deep sand. It took twenty men to help the draft animals force each wagon across these dunes, created by sand blown here from the nearby Rio Salado.

18 miles beyond the sandhills they passed Socorro, the largest community since Santa Fe, and on October 31 they camped 3 miles to the south.

About 10 miles south of Socorro, at the San Antonio exit, travelers might wish to exit east and pick up Highway 1, which follows much closer the old trail for about 18 miles and then connects again with I-25 at the San Marcial interchange.

Near San Antonio, the road south becomes much more difficult. Also in this area, about 30 miles south of Socorro, Battalion member James Hampton died on November 3.

276   Fort Craig Historic Site

East of I-25, 20 miles south of San Antonio, Socorro County
In 1854 the government built Fort Craig in Red Canyon near the Rio Grande to protect merchants and emigrants who began to pass this way in greater numbers subsequent to the American annexation following the Mexican War. The fort postdates the MB, its ruins are right on the old trail and interesting to visit.

To do so proceed south for 9 miles beyond the San Marcial interchange to the Magdalena interchange, exit and return north on a service road for 4 miles to a little-used road going due east. (This road goes right by the very tall and prominent Fort Craig Microwave Relay Mast.) Keep going east for 4 miles on a rough road to an information sign directing you to the fort's ruins. Then return to the Magdalena interchange. Just south of Fort Craig what few tracks of the old trail remains have been inundated by the 40-mile long Elephant Butte Reservoir, the second largest body of impounded water in the world.

Elephant Butte Historic Landmark 277

Just east of Truth or Consequences, Sierra County,
near the Elephant Butte Dam off Highway 51

Elephant Butte, now partly covered by the Elephant Butte Reservoir, is supposed to resemble an elephant lying on its side. Use your imagination! It was undoubtedly noted by the MB.

Today the best view of this landmark is near the Elephant Butte Dam. From this vantage point the traveler can see the increasingly hilly and rugged terrain stretching to the south. Near here General Kearny sent his wagons back to Santa Fe and thus unencumbered and able to make better time, the army turned directly west through the Black Range Mountains towards the Gila River. Kearny, however, ordered Colonel Cooke and the MB to keep their wagons and make a wagon road through the desert to California. That Cooke and the MB actually succeeded in doing so is one of the great accomplishments of the westward migration.

Truth or Consequences Historic Site 278

At Williamsburg near Truth or Consequences,
Sierra County

Approximately where the tiny community of Williamsburg off I-25 is today, General Kearny turned west to the Gila River. It was also here that the MB sent the third Sick Detachment of fifty-eight men back to winter at Fort Pueblo in Colorado (see 250 and 271 above). This left a battalion of 339 trail-hardened men (and several women) to forge a road through the wildness. (Truth or Consequences, named after a popular radio show in 1950, was previously known as Hot Springs.)

279   Rio Grande Historic Site / Marker

Near Hatch, Dona Ana County

By following the Rio Grande this far south, the MB was able to avoid the Black Range Mountains and proceed west across relatively smooth land towards the Gila River in present-day Arizona. Modern travelers should continue south to Hatch on I-25 and then take Highway 26 west towards Deming.

Just south of Hatch a New Mexico historical marker commemorating this passing of the MB is scheduled to be erected in the near future.

MORMON BATTALION

The Mormon Battalion, composed of 500 volunteers, left Council Bluffs, Iowa, June 5, 1846, as part of the expeditionary force of Brigadier General Kearny. The battalion followed the Santa Fe Trail to Santa Fe and down the Rio Grande near here, where it turned west. The 2000 mile march ended in San Diego, California, January 30, 1847.

The old trail west of the Rio Grande is north of the highway and best explored from the air. Here the country becomes increasingly more arid and desolate. The string of little Mexican villages along the Rio Grande and the Royal Road was left behind. West of the Rio Grande the MB found bits and pieces of old Indian, Spanish, and mining trails, which they wove into their new wagon road. The next historic site is 30 desolate miles west.

280   Cookes Spring / Fort Cummings Historic Site / Marker

In Luna County, 30 miles west of Hatch,
in sec. 23, T21S, R8W

This is one of the few places between Hatch and Deming, a distance of 47 miles, where the old trail can be reached with any convenience, and even here you have to drive 6 miles on what is at best a ranch road, but it can be done with care and is worth it.

This well-known spring was a vital water source that the MB had to reach. Later Fort Cummings (1863–84) was built here and the site also became a Butterfield Stage station.

To reach this site drive west from Hatch about 30 miles on Highway

26. At a place known as Florida on county maps there are a house with some cattle pens and a dirt road to the north forming a tee intersection with Highway 26. Some 6 miles along this road are the ruins of Fort Cummings, marked by the DAR in 1935. Dominating the scene is the 8,400-foot high Cookes Peak to the northeast.

The famous Cookes Spring is located one-quarter of a mile almost due south of the ruins of Fort Cummings, an easy walk. The spring, capped years ago by railroad interests, is covered by a decaying large wooden gazebo structure that can be seen clearly from the old fort. In 1980 the Mormon church placed a marker here and the site is worth the short walk; you can also drive there.

THE MORMON BATTALION / 1846–1847

Under the command of Lt. Col. P. St. George Cooke, the U.S. Army's "Mormon Battalion" camped at Cooke's Springs on November 16, 1846. 500 Mormon volunteers blazed a trail over 1100 [2000] miles from Council Bluffs, Iowa, to San Diego, California during the war with Mexico. "History will be searched in vain for an equal march of infantry."

Return to Highway 26.

Petroglyphs Historic Site 281

14 miles north of Deming, Luna County,
in the SE 1/4, SW 1/4, sec. 29, T21S, R8W

On November 17, 1846, Standage, a member of the MB, recorded that 3 miles beyond Cookes Spring they found "proof of the Nephites [American Indians] once living here. Large entrances into the rocks and several pestles and mortars found made of rock. . . . We found a great many hierogliphics engraven in the rocks which . . . I take for good circumstantial evidence of the. . . Book of Mormon" (compare to site 294).

While these mortars and petroglyphs are much too late to be in any way connected with the Book of Mormon, they are of great interest and may still be found by the curious and adventurous—with time and a four-wheel drive vehicle, and Deming East and Massacre Peak 7.5 minute quadrangle maps. Return to Highway 26.

282　　　　　　　　**Mormon Battalion Marker**

On U.S. 180, 20 miles northwest of Deming, Luna County
In Deming, 15 miles from Florida, turn northwest towards Silver City
on U.S. 180 for about 20 miles. To the east of the road is a DAR marker.

> Here crossed the first road to southern California opened
> for wagons by Capt. Cooke, who passed here in command of
> the Mormon Battalion, Nov. 1846. Later it became the Cali-
> fornia Emigrant road. From 1858–1861, the route of the But-
> terfield Overland Mail, St. Louis to San Francisco, the longest
> land mail route ever attempted.
>
> Erected by the Butterfield Trail Chapter, D.A.R., Deming,
> N.M.-Oct. 1933.

Return to Deming.

Between Deming and the Arizona state line 110 miles to the southwest, the MB blazed a trail through some beautiful and frighteningly
desolate land, most of which is difficult even to approximate without
ORVs, good maps, and even guides. From here the traveler has three
options to reach the next historic site on the SFT, the San Bernardino
Ranch in Arizona (see 283 and 284 below).

West of Deming, on I-10 a New Mexico historical marker is scheduled
to be erected with the following text: "COOKE'S WAGON ROAD: In 1846,
while leading the Mormon Battalion to California during the Mexican
War, Lt. Col. Philip St. George Cooke blazed the first wagon road from
New Mexico to the West Coast. The potential of the route for railroad
construction was one of the reasons for the Gadsden Purchase in 1854.
Cooke entered Arizona through Guadalupe Canyon" (see 283 below
for road directions west of Deming).

Arizona
(see map 17)

Thanks to the Boy Scouts of America (BSA) and that fact that the Butterfield Overland Mail Road followed much of the Mormon Battalion
Trail in Arizona, the route of the MB across this state is relatively well
known and marked. Across Cochise County, for example, the BSA have
erected six trail monuments.

San Bernadino Ranch and   283, 284
Guadalupe Canyon / Markers

16 miles east of Douglas, Cochise County

The traveler has three options to reach the San Bernadino Ranch area from Deming. With the proper Hidalgo County, New Mexico and Cochise County, Arizona (sheet 7) maps, an ORV, and luck, you can attempt to follow the MB. Another option is to take I-10 out of Deming west to U.S. 80 for a total of 160 miles to Douglas, Arizona, and approach the area from the west.

There is a third option, which is a compromise between the first and second. It hardly follows the old trail, but is much closer than I-10. From Deming take I-10 for 33 miles west to Highway 81, go south 19 miles to Hachita (12 miles south on Highway 81 you will pass Black Mountain to the west; the MB passed this landmark on its west side). From Hachita take Highway 9 for 30 miles west to Animas. (About 6 miles west of Hachita you will cross the route of the MB.) From Animas continue 14 miles west on Highway 9 to U.S. 80 at the Arizona state line. Drive on to Douglas, 47 miles farther.

From Douglas go east on Fifteenth Street (which soon becomes the Geronimo Trail), a rough, gravel road for about 16 miles. Here on the edge of the huge San Bernardino Land Grant to the south of the road is an LDS marker, almost on the Mexican border, erected by the Boy Scouts of Douglas.

MORMON BATTALION
LDS Church / San Bernardino / Ranch / Rest camp / Dec. 3, 1846 / Erected 1960 / By Troop 27.

About 4 miles farther on, to the south of the road is another LDS Scout marker erected in 1933.

MORMON BATTALION / Passed here / in 1846 / erected by / LDS Scouts / Douglas, Ariz. / 1933.

About 3 miles beyond this marker there is a wye intersection. Take the right-hand fork and the mouth of Guadalupe Canyon is some 9 desolate miles ahead. This is the canyon Cooke pushed the MB through (because his guides missed the pass); even today it is difficult to drive and ORVs and good maps are strongly advised. (I did, however, once push a Camero several miles into the canyon.) With luck the traveler can follow the canyon all the way back into New Mexico. Return to Douglas.

285   Elisha Smith Historic Marker

Off U.S. 80, 10 miles west of Douglas, Cochise County
Drive 10 miles west of Douglas on U.S. 80 to Paul Spur where a road leads to the south. To the left of this intersection is another concrete Boy Scout marker. This one commemorates the death near here of Elisha Smith, a MB teamster.

MORMON BATTALION

LDS Church / Smith grave / two miles south / buried / Dec. 7, 1846 / Erected 1960 / By Troop 27.

286   San Pedro River

One-half mile east of Palominas, Cochise County
All the way from the Rio Grande the MB had been marching towards the San Pedro, a major source of water, which they followed north some 50 miles. From the Elisha Smith marker (see 285 above), there are two ways to reach the San Pedro River. The shorter route, which roughly parallels the old trail, is fairly easy to drive, but a Cochise County map (sheet 8) is recommended. Take a gravel road next to the Smith marker west for about 10 miles along the Mexican border to Bisbee Junction, then west 4 miles along Purdy Lane to Country Club Road (do not turn on the Naco Road; keep going 1 mile west), which goes north 2 miles to Highway 92, then turn west and drive 10 miles to the little town of Palominas. The longer, but much easier way is to remain on U.S. 80 (from the Smith marker), go 12 miles west to Highway 92, then to Palominas where the road crosses the river 0.5 mile east of town.

287   Battle of the Bulls Historic Site / Marker

10 miles southwest of Tombstone, Cochise County,
in sec. 1, T21S, R21E
From Palominas take the main road, Palominas Road, for 4 miles north along the San Pedro Valley, to Hereford Road, then turn west for 4 miles

and take a section-line road for 11 miles north to a tee intersection with a road from Sierra Vista, turn right for 2.2 miles, cross the San Pedro River, and the Battle of the Bulls marker is east of the road one-quarter of a mile beyond the river.

This marker commemorates a famous incident, the only "battle" the MB participated in during the entire Mexican War. After they passed the San Bernardino Ranch (see 283 above) the battalion noticed many wild cattle, cattle that had escaped from the ranch and had bred prolifically. At this crossing of the San Pedro River, known locally as the Narrows, some of these wild bulls decided to attack the battalion, probably because the men had been shooting at them. Before the attack was over several mules were gored, two wagons damaged, and two men wounded; at least twenty bulls were also killed.

MORMON BATTALION

LDS Church / The Narrows / Dec. 12, 1846 / Battle of / the Bulls / Erected 1960 / by Post 16.

From the Battle of the Bulls marker continue northeast along the same road to the famous old town of Tombstone, very touristy, but worth a visit.

Mormon Battalion Historic Marker 288

On U.S. 80, east end of St. David, Cochise County
From Tombstone take U.S. 80 for 19 miles north to St. David, a city founded on the San Pedro River in 1877 by P. C. Merrill of the MB. Here about 0.5 mile east of the high school on the east side of the road is another concrete Boy Scout marker.

MORMON BATTALION

LDS Church / Camp Dec. 13, 1846 / Capt. P. C. Merrill / returned to / San Pedro 1877 / Erected 1860 / By Troop 24.

From near St. David, travelers are also following rather closely the famous Butterfield Overland Mail trail that started in St. Louis and Memphis in 1858 and ran 2,795 miles to San Francisco via El Paso. Near St. David, Butterfield took advantage of the wagon road made by the MB and followed it into California. For this reason the trail west of here is generally much better known and marked than the trail between the Rio Grande and the San Pedro.

289   Mormon Battalion Historic Marker

On U.S. 80, west end of Benson, Cochise County

Take U.S 80 for 6 miles north to Benson, where on the western end of town in a small pull-off north of the road is the last of the six concrete Boy Scout markers.

MORMON BATTALION

LDS Church / Dec. 14, 1846 / Last camp on / San Pedro / Turned west / toward Tucson / Erected 1960 / By Patrol 27.

290   Mormon Battalion Marker

On South Sixth Avenue, Tucson, Pima County

Continue west on U.S. 80, which soon becomes I-10, for about 46 miles to Tucson. The route of the old MBT lies north of the highway about where the tracks of the Southern Pacific Railroad are today. Consequently there is almost nothing of interest to see.

In Tucson take the South Sixth Avenue exit and go several blocks north to Armory Park, near the main public library. Near the north end of this park is a LDS marker.

TO THE

MORMON BATTALION

which, under command of / Col. Cooke, in the course of / their 2,000 mile infantry / march to the Pacific Coast, / arrived and raised the first / American flag in Tucson. / DECEMBER 16, 1846. / Erection supervised by / M-MEN AND GLEANER GIRLS / of the / Central Arizona District / of the / CHURCH OF JESUS CHRIST / OF LATTER-DAY SAINTS / JUNE 13, 1937.

That part of old Tucson which the MB visited was known as the Presidio and was located near the intersection of modern Main Street and Alameda. Tucson was the last Mexican outpost on the trail to California. Also, about 6 miles south of Tucson on I-19 is the famous San Xavier del Bac Mission, which was seen and noticed from a distance, but not visited by the MB. It should not be missed.

Mormon Battalion Trail Marker   291

Picacho Peak State Park, Pinal County

Return to I-10 and go about 42 miles north. Once again the old trail is generally where the Southern Pacific Railroad tracks are and there is little to see except the Santa Cruz River, which provided some water for the Battalion. On December 17 the Battalion made camp near the foot of Picacho Peak, a famous landmark that can be seen for miles. Today the area is a state park, near the entrance of which is a handsome trail marker erected by some Mormons of Mesa, Arizona.

MORMON BATTALION TRAIL

The Mormon Battalion of the U.S. Army camped here en-route to California December 17, 1846 during the war with Mexico. On the longest infantry march of record, they were first to unfurl the flag of the United States in Tucson. [The names of those responsible for this marker take up the rest of the plaque.]

Mormon Battalion Historic Marker   292

On Highway 93, Casa Grande, Pinal County

Stay on I-10 for about 15 miles northwest to the Casa Grande interchange; there pick up Highway 93 and continue northwest and then north for 8 miles. There is a white monument west of the road that was erected by some Mormons from Mesa, Arizona, to commemorate a Battalion camp on December 20. That the actual campsite is at least 8 miles to the north is not indicated.

IN HONOR OF THE MORMON BATTALION which camped here [really 8 miles north of here] Dec. 20, 1846 en route to Cal. War with Mexico. [As with the Picacho Peak marker, this one is largely devoted to the names of those who erected it.]

From Casa Grande (when there are some impressive Indian ruins), the traveler has several options for visiting one of the most interesting sites along the whole MBT—a several-mile stretch of original trail east of Gila Bend (see 293 below). There is, however, no easy option. Each way requires driving a long stretch of dirt and desolate roads.

293   The Mormon Battalion Trail Historic Site/Markers

20 miles east of Gila Bend, Maricopa County,
on a dirt road in sec. 27, T4S, R2W

The most convenient way, perhaps (be sure to have a Maricopa County map, sheet 8) is to go west of Casa Grande on Highway 84 and on I-8 to Gila Bend, which is 62 miles west and then backtrack on a dirt road toward Mobile for 16 miles to an intersection with a dirt trail going north. At this intersection is a wooden sign reading BUTTERFIELD TRAIL. There is also a second wooden sign.

> MORMON BATTALION TRAIL (4.3 miles)/ In December 1846 360/ Mormon soldiers marched/ enroute to San Diego./ They blazed the Butterfield Stage Trail.

This 4.3-mile dirt road is very, very rough, but can be made in an ordinary passenger car with careful driving. Along this track are several directional arrows, so do not get discouraged. At the end of 4.3 miles, there are several wooden signs pointing the way west along the MBT-Butterfield Trail. Here travelers can take a several-mile hike or take their chances trying to drive another track. An ORV is advised. The most informative of the several signs reads:

> MORMON BATTALION TRAIL—Five miles East. / 360 Mormon soldiers camped/ on December 25, 1846. / They marched over 2,000/ miles enroute to San Diego/ and blazed the Butter-/ field Stage Trail.

This section of the old trail has been designated as an official Boy Scout Butterfield Stage Hiking Trail. For information write: Theodore Roosevelt BSA Council, P.O. Box 7278, Pheonix, AZ. 85011.

The most historic way to reach this trail site requires Pinal County maps (sheets 1 and 2) and a Maricopa County map (sheet 8) and the willingness to drive more than 40 utterly desolate miles on a dirt road. It is, however, well worth the effort. To do so continue north of the Casa Grande monument on Highway 93 for 6 miles to Highway 387, follow this for 7 miles to Highway 87. (About 5 miles east on this road is Thin Mountain. The MB trail crosses Highway 387 just west of this mountain. Some say ruts can be found, but I did not succeed in finding any.) Turn left on Highway 87 towards the village of Sacaton for 8 miles northwest. Before following the gravel road No. 1 off Highway 87 to Sacaton, however, it is a good idea to go about 2 miles beyond this gravel road and cross the Gila River. This is one of the few places where it is convenient to take a good look at this strange river, which consists mainly of sand and which the MB followed, more or less, over 200 miles to present-day Yuma, Arizona.

Return to gravel road No. 1 and go to Sacaton. It was near here on the Gila River that the MB traded with some Pima Indians and finally picked up General Kearny's trail, which they followed on to San Diego. Keep going northwest for 6 miles to Casa Blanca interchange, near Bapchule. Cross I-10 and take the Casa Blanca Road, through the town of Casa Blanca, 10 miles due west to the Maricopa Road. Turn south on the Maricopa Road and go 6 miles to the town of Maricopa. Here in Maricopa the traveler picks up the more than 40-mile long, utterly desolate dirt road to Gila Bend via Mobile. Approximately 24 miles west of Maricopa, this road brings the traveler to the same intersection with the dirt track from the north already described.

There is still one other way to visit this historic site. Take the Casa Grande–Maricopa Highway northwest of Casa Grande for 20 miles to Maricopa and continue as described above. (Good luck with whichever route you take, and watch your maps.)

There used to be a trail marker 3.1 miles north of the I-8 overpass in Gila Bend on U.S. 80, but it has been destroyed. The vandalized site can be located west of the road.

Painted Rock Historic Park / Marker   294

Painted Rock Historic Park, Maricopa County
Take I-8 west from Gila Bend for 14 miles to the Painted Rock interchange, turn north on a gravel road for 11 miles to the park area. Near the park entrance the Mormon Battalion, Inc., of Salt Lake City, Utah, placed a small metal marker in 1983 commemorating the MBT.

U.S. MORMON BATTALION TRAIL / 1846–1848.

Near this marker is a fenced area protecting a pile of basalt boulders marked with Indian petroglyphs, which may be a thousand years old. In at least two places along the trail in New Mexico and Arizona, members of the MB noticed these petroglyphs, which they again "took as good evidence of the Book of Mormon" (see 280 above), a bit of wishful, but understandable thinking on their part.

There is a second MB marker in this park, located about 100 feet west of the first marker. More of an information kiosk than a marker, it presents extensive text about the history of the Mormon Battalion along with an excellent map of the whole trail from Iowa to California. It was placed there by the U.S. Mormon Battalion, Company A, Mesa Arizona.

A mile due west of the park on a dirt road are the ruins of a Butterfield Stage station south of the road. Return to I-8.

295   The Oatman Grave Historic Site

7 miles west of Painted Rock Historic Park,
Maricopa County, in sec. 11, T5S, R9W

In 1851 the Royce Oatman family of Illinois joined a splinter sect of the Mormon church, the Brewsterites, and followed James C. Brewster into New Mexico. There the father caught California gold fever and unwisely tried to take his family there alone. Atop this mesa on February 18, 1851, the Yavapais Indians massacred most of the family and captured two daughters, Olive and Mary Ann. Olive lived to help write a book about her ordeal, *Captivity of the Oatman Girls* (1857).

I do not encourage anyone to try and reach this grave, but I will give instructions. While it is only 7 miles west of the park, there is no bridge across the Gila River, which must be crossed twice. I tried and failed. The easiest way is to return to the Painted Rock interchange on I-8, go 15 miles west to the Sentinel interchange where there is a gas station. Before you ask directions you should have an ORV, a Maricopa County map (sheet 9), and water, and even then everyone will try and dissuade you from trying to find the grave. If you persist, take a ranch "road" north for 9 miles. Then, if you have not bottomed out or become stuck, watch carefully for the very faint trace of a track going left from the "road." It is easy to miss, and perhaps that is just as well. From here it is best to walk the 2 miles to the massacre and grave site.

This 2-mile track will take you to the top of Oatman Flat (Mesa). Look around and you will see a plain metal white cross. This is where the massacre of the Oatman family probably took place. Due east of the cross you can see trail tracks in solid rock coming up the flat. The family gravestone is about one-quarter of a mile down the flat to the east through a wooded area. Return to I-8.

The Colorado River Crossing Historic Site   296

Yuma, Yuma County, near the Morelos Dam

Between Painted Rock State Park (or Oatman Flat) and Yuma, for 90 miles west on I-80 there is little of interest to see. The trail is always north of the interstate, following the south bank of the Gila River.

As yet there is no marker in Yuma commemorating the MB, which crossed the Colorado River 8 miles downstream from the I-8 bridge, somewhere near Moleros Dam, but it is hardly worth the effort to drive here. If one is determined, however, take Ninth Street in Yuma to the river.

In the Yuma Crossing Park, located where I-8 crosses the River, there is a marker commemorating this crossing and there is talk of putting a MB marker in this same park. Travelers should take I-8 into California.

The Mormon Battalion, Inc., has developed a Mormon Battalion Bicycle Trail that runs for 250 miles from Yuma, Arizona, to San Diego, California. Information may be obtained from: Maynard R. Olsen, 10961 Rapatee Court, La Mesa, CA. 92041.

California
(see map 18)

Once the MB crossed the Colorado River at Yuma, it entered present-day Mexico and remained there for about 50 miles before turning north into modern California, a few miles west of El Centro. Travelers can approximate this route by taking Highway 98 off I-8 and going to El Centro via Calexico, but it is hardly worth the effort. One may as well stay on I-8 the entire 51 miles from Yuma to El Centro. There is one point of interest, however, along this 50 miles. About 17 miles into California, start looking for a sand dune area that looks like the Sahara. Many Hollywood desert epics were made here.

297   Mormon Battalion Marker

West of El Centro, Imperial County, on I-8,
10 miles west of the Highway 111 interchange

A marker, erected in 1978 by the Mormon Battalion, Inc., of Salt Lake City, Utah commemorates the Mormon Battalion Trail, which crossed present-day I-8 about 7 miles farther west. The marker is located in the westbound rest area off I-8.

MONUMENT

On Friday, January 15, 1847, the Mormon Battalion, a volunteer unit of the Army of the West, crossed Interstate Highway 8 approximately seven miles west of this point. Lieutenant Colonel Philip St. George Cooke commanded this battalion when the United States was at war with Mexico. They made their historic march from Council Bluffs, Iowa, to San Diego on the Pacific Coast. This being regarded as the world's greatest march of infantry of over 2,000 miles. The first wheels that traversed this area, now Imperial County, California, were by the battalion supply wagons opening the first southern route west.

From here to the next historic site, continue west on I-8 for 19 miles to the Ocotillo exit and turn north on Highway S-2 up through the Anza-Borrego Desert State Park.

298, 299   Old Trail and Palm Spring Historic Sites

18 miles north of I-8 on Highway S-2, San Diego County

Here there is a road sign commemorating the GREAT SOUTHERN OVERLAND ROUTE OF 1849, for it is here that Highway S-2 intersects the Mormon Battalion Trail and the Butterfield Stage Trail. From here the modern traveler can follow the old trail rather closely for about 84 miles north to near Temecula.

A few miles beyond this road sign is another sign pointing east to PALM SPRING, a well-known camping site on this trail. Travelers can drive from this sign towards the old spring, but most of the time the track is simply in the deep sand bed of the dry Vallecito Creek. To many it will not be worth the effort or risk.

Vallecito Stage Station Historic Site 300

On Highway S-2, 4 miles west of
Aqua Caliente Springs, Imperial County

Here is to be seen the only fully restored Butterfield Stage station along that part of the Mormon Battalion Trail later used by Butterfield. Near here the MB camped in 1847.

From near Aqua Caliente north to Warner's Ranch is the official U.S. Mormon Battalion Boy Scout Hiking Trail. Information may be obtained by writing to: San Diego County Council, BSA, 1207 Upas St., San Diego, CA. 92103.

Box Canyon Historic Site / Markers 301

10 miles west of the Vallecito Stage station on Highway S-2

Here is one of the most famous sites along the entire 2,000-mile length of the Mormon Battalion Trail—the trail cuts in Box Canyon. On January 12, 1847, the Battalion found itself boxed in this narrow defile and had to widen the canyon by about a foot with a few hand tools to get the wagons through. These cuts are still clearly visible, well marked and preserved, and must be seen. They can be viewed from an observation platform and a short path leads down to them. In 1953 San Diego County declared the site a state registered landmark and erected a marker here.

BOX CANYON

The old way variously known as Sonora, Colorado River, or Southern Emigrant Trail and later as Butterfield Overland Mail Route traversed Box Canyon just east of here. January 12, 1847, the Mormon Battalion under command of Lt. Col. Philip St. G. Cooke using hand tools hewed a passage through the rocky walls of the narrow gorge for their wagons and opened the first road into southern California.

At the observation platform is another information sign.

BOX CANYON

Looking directly across the canyon, you will see traces of two roads, the upper one was built by the Mormon Battalion in 1847. The lower one is more recent. A short walk to your left and down slope will reveal the reason for the roads.

Also on this observation platform is a marker featuring, under glass, hand-lettered text and colored illustrations (it is titled "Box Canyon: A Window to the Past on the Southern Emigrant Trail") featuring the Mormon Battalion, General Kearny and Kit Carson, the gold rush, Butterfield Stage, and cattlemen.

302   Warner Ranch Historic Site / Marker

26 miles beyond Box Canyon
near intersection of S-2 and Highway 79

Continue north along S-2 to the locally known Scissors Crossroads and pick up Highway 79 north. After about 26 total miles the traveler approaches an intersection with Highway 79. Just before reaching this intersection, there is a historical marker commemorating the Warner ranch house east of the road. The original building, where the MB rested in 1847, still stands, but it is a disgrace, held together by corrugated sheet metal and bailing wire. San Diego County placed the marker here in 1964.

WARNER RANCH HOUSE

In 1844, Gov. Manuel Micheltorena granted 44,322 acres to Juan Jose Warner who built this house. Gen. Kearny passed here in 1846; Mormon Battalion in 1847. First Butterfield stage stopped at this ranch on Oct. 6, 1858 enroute from Tipton, Mo. to San Francisco; 2600 miles, time 24 days. This was the southern overland route into California.

Just beyond this marker turn right on Highway 79 and follow it for some 17 miles north to Oak Grove, where the remains of an old Butterfield Stage station have been incorporated into a store and bar. There is a marker here. From Oak Grove continue north for 25 miles to an intersection with I-15 near Temecula. Here the MB turned south towards San Diego and the later Butterfield Trail continued north to San Francisco.

303   The San Luis Rey Mission Historic Site / Marker

On Highway 76, 4 miles east of Oceanside,
San Diego County

Near Temecula take I-15 south for about 11 miles to Highway 76. (Although no evidence of the old trail exists, modern travelers are close to it from near Temecula all the way to San Diego.) Turn west on Highway 76 and follow the San Luis Rey River for 14 miles to the restored Franciscan mission of San Luis Rey de Francis north of the highway. This is one of the twenty-one Spanish missions founded between San Diego and San Francisco along an old *El Camino Real* or Royal Road. This mission was founded in 1789.

When the MB camped here in February 1847 the mission had already been secularized and abandoned. It is worth a visit and there is a wooden marker on its grounds near the main entrance to the mission.

> Captain Fremont took possession of Mission San Luis Rey
> in August of 1846. The Mormon Battalion under Lt. Cooke
> camped at Mission San Luis Rey in Feb. 1847.

From the mission the MB pushed on 1 more mile, where from a rise they could just barely see the Pacific Ocean 3 miles distant. You can get the same view today by turning south, less than a mile west of the mission, onto Highway S-11, which is also known by its much older name, *El Camino Real*. (The best place to see the ocean is near a street sign reading Vista Oceana.) This is the Royal Road the battalion followed all the way to San Diego. Modern travelers can follow *El Camino Real* for about 15 miles south to Encinitas. Thereafter you may as well pick up I-5 towards San Diego.

The Mormon Battalion Memorial Area / Markers   304

2510 Juan Street in Old Town, San Diego, *San Diego County (take the I-8 exit off I-5)*

At 2510 Juan Street is located the Mormon Battalion Memorial Visitors' Center. Admission is free and the center features free films, literature, maps, and dioramas pertaining to the trail. It is worth a visit.

Within easy walking distance is an extensive outdoor memorial to the MB. Here, at the crest of Presidio Park, there is a statue of a battalion member, a flagpole and cannon, and five memorial plaques, including the only one dedicated to women of the Mormon Battalion. It was erected by the Daughters of Utah Pioneers in 1959, the 257th such marker placed by that society.

> Mormon women were anxious to reach the glorious west
> and any means offered seemed an answer to prayer to help

them on their way. It was learned four laundresses would be allowed each of the five companies. The wives of the soldiers made application and twenty were chosen. Men who could meet the expenses were permitted to take their families. Hence nearly 80 women and children accompanied the battalion. They endured the hardships of the journey knowing hunger and thirst. Four wives, Susan M. Davis, Lydia Hunter, Phoebe O. P. Brown, and Melissa Coray traveled the entire distance arriving in San Diego 20 January 1847. Mrs. Hunter gave birth to a son April 20, 1847, first L.D.S. child born in San Diego. She died two weeks later.

This area all around the Presidio Park is also an official Boy Scout hiking trail. For information write the Scout Council referred to at 300 above.

Although San Diego was the official end of the Mormon Battalion Trail, two other historic sites and markers in California are worth mentioning.

305   Fort Moore Memorial

Los Angeles

A huge monument close to City Hall, nearly one block in length, commemorates the presence of some members of the MB who were for a time in Los Angeles.

306   Santa Fe and Salt Lake Trail/Marker

12 miles northwest of San Bernardino, San Bernardino County, in the Cajon pass at the junction of I-15 and Highway 138, just to the southeast on a dead-end service road.

An unusual twelve-foot high marker, erected in 1917, commemorates members of the MB who trekked east from California to the Valley of the Great Salt Lake and some Mormons who later migrated to California along this part of the Old Spanish Trail.

SANTA FE AND SALT LAKE TRAIL, 1848

Erected in honor of the brave pioneers of California in 1917.

XXV

The Santa Fe-Mormon Battalion Mountain Route in New Mexico, Colorado, and Kansas

The Mountain Branch of the SFT is about 100 miles longer than the Cimarron Cutoff, but for travelers there were more sources of water, fewer Indian troubles, and Bent's Fort, which provided a rest stop, security, and supplies. This branch does not cross the Arkansas River in the area of Cimarron and Ingalls, Kansas (see trail XXIV, 250), but continues west along the river to Bent's Fort, near present-day La Junta, Colorado, crosses the river there and heads for the Raton Pass on the present-day New Mexico state line, continuing south to its junction with the Cimarron Cutoff at Watrous (La Junta), New Mexico (see trail XXIV, 265). It was this Mountain Branch that the first Sick Detachment of the MB followed west from Ingalls to Fort Pueblo via Bent's Old Fort (see trail XXIV, 250) and that the second and third Sick Detachments took north from near Santa Fe and from today's Truth of Consequences, New Mexico (see trail XXIV, 278).

This branch is usually presented going south from Ingalls to Watrous. Since most Mormons followed the trail north from Watrous, however, I have chosen to present the trail in that direction starting at Watrous.

New Mexico
(see map 15)

The DAR has placed six gray granite markers along the Mountain Branch of this trail in New Mexico—all reading: "Santa Fe Trail / Mountain Branch / 1822–72 / Erected by the / Daughters of the / American Revolution / and the / State of New Mexico / 1909."

All but about 30 miles of the 110 miles of this trail in New Mexico can be followed closely and conveniently.

307   Fort Union Historic Site

On Highway 477, 8 miles north of Watrous, Mora County

Fort Union was established in 1851 as the military headquarters of the New Mexico Territory. Today the impressive ruins of this huge installation are preserved as the Fort Union National Monument and must be visited.

Of special interest are the remains of some one-time spectacular trail ruts behind the old hospital. Other, much better ruts can be seen east of Highway 477, just north of the two-mile marker. From here it is almost impossible to follow the trail, which runs northward for some 30 miles to Rayado. Return to I-25 at Watrous and go north 45 miles to Springer (see trail XXIV, 261).

308   Rayado Marker / Ruts

On Highways 199 and 21,
23 miles west of Springer, Colfax County

Turn west at Springer and follow Highways 199 and 21 for 23 miles to the little town of Rayado, founded in 1848. At the south end of town, west of the road, is a home of Kit Carson, restored too grandly. In front of this place is a DAR marker. At the northern end of town, where the road turns sharply to the left, are some badly eroded ruts coming down an incline to the right of the road.

309   Philmont Scout Ranch / Marker

On Highway 21, 7 miles north of Rayado, Colfax County

What is now a famous national Boy Scout camp was once the 127,000-acre private estate of Waite Phillips (of Phillips Oil), who donated the land to the Scouts. His former home is most impressive, done in Mediterranean style. North of the road is a library with a DAR marker in front.

310   Cimarron Historic Site / Marker

On U.S. 64, 5 miles north of Philmont, Colfax County

Settled as early as the mid-1840s, Cimarron by the 1850s was an important stop on the Mountain Branch of the SFT and there are many old trail sites left in the community. There is a DAR marker at the northwest corner of the St. James Hotel, on Highway 21, usually hidden by vines.

Two other historical signs can be found on both sides of U.S. 64, just east of its intersection with Highway 21. Of most interest are the trail ruts east of town. As there are no services along the 41 miles from Cimarron to Raton, travelers should get gas before setting out to the next site.

Santa Fe Trail–Mormon Battalion Trail Ruts   311

South of U.S. 64, 2 miles east of Cimarron, Colfax County
About 2 miles east of Cimarron, start looking for miles of excellent ruts south of U.S. 64. For best viewing, travelers should try to hop the fence and walk about 100 feet south, then look east into miles of ruts.

Ghost Town of Colfax/Marker   312

On U.S. 64, 12 miles northeast of Cimarron, Colfax County
Near the Vermejo River and the Santa Fe Railroad is the ghost town of Colfax. Just beyond the river is a wye intersection in the center of which is a DAR marker.

Between Colfax and Raton there is little to see for 30 miles. At the Hoxie Junction of U.S. 64 and old U.S. 85 is a recently restored SFT sign.

SANTA FE TRAIL/ William Becknell, the first Santa Fe Trail trader, entered Santa Fe in 1821 after Mexico became independent from Spain and opened its frontier to foreign traders. The Mountain Branch over Raton Pass divided here. One fork turned west to Cimarron, then south and joined a more direct route at Rayado.

For more information on William Becknell, see trail XXVII.

Raton Ruts/Marker   313

Raton, Colfax County
Exit off I-25 into downtown Raton, a Santa Fe Railroad community established in 1879. At the southwest corner of a small park at Second and Savage streets is a DAR marker. North of the park just south of the

Melody Land Motel is a traffic light. Take the unmarked street to the west of the light (here a small sign reads "Historic Old Raton Pass") for a block or two, and you will see some ruts coming off a hill. This is the original pass. Then return to I-25.

314   ## Raton Pass Summit Historic Site / Marker

On I-25, 5 miles north of Raton, Colfax County,
on the Colorado state line

Before reaching the 7,881-foot-high summit of the Raton Pass you should look back several times to the south at majestic mesas rising above the New Mexico plains. This view is just one of the reasons New Mexico is called the Land of Enchantment. At the summit, to the northwest you can see the noted landmark called the Spanish Peaks or Breasts of the World of the Sangre de Cristo Mountains. Also at this summit, unfortunately only off the southbound lane of I-25, is a Welcome Center and two markers commemorating the SFT and Raton Pass. The most informative one reads:

RATON PASS

This important pass on the Mountain Branch of the Santa
Fe Trail was used by Brigadier General Stephen Watts Kearny
for his 1846 invasion of New Mexico, and by the Colorado
Volunteers who defeated the Confederates in 1862. Richens
L. "Uncle Dick" Wooten [Wootton] operated a toll road from
1866 to 1879, when the Santa Fe Railroad crossed the pass.

The Mormon Battalion of Kearny's Army of the West did not use this pass; it proceeded via the Cimarron Cutoff. Two of the three Sick Detachments of the Mormon Battalion came this way, however. This pass is a registered national historic landmark and its name is Spanish for *mouse*.

On the Colorado side of the Welcome Center are three informative signs about the pass and general area. And just at the summit is a Welcome to Colorful Colorado sign. Trinidad, Colorado, is only 10 miles away on I-25.

Bent's Old Fort, now restored, was an important stop along the Mountain Route of the Santa Fe Trail. This typical pioneer wagon is located at the fort. Photos by Violet Kimball. *See trail XXV, 321.*

Madonna of the Trails statues commemorate the courage and survival of all pioneer women. *See trail XXV, 327.*

Colorado
(see map 11)

There are approximately 192 miles of the Mountain Branch of the SFT in Colorado, almost all of them rather easy to follow. Highways I-25, U.S. 350, and U.S. 50 approximate it closely, and there are at least fourteen gray granite DAR trail markers, most of which are easy to locate, and most of them read the same: "Santa Fe Trail / 1822–72 / Marked by the / Daughters of the / American Revolution / and the State of Colorado / 1908."

The first Sick Detachment of the MB (see trail XXIV, 250) followed the SFT in Colorado west from near Cimarron, Kansas, along the Arkansas River to La Junta (where the SFT turned southwest), and continued northwest along the same river about 70 miles to Fort Pueblo, where the sick spent the winter of 1846–47. The second and third Sick Detachments (see trail XXIV, 271 and 278) followed the SFT in Colorado from Raton Pass to Bent's Old Fort, and then followed the first Sick Detachment west up the Arkansas River to Fort Pueblo (see site 321).

Trinidad Markers   315

Trinidad, Las Animas County

Trinidad is marked by the 10,000-foot high Fisher's Peak (formerly Raton Peak), an important landmark in trail days. Trinidad sits at its base.

The city's Main Street is the route of the old trail. On the northwest corner of the intersection of Main and Commercial streets is the Old Columbian Hotel, to which is affixed a SFT marker with extensive text. Also, the largest DAR marker on the SFT in Colorado is in small Kit Carson Park on San Pedro Avenue between Kansas and Topeka streets.

From Trinidad the easy way to the next historic site is to take U.S. 350 north for 36 miles. There is, however, a recommended side route, one which permits the traveler to more closely follow the old trail for 12 miles along Purgatoire River and to visit two little-known and rarely seen trail markers. To do this simply drive north of Trinidad on Highway 239 for 3.5 miles from town center to the crossroads known as El Moro. At the only intersection in this hamlet, turn right to the first residence on the right, which belongs to the Tortorelli family. There, in their backyard behind a small cinder-block building is a white granite SFT marker about twice as big as other such DAR markers.

Santa Fe Trail / 1822–1872 / placed by / Colorado Chapter, Denver / Daughters of the / American Revolution / November, 1908.

This marker was put in this seemingly out-of-the-way spot because back in 1908 this was the site of a railroad station on the Santa Fe Railroad and was then a prominent place.

Continue north another 7 miles to the village of Hoehne, near which there is another DAR marker to the SFT. Turn left into town, cross the railroad tracks, drive through town to County Road 83.3, turn right about 0.5 miles to a wye in the road, turn right again and go 0.4 miles. The marker is to the left (north) side of the road. To the south you get a dramatic view of the twin Spanish Peaks. (Eight miles due west of Hoehne is U.S. 85. To the south of the road just before reaching U.S. 85 is a sign reading "Hoehne / located on the Santa Fe Trail / 8 miles.") Return to road 239 and continue north for 4 miles to an intersection with U.S. 350, the main road between Trinidad and La Junta. For 80 miles, between Trinidad and La Junta, there are few road services of any kind, so check your gas. This utterly desolate stretch of country looks very much like it did long ago when wagons followed the trail.

316   Hole-in-the-Rock Historic Site

On U.S. 350, at Thatcher, Las Animas County,
36 miles northeast of Trinidad

Take U.S. 350 for 36 miles northeast to nearly deserted Thatcher, a one-time railroad community on the Santa Fe Railroad. At the only intersection in Thatcher, turn west off U.S. 350 onto a gravel road, cross the railroad tracks and pass the abandoned two-story school, and go to a small wooden bridge over Timpas Creek. One-quarter of a mile north along this creek is a small rocky "canyon." This is Hole-in-the-Rock, where water was always found in trail days. Return to U.S. 350, and soon you will enter the Comanche National Grassland of the U.S. Forest Service.

Iron Springs Stage Station Historic Site / Marker 317

5 miles south of Ayer, Otero County, in sec. 17, T27S, R58W
Exactly 16.1 miles northeast of Thatcher is a dirt road turning to the right (due south), marked by a metal sign in the shape of a cow. Go down this road exactly 0.5 mile. With sharp eyes you might be able to spot a low, gray granite DAR marker some 200 yards to the right, or due west. Some faint trail ruts can also be seen near this marker. Then return to U.S. 350.

Santa Fe Trail Marker 318

Approximately 7 miles northeast of the
Iron Springs marker (317 above), Otero County
Continue on U.S. 350 towards La Junta. About 7 miles beyond the Iron Springs, there is a DAR marker west of the road near mile marker 51.

Santa Fe Trail Marker 319

Approximately 11 miles northeast of the marker 318 (above),
Otero County
Continue on U.S. 350 towards La Junta. About 5 miles before reaching La Junta, or about 11 miles beyond the last marker, there is another DAR marker to the west of the road just north of a telephone pole. Here the SFT crosses present-day U.S. 350 to pick up Timpas Creek, which it follows to Hole-in-the-Rock (see 316 above).

La Junta Marker 320

Court House Square, La Junta, Otero County
On the northwest corner of the Court House Square on Third Street is an unusual shield-shaped DAR marker to the SFT.

Bent's Old Fort Historic Site / Marker 321

On Highway 194, 8 miles east of La Junta, Otero County
Bent's Old Fort is the most famous site on the Mountain Route of the SFT. Established in 1833–34 and abandoned in 1849, it was faithfully

restored in 1976 by the National Park Service and is probably the most perfectly restored of all western fortified establishments—even including a billard room, trade goods, and the wash room. It is now a national historic site, worth a visit by everyone traveling along the old trails. It was a private fort, not a military establishment, and all three Sick Detachments (among them my great-grandfather with one of his wives) visited it. Just east of the main entrance to this fort is the old, arched cobblestone gateway. Here are three historic markers.

Before following the Mountain Branch of the SFT east from Bent's Old Fort, it is appropriate here to describe briefly the route that the three Sick Detachments of the MB took from Bent's Old Fort to Fort Pueblo. Other Mormons also followed this route, for example, one "Texas Company," in 1856. This trail, known subsequently as part of the Cherokee Trail of 1849, simply followed the left bank of the Arkansas River for about 72 miles upstream to the west. Today Highways 194, 50, and 96 parallel this old trail closely, but there is little to see of any interest except perhaps the historical marker to Fort Reynolds (1867–72), which protected settlers from hostile Indians. The marker was erected in 1932 by the State Historical Society of Colorado and is located 3 miles east of Avondale, Pueblo County, to the north of U.S. 50.

Between Bent's Old Fort and Ingalls, Kansas (170 miles to the east), most of the Mormon traffic moved westward. Since this guide has been following the Mountain Branch eastward, you should continue in that direction.

322–324   Las Animas Area Markers

There are five DAR markers in Bent County, three of which are near Las Animas. The first one is in Las Animas, 12 miles east of Bent's Fort, just east of the junction of Highway 194 and U.S. 50, north of U.S. 50 near the Alpine Inn. The second marker is 2 miles east on U.S. 50 at the northeast corner of the junction of U.S. 50 with County Road 13. The third one is another 2 miles east on U.S. 50, then turn right (south) on the road leading to the Fort Lyon Hospital. Six-tenths of a mile down this road, the DAR marker is to the west, most likely hidden by weeds. Then return to U.S. 50.

Santa Fe Trail Marker / Ruts 325

Near Hasty, Bent County

10 miles east of the road to the Fort Lyon Hospital is Hasty. Turn south on Highway 260 towards the Martin Reservoir. In 1.8 miles the road forks; take the right-hand fork (which really continues straight ahead) for about 0.1 mile, then turn right and drive 0.1 mile to a sign referring to some SFT ruts. Follow this road to a fenced area with a turnstile at the entrance. A DAR marker, usually nearly hidden by tall grasses, is located in the middle of some very faint trail ruts. To continue to the next site, return to U.S. 50.

Bent's New Fort / Markers 326

Off U.S. 50, 11 miles east of Hasty, Bent County

Bent's Old Fort was abandoned in 1849 and a new, stone fort was built in 1853 east of Hasty to serve as a way station on the SFT. Eleven miles east of Hasty turn south off U.S. 50 onto a dirt road, Highway 35. Go south for 1 mile, turn east for 0.2 mile. Turn right, park, and hike 0.2 mile to the site, where there is a DAR marker (near a telephone pole). A second monument about nine feet tall is nearby, erected in 1940 by the State Historical Society of Colorado.

> The site of / Bent's New Fort / built by William W. / Bent in 1853 / as an Indian trading post. / Sold to U.S. Government 1859. / Buildings added one mile west / and named Fort Wise in 1860. / Renamed Fort Lyon in 1861. / Fort moved farther west, 1867.

Return to U.S. 50.

Lamar Marker 327

On U.S. 385, 8 miles east of the turn-off to
Bent's New Fort, at Lamar, Prowers County

Take U.S. 50 east to Lamar, turn south on U.S. 50 / 385; just beyond this turn is a pull-off east of 385 where there is a DAR marker. In addition, there is a Madonna of the Trails statue on Main Street in Lamar. Cross the Arkansas River and take U.S. 50 east to travel to the next site.

328   **Amity Marker**

On U.S. 50, 24 miles east of Lamar,
or 6 miles east of Granada, Prowers County

Drive 24 miles east of Lamar on U.S. 50 to Amity, Prowers County (too small to be shown on regular maps). One and one-half miles beyond the bridge across the Arkansas River is an intersection in Amity. The DAR marker is 75 yards east of this intersection, south of U.S. 50, close to a fence and most likely hidden by weeds.

329   **Santa Fe Trail Marker on State Line**

About 8.5 miles east of Amity, Prowers County,
on the state line

Just north of U.S. 50 at the Colorado-Kansas state line is the last of the gray DAR markers in Colorado commemorating the SFT.

Kansas
(see map 14)

From the Colorado state line the Mountain Branch of the SFT extends east for 94 miles to Ingalls, Gray County—the beginning of the Cimarron Cutoff (see trail XXIV, 250). The DAR placed at least eight red granite markers along this section of the SFT early in the century.

330   **Santa Fe Trail Marker at Syracuse**

On U.S. 50, in front of the
Hamilton County Museum in Syracuse

About 17 miles east of the Colorado state line on U.S. 50 is Syracuse. In front of the Hamilton County Museum, north of the road, is a DAR marker.

Santa Fe Trail Marker at Kendall   331

On U.S. 50 in Kendall, Hamilton County

Eleven miles east of Syracuse is the village of Kendall. Turn south into the town; the DAR marker is one block north of the railroad tracks, west of the road.

Chouteau's Island Santa Fe Trail Marker   332

On old Lakin Road, Kearny County, in sec. 15, T25S, R37W

From Kendall immediately north of the railroad tracks is a dirt road, the old road to Lakin going east. Follow this desolate road for 10 miles; about 0.4 mile beyond an intersection with a dirt road coming from the north, south of the Lakin Road is a DAR marker commemorating the site of Chouteau's Island, 0.5 mile south of this marker in the Arkansas River. This island, like Grand Island in the Platte River, no longer exists, but it was a famous landmark in trail days and was duly noted in the SFT survey of 1826–27.

It took its name from the fact that in 1816 August P. Chouteau and a fur trading party were attacked here by Pawnees and fled to the island for protection (see 333 below).

Indian Lookout Site / Marker   333

2 miles east of marker 332 (above), north of the road

About 2 miles east of the Chouteau Island marker, north of the road, is a rather prominent land feature usually called the Indian Mound. It is distinct and clearly visible, but must be carefully looked for. It is north of a good-sized irrigation ditch and therefore not easily climbed. Atop this bluff of the Arkansas River is yet another DAR marker.

Continue east about 1 mile to another dirt road going north and go north 3 miles, back to U.S. 50, and turn east towards Lakin.

Chouteau's Island Information Sign   334

On U.S. 50, 1.5 miles west of Lakin, Kearny County

From the point where you rejoin U.S. 50, go 2 miles east, where there is a Kansas historical marker in a roadside park south of U.S. 50.

CHOUTEAU'S ISLAND

In the spring of 1816 August P. Chouteau's hunting party traveling east with a winter's catch of furs was attacked near the Arkansas River by 200 Pawnees. Retreating to what was once an Island five miles southwest of this marker the hunters beat them off with the loss of only one man. In 1825, increased travel on the Santa Fe Trail brought a government survey and Chouteau's Island was listed as a turning off place for the dangerous "Jornada" to the Cimarron. For a time the river here was the Mexican boundary. . . .

335   Santa Fe Trail Marker in Lakin

On Court House Square, Lakin, Kearny County
In Lakin turn right on Highway 25, go two blocks to the DAR marker on the grounds of the courthouse. Then return to U.S. 50.

336   Santa Fe Trail Ruts (P)

4 miles east of Lakin, north of U.S. 50 in sec. 8., T24S, R36W
From Lakin go northeast for 3.5 miles on U.S. 50. Where the highway turns directly east, start looking to the north for a small lake behind an earthen dam. The ruts are east of the lake, between the lake and the highway, running east and west. They can be seen easily and well from the highway, so there is no need to trespass.

337   Santa Fe Trail Marker in Deerfield

In Deerfield city park, Kearny County
In Deerfield, turn south towards town center and the park will be on the right; there is a marker here. Then return to U.S. 50 and go two miles to the Finney County line. Fourteen miles east is Garden City. (Watch your speedometer in Finney County. One of the few speeding tickets I ever received while trailing was given to me here, and it set me back $90.00.)

Santa Fe Trail Markers in Garden City   338

On U.S. 50 at the east end of Garden City, Finney County
On the east end of this community, south of U.S. 50 is a pull-off with two markers. One is a typical red granite DAR marker. The other is a Kansas historical marker about "The Indian and the Buffalo," which provides the best short account of the Plains Indians' dependence on the buffalo I have ever read. It deserves to be printed here in full.

THE INDIAN AND THE BUFFALO

The buffalo was the department store of the Plains Indian. The flesh was food, the blood was drink, skins furnished wigwams, robes made blankets and beds, dressed hides supplied moccasins and clothing, hair was twisted into ropes, rawhide bound tools to handles, greenhides made pots for cooking over buffalo chip fires, hides from bulls' necks made shields that would turn arrows, ribs were runners for dog-drawn sleds, small bones were awls and needles, from hooves came glue for feathering arrows, from sinews came thread and bow strings, from horns came bows, cups, spoons, and even from gall stones a "medicine" paint was made. When the millions of buffalo that roamed the prairie were exterminated the Plains Tribes were starved into submission. A few small herds saved the buffalo from extinction and there are now more than 22,000 in North America game preserves. A herd may be seen just south of Garden City.

To see this herd turn back west to U.S. 83 and go south for 2 miles, across the Arkansas River. Here to the right is the Garden City Buffalo Preserve. No one is present, so just follow the signs and hope to see some buffalo.

Twelve miles east of the Indian and Buffalo sign in Garden City is Pierceville where a DAR marker used to be on the school grounds. The town is 1 mile from the Grey County line. And 12 miles east into Grey County brings us full circle, right back to the Cimarron Crossing at Ingalls (see trail XXIV, 250).

TRAILS XXVI–XXVII

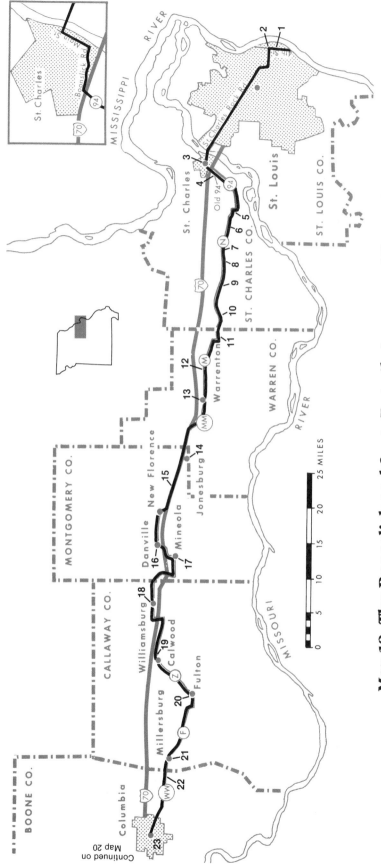

Map 19. The Boonslick and Santa Fe trails in eastern Missouri

On the Boonslick Trail, there is a trail marker at each numbered site 1–26.

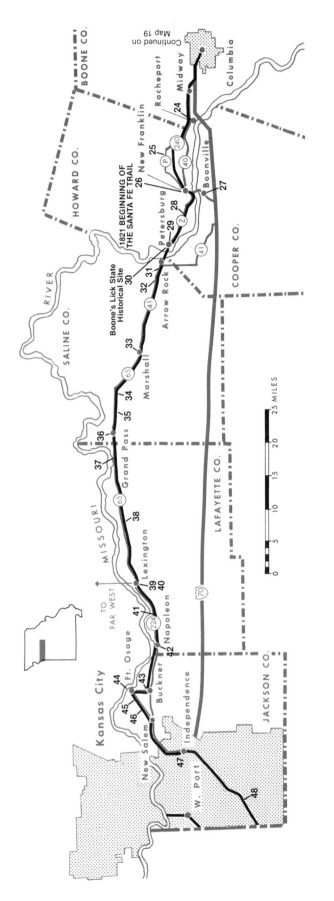

Map 20. The Boonslick and Santa Fe trails in western Missouri

On the Santa Fe Trail in Missouri, there is a trail marker at each numbered site 26–48.

XXVI

The Boonslick Trail in Missouri, 1831–39

(see maps 19 and 20)

The Boonslick Trail was the granddad of all trans-Mississippi trails to the Far West. Originally a trace used by Indians and trappers, it became an important trail in 1764 when St. Louis was established as a fur trading center. Out of the Boonslick Trail grew the more famous Santa Fe, California, and Oregon trails. Part of the Boonslick Trail is also designated as the Lewis and Clark Trail.

The trail, known by the Boonslick name since 1807, derives its designation from the fact that in 1805 the famous frontiersman Daniel Boone and his son extended the trail to some salt springs, an animal licking place, in Howard County, Missouri, at present-day Boone's Lick State Historic Site (10 miles northwest of New Franklin). By 1817 old Franklin, which was later washed away by the river and no longer exists, had been established on the Missouri River and became the functional terminus of the Boonslick Trail.

The first Mormons to use this trail were Parley P. Pratt and four other missionaries who left Kirtland, Ohio, early in 1831 to preach to some American Indians immediately west of Independence, Missouri, across the Missouri River in Indian Territory. Their success with the Shawnees and Delawares was minimal, but those missionaries were the first Mormons in what was soon to become one of the main centers of the church—Jackson County, Missouri.

Joseph Smith himself visited Jackson County during the summer of 1831. He traveled from Kirtland and walked the entire 240 miles from St. Louis to Jackson County. The following spring Smith again had business in Jackson County, and that time he went all the way by regular coach. After that there are few specific references to Mormons using this road, but for as long as they traveled between St. Louis and western Missouri—until forced out of the state by mobs during the winter of 1838–39—this is the way they went.

In 1913 the DAR marked the route between St. Louis and New Franklin with thirty-three large, red granite markers, most of them appearing today as if they had only recently been erected. This means that along the 175 miles between St. Louis and New Franklin, the Boonslick Trail is marked approximately every 5 miles; it is one of the best marked of all western trails. Since most of these markers are easy to locate, we have a unique opportunity to follow closely this old historic and important trail. Unfortunately, however, almost nothing remains of the old trail itself or of the stage stops along its course. Other than the countryside and the DAR markers, there is little to see today.

Because there are so many markers, mostly along county roads, the designations of which change from county to county, I have decided present this trail county by county, marker by marker. Almost all of these thirty-three DAR markers read the same: "Boone's Lick Road / Marked by the / Daughters of the / American Revolution / and the / State of Missouri / 1913," differing only with a one-line inscription naming the site so commemorated. I have added the approximate date that each of these sites came into existence, showing that most of the stage stations, taverns, forts, communities, river ports, springs, farms, churches, and places of business existed at the time of the Mormon use of this trail.

1, 2   The Boonslick Trail in St. Louis County

At one time there were three DAR markers in St. Louis County, but two have disappeared because of urban sprawl. The most important one, however, remains.

Travelers should start at the Old Court House in St. Louis, first visiting the famous St. Louis Arch and the Jefferson National Expansion Museum and the Old Court House. The marker is now located on Fifth Street directly west and behind the Old Court House.

ST. CHARLES ROCK ROAD / BOONSLICK ROAD / ST. LOUIS
First trail west / started near this corner 1764 / Marked by the / Daughters of the / American Revolution / and the / State of Missouri / 1913.

Circle the Old Court House and go north on Fourth Street to Washington Avenue. On the northwest corner of this intersection is a Mormon Pioneer Trail Foundation plaque (on the Missouri Athletic Club building) indicating the site of the first chapel used by the Mormons in St. Louis.

SITE OF THE FIRST MORMON MEETING PLACE IN ST. LOUIS

On this site from 1854 to 1857 stood the building used as the first Mormon church in the St. Louis area.

Beginning in 1831 and during the difficult days of persecution that followed, St. Louis provided an oasis of tolerance, security and religious freedom. It was an economic and cultural metropolis offering homes and employment to thousands of local Mormons and convert-immigrants enroute to western Missouri, Illinois and later to Utah.

This marker is erected in appreciation of the continuing kindness St. Louis has extended to the Church of Jesus Christ of Latter-Day Saints (Mormon).

Mormon Pioneer Trail Foundation, 1975

From here it is possible to zigzag along Washington Avenue, Tucker Boulevard, Martin Luther King Boulevard, and St. Charles Rock Road to follow the old trail to the Missouri River, but it is a long 20 miles of inner-city and surburban traffic, with little of interest to see. Most travelers will prefer to take I-70 downtown to its intersection with St. Charles Rock Road, about 14 miles west (where at one time there was a DAR marker) and take the Rock Road for 6 miles west to St. Charles.

The Boonslick Trail in St. Charles County   3–10

The trail is very easy to follow in St. Charles County and eight markers can be found.

On the southeast corner of the courthouse at Second Street and Jefferson is a handsome trail marker with important text.

THE BOONE'S LICK ROAD

ST. CHARLES TO FRANKLIN

A trace first marked by the Indians. The trail followed by trappers and hunters and by Daniel Boone when he discovered the salt springs, afterwards called Boone's Lick, which gave to this road its name. The main highway out of which grew the Santa Fe Trail, the Salt Lake Trail, and the Great

Oregon Trail. Marked by the Daughters of the American Revolution and the State of Missouri—1913—(Les Petites Cotes—St. Charles 1769).

From the courthouse travelers can visit restored Old St. Charles, the first capitol of Missouri, by walking or driving down South Main Street, which looks pretty much the way it did in the 1830s. To reach South Main Street from the courthouse continue south on Second Street and turn left one block on First Capitol and then south on South Main. At the end of South Main Street turn west on the Boonslick Road (which is the old trail and along which is the recent Boonslick Park) and go 2 miles to Highway 94 (also known as First Capitol Drive), turn left and cross over I-70. The hill you see to the east was very difficult for draft animals.

Just beyond I-70 you will notice Old Highway 94 on the right paralleling new 94. Go 1.5 miles south and exit on Pralle Lane to Old 94. This is the old trail route. Continue south about one-half mile to the St. Charles chapel of the Mormon church on the right, where the Mormon Pioneer Trail Foundation erected a marker in 1980 as part of the Mormon church's sesquicentennial.

BOONSLICK ROAD
First road west, 1764/ used by Joseph Smith/ and the Mormons/ 1831–1839/ 1980.

About 0.8 mile beyond this marker turn back onto new 94 at an intersection. Stay on new 94 about 4 miles to county road N, turn right (west) and follow this road across the county for about 20 miles. Along this 20 miles there are six other markers. The first, to Kountz Fort (1812), is about 0.5 mile along N to the right of the road.

BOONSLICK ROAD
Kountz Fort/ Marked by the/ Daughters of the/ American Revolution and the/ State of Missouri/ 1913.

Since these DAR markers read exactly the same except for the second line, which identifies the site, the full text of most other markers on this trail will not be given. The second, to Gill's Mill (1812), is on the south side of N, 3 miles west of Kountz Fort. The third, to Naylor's Store (1820), is north of N, 4 miles farther. The fourth, to Pond's Fort from

County roads follow the Boonslick Trail in Missouri in much the same direction that it has run since 1807. *See trail XXVI.*

Old St. Charles, Missouri, has been restored to recapture the time when it was the capitol of Missouri. From there, the Boonslick Trail heads west. *See trail XXVI, 3.*

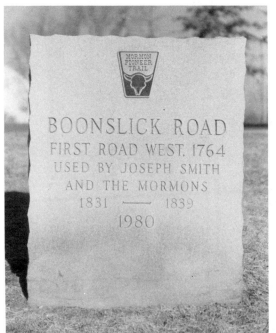

left, This Boonslick Trail marker is located on the Mormon chapel grounds in St. Charles, Missouri. Photo by Violet Kimball. *See trail XXVI, 4. below,* Near the Fulton, Missouri, courthouse, you can see this field stone marked by Daniel Boone, which is believed to be authentic. *See trail XXVI, 20.*

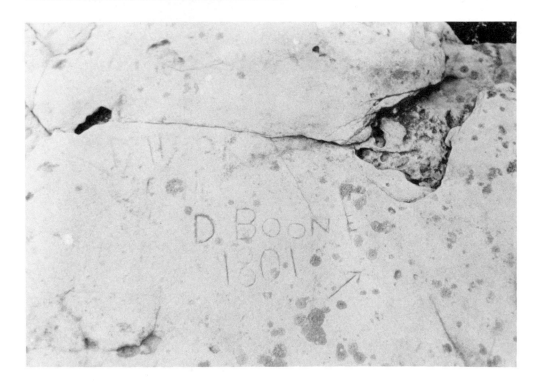

Fort Osage, near Independence, Missouri, was built in 1808 as a trading post. The 1826 survey of the Santa Fe Trail began here. The fort was abandoned in 1827. Photo by Violet Kimball. *See trail XXVII, 44.*

the War of 1812, is south of N, 2.5 miles farther west. About 4 miles beyond the fort at the intersection of roads N and Z is the fifth marker, to Daniel Boone's home. The sixth marker in St. Charles County is 6 miles farther west, south of the road, commemorating Kenner's Tavern (1834).

The Boonslick Trail in Warren County   11–13

There are four markers in Warren County, three of which are easy to find. Also of interest along road M in this county are signs of the historic trail commemorated in modern business names, such as Boon Trail Farm, Boon Trail Offices of Chiropractic, and Boon Trail IGA Food Liner. In Warren County road N becomes OO and the first marker, to Hickory Grove (1809), is 0.6 mile west of the county line south of the road. About 0.5 mile farther west, road OO forms a tee intersection with M; turn north on M. The second marker, to Taylor's Tavern (1816), is north of the road 4 miles along M. The third marker, to Sanders Tavern (1835), is 5 miles farther, north of the courthouse in Warrenton. Main Street in Warrenton is also marked as the Boonslick Trail / Road, and at the courthouse there is a Missouri historical marker about Daniel Boone coming to Missouri in 1799 at age 65 and living at Femme Osage, St. Charles County. The rest of the trail in Warren County may be skipped. Pick up I-70 at Warrenton and go west for 10 miles to the Jonesburg, Montgomery County, exit.

The Boonslick Trial in Montgomery County   14–17

There are four markers in this county and a fifth has disappeared, all easy to locate. Also displaying local recognition of the trail is a large Boonslick Realty sign north of I-70 about 1 mile east of New Florence. The first marker, to Cross Keys Tavern (1829), is on the south side of the Main Street in tiny Jonesburg. To reach the second marker, to Lewiston Trading Post (1826), take I-70 west for 4 miles to the High Hill (or county road F) exit and go west for 1 mile on the service road. The third marker, to Danville (1834), is 7 miles west in little Danville at a truck stop. To reach Danville take either the service road or I-70. The fourth marker, to Loutre Lick Springs (1821), is 3 miles beyond

Danville on road J at Mineola and is one of the prettiest drives along the whole trail. The marker is east of town south of the road across a small stream. Because of the mineral springs, the area was at one time an important health resort.

From here stay on N about 4 miles, cross over I-70, and take the north service road for 4 miles west to Williamsburg, Callaway County.

18–21   The Boonslick Trail in Callaway County

There are five markers in Callaway County, four easy to find. The first one, to Drover's Inn (1836), is 0.2 mile east of Williamsburg, 100 yards north of the road on private property. (It is not worth trying to get any closer.) Return to I-70 and go west 6 miles to the next exit. Turn south on road Z for 2 miles. Here is a marker to Johns Tan Yard; north of the road, just beyond Auxvasse Creek. The third marker is 8 miles south on N in Fulton (1825), where a marker is in front of the courthouse. Near this marker is a large, flat field stone incised with "D. Boon 1801" and an arrow pointing west. It is believed to be authentic, although not at its original site, which was in Fulton on a bluff of Stimson Creek, about 300 yards north of the old trail. The stone was moved here in 1961. The fourth marker in this county, to Millersburg (1829), is north of the road, just east of Millersburg, which is about 12 miles west of Fulton on road F. From here take road WW west 2 miles into Boone County.

22–24   The Boonslick Trail in Boone County

There are five markers in Boone County, three easy to find. The first one, to Vivion's Stage Stop (1827), is south of WW 0.5 mile beyond the county line. From here take WW for 10 miles west to Columbia, to the Smithton (a defunct town, 1821) marker south of Broadway Street near East Parkway.

Return to I-70 and take it and U.S. 40 approximately 9 miles west to county Road J. Exit north and almost immediately take the gravel road marked Old Rocheport Road west for 3.5 miles to Rocheport, founded in 1825 as a riverport. This pretty road suggests what the old trail was probably like. The railroad ended the town's growth, but it is still one of the prettiest places along the old trial. The marker is on Central Street near the main intersection. (Antique shops seem to keep this community alive.)

The Boonslick Trail in Howard County 25–26

There are four trail markers in Howard County, two are easy to find.

From Rocheport, which is right on the county line, take Highway Spur 240 and Highway 240 north for 6 miles to road P, and turn west 2 miles. The marker to Salt Creek Church (1818) sits in the middle of a wye intersection. Stay on P while it twists and turns for 6 miles into New Franklin. An easier way to New Franklin in via U.S. 40.

New Franklin was platted in 1828 to replaced old Franklin, an important river port that was washed away by the mighty Missouri. Here, in the center of the small town, is an impressive monument. Although this marker may be considered to mark the end of the Boonslick Trail, it actually refers to the beginning of the Santa Fe Trail. (For a description of this marker, see trail XXVII, 26). At the rear of the base of this monument, there is a small inscription reading "End of Boon's Lick Trail."

About 10 miles northwest of New Franklin is the original end of the Boonslick Trail, near the salt lick discovered by the Boone family. Today this is the Boone's Lick State Historic Site (see trail XXVII, 30).

Because the Santa Fe Trail, which began here in 1821, is really an extension of the older Boonslick Trail, Travelers should continue following the Santa Fe Trail at least as far as Kansas City, Missouri (see trail XXVII).

XXVII

The Santa Fe Trail in Missouri

(see map 20)

By 1821 old Franklin, Missouri, was a thriving commercial community on the frontier along the Missouri River. In that year a group of traders, led by William Becknell, decided to try to open trade with Santa Fe, the capitol of northern Mexico. (Mexico in 1821 had just won its independence from Spain.) They had heard that because of the city's isolated location the inhabitants of Santa Fe were anxious to trade, even with Yankees.

Becknell forged the Santa Fe Trail and his profits of 1,500 percent were so attractive that many others followed his example; the Santa Fe trail was improved and trade commenced in earnest. Many Mormons from 1831 into the 1850s used this part of the SFT, mainly going to and from St. Louis. After Independence, Missouri (about 100 miles farther west), was founded in 1827, that city became the eastern terminus of the Santa Fe Trail. (For a description of the Santa Fe Trail west of the Independence–Kansas City area, see trail XXIV). Along the 121-mile length of the SFT between New Franklin and Independence (previously known as the Osage Trace) the DAR placed twenty-four markers in 1909. Like the markers along the Boonslick Trail, these markers are inscribed the same: "Santa Fe Trail / 1822–1872 / Marked by the / Daughters of the / American Revolution / and the / State of Missouri / 1909," differing only with one line identifying the site. This trail will be treated county by county. Twenty of the twenty-four markers are easy to find.

26–30   The Santa Fe Trail in Howard County

The first and best of the four markers in Howard County is on Main Street in the middle of New Franklin. It is a bronze plaque on a huge red granite boulder.

Captain William Becknell of Franklin / "Father of the Santa

Fe Trail" / with four companions, led the first organized / trade expedition to Santa Fe / September 1st, 1821 /

FRANKLIN "CRADEL OF THE SANTA FE TRAIL"

1821

This trail / one of the great highways of the world / stretched nearly one thousand miles from / Franklin, Missouri to Santa Fe, New Mexico / "From Civilization to Sundown."

Marked by the / Daughters of the American Revolution / and the / State of Missouri / 1909.

The second marker, 2.5 miles south of New Franklin, east of Highway 5, just north of the bridge to Boonville, marks approximately the site of old Franklin, which the Missouri River washed away.

The third marker, to the Kingsbury Farm (1824), is 4 miles west. Take Highway 87 west, turning left on country road Z. The marker is north of the road 0.5 mile down Z. To reach the fourth marker, to Cooper's Fort, go 6 miles farther west on Z to Petersburg, turn left on a dirt road; the marker is south of the road less than a mile. The traveler is now close to the old ferry across the Missouri River to Arrow Rock, a site that became know as the Santa Fe Crossing.

You are also near the Boone's Lick State Historic Site, site of the original salt lick or spring. To reach this site return to Petersburg and continue northwest 2.5 miles on a dirt road extension of Z to a sign ponting to the site. (Do not turn east on J.) This 17-acre historic site has a picnic area, a short nature trail leading to the salt-water springs, and several information signs. Created in 1960, the park is well worth a visit. Salt springs, or licks, were very important in the settlement of the west as salt was necessary for the preserving of meat, for table use, for livestock, and for the preparation of leather. To continue, return to the Boonville Bridge.

The Santa Fe Trail in Saline County   31–36

Because there is no ferry or bridge across the Missouri River at the Santa Fe Crossing, the traveler must return to the Boonville Bridge and take a 20-mile detour through Cooper County on U.S. 40, I-70, and Highway 41 into Saline County. (Here Highway 41 is also marked as the Lewis and Clark Trail to Marshall, which is 27 miles northwest.)

There are seven DAR markers in Saline County, six of which are easy to locate. The first is west of Highway 41 at the entrance to Arrow Rock State Park, 1 mile beyond the Saline County line.

The site of Arrow Rock, found on maps as early as 1755, was visited by Lewis and Clark in 1804 and by 1829 had become important as a ferry site and assembly point on the Santa Fe Trail. You should not miss the Santa Fe Springs. Continue east on the main road through town. At a tee intersection turn right into the state park. The spring, associated with William Becknell's trading expedition of 1821, is located down through the bluffs on the flat ground left of the road.

The second marker, to Chestnut Hill (c. 1826), is north of Highway 41 a little more than 1 mile north of Arrow Rock. Here faint traces of the SFT may be seen behind the house and permission must be secured to visit them. These are some of the very few SFT ruts along the trail in Missouri, but they are hardly worth the effort to find them. There are some other alleged trail ruts 5 miles west of here in sec. 24, T50N, R20W, behind the Nave Cemetery, but they too are definitely not worth the effort to find.

The third marker is 14 miles west on the northwest corner of the courthouse in Marshall. The next three markers are along U.S. 65 west of Marshall. The fourth, marker number 34, memorializing Kiser's Spring— a favorite camping site, is south of the road about 7.5 miles west of Marshall, near the bridge over the Salt Fork Creek. The fifth marker is south of the road at Malta Bend, 4 miles farther west. And the last marker in Saline County is north of the road in the tiny town of Grand Pass, 4.5 miles beyond Malta Bend. At one time there was a narrow pass here between the Salt Fork Creek and the Missouri River, hence the name.

37–42   The Santa Fe Trail in Lafayette County

There are seven markers in Lafayette County, six of which are easy to locate. The first one is at the Waverly Post Offfice (1845), 2 miles beyond the county line. The second marker is in the Lion's Park at the west end of Dover (1835), south of U.S. 24, 10 miles west of Waverly.

The third and fourth markers are in Lexington, founded in 1822 as a trading post. In the 1830s many Mormons came here from St. Louis on their way to Far West, Caldwell County. The first marker is right next to

260

the Madonna of the Trails monument on Highway 224 just where the road turns southwest down to the Missouri River. The trail marker was moved to this site from a place 8 miles east of Lexington on Highway 24 called Tabo—an American illiteracy by way of Tabeaux from the original French Terre Beau, or Pretty Land. The other marker is about 1 mile west of town center, west of Highway 224 near a small playground. From this marker, the old trail and the modern road parallel the Missouri River, and here is the best view of this river along the entire SFT in Missouri.

The fifth marker is on Main Street in Wellington, 6 miles from Lexington. To reach the last marker in this county, drive 5 miles farther west to Napoleon, turn south on D for about 2 miles to the Ish School; the marker is on the school grounds. Return to U.S. 24 and drive for 2 miles to the county line.

The Santa Fe Trail in Jackson County   43–47 (to Independence)

Of the six markers along the last stretch of the SFT in Missouri, five are easy to locate. The first one is 5 miles west of the county line, in Buckner at the southeast corner of the intersection of U.S. 24 and road BB. This marker is not one of the red granite DAR markers from 1909. It is a large, three-panel marker of white granite erected by the DAR in 1913.

> Santa Fe Trail / 1822–72 / Government Reservation / 1808
> Marked by the / Daughters of the / American Revolution /
> of Fort Osage Township
> Cross State Highway / Buckner 1876 / Jackson County Mo.

The second marker is at Fort Osage, 3 miles north of this white granite marker. It is located on the east side of the old Sibley Cemetery just before reaching the entrance to the fort. Fort Osage was established in 1808 on high bluffs above the Missouri River. It has been well restored and is certainly worth a visit. From here the 1826 survey of the SFT commenced (see trail XXIV, 255).

The next marker is on Blue Mills Road. About 1 mile due south of the old fort is Blue Mills Road going straight west. Four miles down the road is Six-Mile Church, founded in 1825; the marker is south of the road. The next marker is 5 miles farther along Blue Mills Road near the Salem Church (founded 1826), in a pull-off north of the intersection of Blue Mills Road with U.S. 224. The final marker is on the grounds of the courthouse in Independence, 5 miles away.

Mormon use of this section of the SFT generally ended here at Independence, an important Mormon center from 1831 to 1833. In 1846 the Mormon Battalion also followed the SFT (see trail XXIV), but they used a military variant from Fort Leavenworth that completely bypassed the Independence area. Later in the 1850s some Mormons again used part of the SFT, but they picked it up at Westport (in present-day Kansas City, see trail XXIV) and also bypassed Independence.

There are several variants of the SFT west of the the Independence courthouse through Greater Kansas City—some rather difficult to follow. For a detailed study of these, see Gregory Franzwa's *Oregon Trail Revisited*, or Marc Simmons's *Following the Santa Fe Trail*. In this book I shall present only the main route. (I suggest you acquire a Kansas City map.) To follow it, pick up Osage Street going south from near the courthouse to Twenty-third Street, turn west to McCoy, then south (where eventually McCoy becomes Santa Fe Road) to an intersection with Thirty-ninth Street, turn west to Blue Ridge Boulevard, then south. At Sixty-sixth Street there is a DAR marker commemorating "Aunt Sophy's Cabin"; keep going to Seventy-second Street, where there is another DAR marker commemorating the Cave Spring campground. Keep going south to Eighty-seventh Street. Turn west a bit to Santa Fe Road and go south again to Ninty-third Street, then west to Hillcrest Road. Turn south to Red Bridge Road, then west to W. E. Minor Park, where there is a DAR marker, an information sign, and some excellent trail ruts.

48   Santa Fe Trail Historic Site / Ruts / Markers

W. E. Minor Park off Red Bridge Road, Kansas City
Here are the best SFT Ruts in Missouri and some of the best along the entire trail. In the parking lot is an excellent map of the SFT with text. The ruts and DAR markers are about 100 yards south along a wire fence. (The map has recently been vandalized.)

Continue west on Red Bridge Road to Holmes Road, then south again to the Santa Fe Trail, turn west to the state line at State Line Road, where there is a DAR marker. This is the end of the SFT in Missouri.

From here the traveler has at least two options. You can either drive 9 miles north to old Westport (see trail XXIV, 137) and pick up this section of the SFT, or go about 2 miles north to I-435 and go west to U.S. 56 and pick up the SFT near Gardner (see trail XXIV).

TRAIL XXVIII

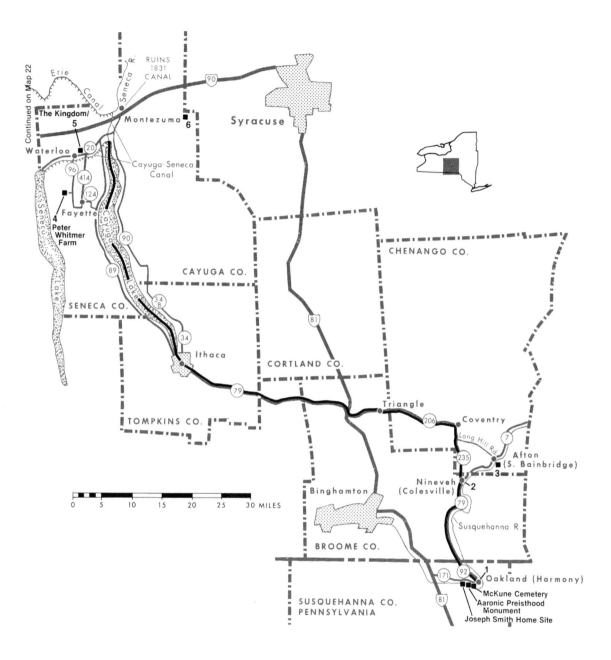

Erie Canal

RUINS
1831
CANAL

Seneca R.

90

Continued on Map 22

The Kingdom/
5

Montezuma 6

Syracuse

Waterloo 20

96

Cayuga-Seneca
Canal

414

124

Fayette

4
Peter
Whitmer
Farm

Seneca Lake

Cayuga Lake

90

CHENANGO CO.

89

CAYUGA CO.

SENECA CO.

34
B

34

Ithaca

CORTLAND CO.

81

79

TOMPKINS CO.

Triangle

206   Coventry

Long Hill Rd.

7

Afton
(S. Bainbridge)

235

3

Nineveh
(Colesville)   2

Binghamton

79

Susquehanna R.

BROOME CO.

17   92

1

Oakland (Harmony)

81

McKune Cemetery

Aaronic Preisthood
Monument

Joseph Smith Home Site

SUSQUEHANNA CO.
PENNSYLVANIA

0   5   10   15   20   25   30 MILES

Map 21. The First Mormon Road West in west-central New York, 1831

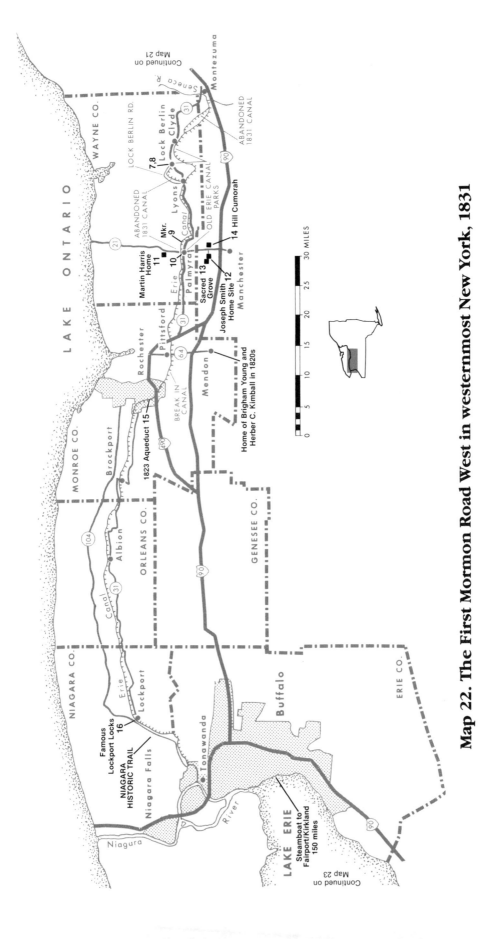

Map 22. The First Mormon Road West in westernmost New York, 1831

XXVIII

The First Mormon Road West: Across New York in 1831

(see maps 21 and 22)

The first Mormon road west left more of a boat's wake than a wagon's rut, because it traversed mostly water. The Mormon church had barely been established in a few counties of western New York and northern Pennsylvania when Joseph Smith said it was God's will that the church remove to Ohio. Smith himself left Fayette Township, Seneca County, New York, for Kirtland, Ohio, in January 1831 and advised the nearly 200 Mormons left behind to join him when they could.

These Mormons separated into three groups and were soon on the way to Kirtland, using all or parts of a route that started near the New York–Pennsylvania line, passed through Ithaca, up Cayuga Lake, then west to Buffalo, New York, along the Cayuga-Seneca Canal and the famous Erie Canal for a total of about 275 miles. From Buffalo they took a Lake Erie steamer for 150 miles southwest to Fairport Harbor at Painseville, Ohio, only 11 miles from Kirtland.

I know of no markers of any kind along this route referring to the Mormons or anyone else traveling this way. There are, however, some markers referring to Mormon history, for this road does pass through several places very important in early New York and Mormon history. Today following this old route is easy, pleasant, and interesting.

Oakland Historic Area Markers   1

Oakland, Susquehanna County, Pennsylvania

It is convenient to reach this area from Binghamton, New York. Take I-81 out of Binghamton south for 15 miles to Highway 171, then go east for 8 miles to Oakland, which was known as Harmony to the early Mormons. Here in a small roadside park immediately west of the McKune Cemetery and south of the road are two markers, one information sign, and one monument commemorating the Joseph Smith home site where much of the Book of Mormon was translated, the restoration of the Aaronic Priesthood (lesser administrative orders in the Mormon church), and some Smith family burials. Also in the small cemetery are three graves—one is that of an unnamed infant son of Joseph and Emma Smith and the other two are of Emma Smith's parents. In this cemetery is an official New York State marker.

JOSEPH SMITH
The founder of Mormonism lived in this vicinity about 1825–29. His infant son is buried in the cemetery. Much of the translation of the "Golden Plates" for the Book of Mormon was done nearby.

2   Nineveh Historic Site

Nineveh, Broome County
Take Highway 92 north from Oakland for about 5 miles to the New York state line. Here the road becomes Highway 79. Follow it some for 19 miles along the lovely Susquehanna River valley to Nineveh on Highway 7.

In the 1830s Nineveh was known as Colesville, the location of the first branch (congregation) of the Mormon church. This branch was one of the three groups of Mormons that followed their prophet west into Ohio.

3   Afton Historic Area Marker

Afton, Chenango County
Take Highway 7 north from Nineveh for 5 miles to Afton, which early Mormons knew as South Bainbridge. Here Joseph Smith married Emma Hale. The home where the marriage took place stood until 1948. To visit the site take Highway 41 south from Afton to the Afton Fairgrounds. Here in front of the fairgrounds is a 1932 New York State Education Department marker commemorating this marriage.

MORMON HOUSE
Joseph Smith, founder of the Mormon Church was married in this house January 18, 1827 to Emily [Emma] Hale.

From Afton the early Mormons went some 60 miles to Ithaca. To follow them today, take Spring Street northwest out of Afton. This becomes the Long Hill Road to Coventry, Chenango County. From here take Highway 206 to Triangle, Broome County, and then Highway 79 to Ithaca.

In Ithaca the Mormons booked passage on Cayuga Lake steamers and sailed the 45-mile length of this Finger Lake north to an intersection with the Cayuga and Seneca Canal. (According to an Iroquois Indian legend the five Finger Lakes in this area were formed when the Great Spirit placed his hand on the earth, designating this place as a chosen spot.)

Peter Whitmer Farm Historic Site   4

Near Fayette, Seneca County

To reach the old (and the new) Cayuga and Seneca Canal, modern travelers must drive, rather than sail, along Lake Cayuga. To do so take Highway 89 north from Ithaca. En route it is convenient to visit the Peter Whitmer Farm historic area.

Go north about 30 miles on Highway 89 and turn west to the village of Fayette. Go several miles west on Highway 336 to Highway 96 and turn north for 4 miles, then west into the farm. (Along the roads are several large signs giving directions and announcing that you are in Historic Mormon Country.)

Here in the farm area there is a colonial-style visitors' center, a large monument to the Book of Mormon, and the restored Whitmer family log cabin in which the Mormon church was officially organized on April 6, 1830. To continue, return to Highway 96.

The Kingdom Historic Site   5

East of Waterloo, Seneca County

Take Highway 96 for about 6 miles north from the Peter Whitmer farm to Waterloo. In 1830 Joseph Smith's parents lived 2 miles east of this village at a place then known as The Kingdom. Today on U.S. 5/20 a large Kingdom Plaza Shopping Center and a historical marker located 1 mile east of the shopping center and commemorating the Kingdom cemetery are all that mark this vanished settlement. Along this stretch of the road you can see the modern Cayuga and Seneca Canal, which ran in front of the Smith home and which some of the early Mormons used on their way to Buffalo.

Continue east on U.S. 5 / 20 for about 9 miles to Highway 90, which is reached just across the Seneca County line, and take it north for about 4 miles to another village, Montezuma.

6   Montezuma Historic Site / Marker

Montezuma, Cayuga County

In the 1830s the Cayuga and Seneca Canal met the Erie Canal at Montezuma where passengers transferred to the Erie. This canal, connecting the Hudson River with the Great Lakes, was one of the great engineering feats of its day and was very important in the opening up of the West. Its total length was 363 miles.

Today you can see the extensive remains of this old canal point of intersection, and there is a 1935 New York State Education Department historical marker here.

OLD ERIE CANAL

Completed from Utica to / here 1819. The "Montezuma" / built here was the first / boat in the canal. Took / passengers to Syracuse 1820.

From here the various groups of Mormons followed the Erie Canal more than 160 miles west to Buffalo.

Travel by canal boat was considered more convenient, cheaper, and more comfortable than overland travel. By law the horse-drawn boats were restricted to four miles per hour, or to an absolute maximum of ninety-four miles a day. Long delays in going through many locks, however, cut their real average to about fifty miles a day. (Most canal traffic ended by the 1840s because railroads were much faster, averaging fifteen miles an hour.)

During the day passengers stayed below in the main cabin or sat outside on the roof of the cabin, where they had an unobstructed view of all they passed. If one felt the need to stretch one's legs it was possible to jump off the boat onto the bank, walk a spell, and leap back on. Three substantial meals were served every day, and additional supplies and

Grave of the infant son of Joseph and Emma Smith, in Oakland, Pennsylvania. *See trail XXVIII, 1.*

The Mormons first traveled west along the Erie Canal, viewed here in Old Erie Canal Park, Palmyra, New York. The Palmyra area is important in early Mormon history. *See trail XXVIII, 11.*

At Lockport, the Erie Canal passes through five locks to raise the water level fifty-six feet. In all, boats were lifted 179 feet by locks all along the canal. *See trail XXVIII, 16.*

refreshments could be obtained along the route while the boat went through the locks. At night, cabin areas were usually divided into male and female sections. Bunks, three and four tiers high, were lowered from the cabin sides and provided reasonably tolerable sleeping conditions.

The Erie Canal has been enlarged and improved twice since the early Mormons used it. Referred to affectionately as Clinton's Ditch (it was built by De Witt Clinton between 1817 and 1825), it was forty feet wide and four feet deep. During the 1840s and 1850s most of this canal was improved and enlarged to seventy feet wide and seven feet deep, and during the early twentieth century it was again enlarged, this time to seventy-five feet wide and twelve feet deep, and was rechristened the New York State Barge—Erie Canal. In general, all three canals followed the same route with few changes; because rebuilding obliterated the earlier canals, only bits and pieces of the Clinton's Ditch of pioneer times are still visible. Modern travelers should make an effort to see some of these bits and pieces.

Old Erie Canal Historic Sites   7, 8

To reach some of these historic sites go north and west from Monte-zuma for 20 miles on Highway 31 (a road that closely parallels the Erie Canal all the way to Buffalo) to Clyde, Wayne County, and continue west on Highway 31 about 5 miles to the tiny village of Lock Berlin. Here the Old Erie Canal Park on Gansz Road must not be missed. Also ask for directions to the back country Lock Berlin Road, which for several miles follows the still faintly visible ruins of the original Erie Canal into the community of Lyons. What is left of the old canal is often to the left of the road and looks like an abandoned irrigation ditch—not much is left of its original forty foot width. From Lyons continue on Highway 31 for 15 miles west to Palmyra.

Palmyra Area Historic Sites   9–14

In and near Palmyra, Wayne County

Around Palmyra is one of the most historic areas in all this Historic Mormon Country. To the north of the road just before reaching Palmyra (from the east) is an official New York State historical marker regarding the Palmyra area. In and near Palmyra are six very easy to find historic sites—either on Main Street or along Highway 21, which runs at right angles to Main Street. Free guides to the whole area may be obtained at any of the six sites.

Perhaps the first stop should be in downtown Palmyra on Main Street (Highway 31) on the north side where in a block of buildings known as Exchange Row was the E. B. Grandin Printing Shop. It was here that the first edition of the Book of Mormon was printed in 1830.

Continue west on Main Street to Highway 21. Turn north to another of the Old Erie Canal Parks. A mile or so north of this is the Martin Harris home, where an interesting exhibit can be seen. Harris was an early Mormon leader best known for having mortgaged his farm to finance the printing of the Book of Mormon.

Turn around and go south on Highway 21 back through Palmyra and follow large signs, first to the Joseph Smith home and the Sacred Grove, and then to the Hill Cumorah. All three are worth visiting.

Beyond Palmyra a few remnants of the old canal are visible. One of the best is in downtown Rochester, about 25 miles west on Highway 31.

15   Rochester Historic Aqueduct

South Street Rochester, Monroe County

In the center of modern Rochester, South Street crosses the Genesee River. The modern street is built right on top of the 802-foot long stone aqueduct of 1823 that carried the Erie Canal across the Genesee River. This is the most impressive remnant of the whole Erie Canal.

For an interesting side trip, drive about 12 miles south of Rochester on Highway 64 to Mendon, Monroe County, one-time home of early Mormon apostles Brigham Young and Heber C. Kimball. Directions for a self-guided tour of the area may be obtained at the Valentown Museum, Fishers, New York, near Mendon.

16   Historic Lockport Locks

Lockport, Niagara County

From Rochester west, Highway 31 follows the route of the old and new canal rather well for some 60 miles to Lockport. Along the road at places such as Brockport, Albion, and Medina the canal may be viewed with ease.

At Lockport are the most impressive set of locks along the Erie Canal. Between Montezuma and Buffalo, canal boats were lifted a total of 179 feet by locks at Clyde, Lyons, Brighton, Rochester, and Lockport. At Lockport a series of five seperate locks were necessary to raise the boats fifty-six of those feet. Here, near the center of town, the ruins of the old as well as the new locks may be seen.

From Lockport travelers can follow the lovely Niagara Historic Trail to Buffalo via Tonawanda. In Buffalo the traveler is advised to visit the impressive, interesting, and informative Old Canal Days exhibit in the Buffalo Historical Museum in Delaware Park, north of downtown. Here at Buffalo the Mormons transferred to Lake Erie steamers and continued by water to Fairport Harbor, only 11 miles from Kirtland, Ohio. In theory, those Mormons who went to Ohio from Ithaca via Lake Cayuga, the Cayuga and Seneca Canal, the Erie Canal, and Lake Erie to Fairport could have done so without setting foot on land. For those today who wish to follow the Mormons west from Buffalo, take I-90 for 175 miles southwest to Kirtland, Ohio (see trail XXIX).

TRAIL XXIX

Map 23. The Zion's Camp Trail in northeastern Ohio, 1834

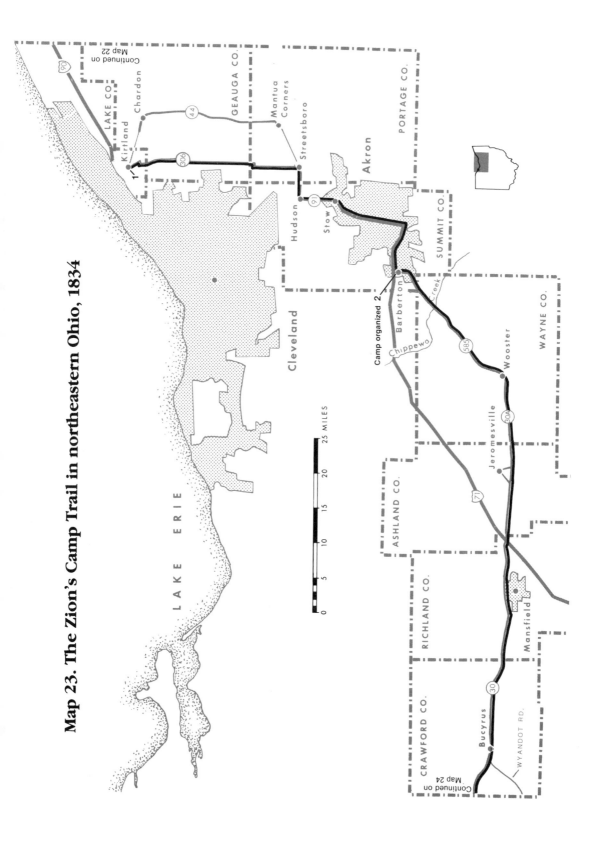

LAKE ERIE

Cleveland

Akron

LAKE CO.

GEAUGA CO.

PORTAGE CO.

SUMMIT CO.

WAYNE CO.

ASHLAND CO.

RICHLAND CO.

CRAWFORD CO.

Kirtland

Chardon

Mantua Corners

Streetsboro

Hudson

Stow

Barberton

Chippewa

Creek

Wooster

Jeromesville

Mansfield

Bucyrus

Camp organized 2

WYANDOT RD.

Continued on Map 22

Continued on Map 24

90

306

44

8

585

30A

71

30

0 5 10 15 20 25 MILES

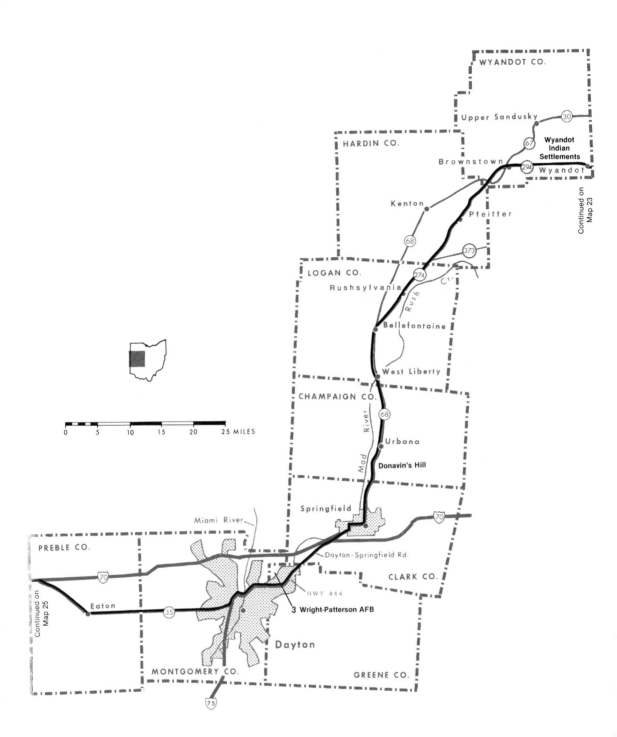

Map 24. The Zion's Camp Trail in west-central Ohio, 1834

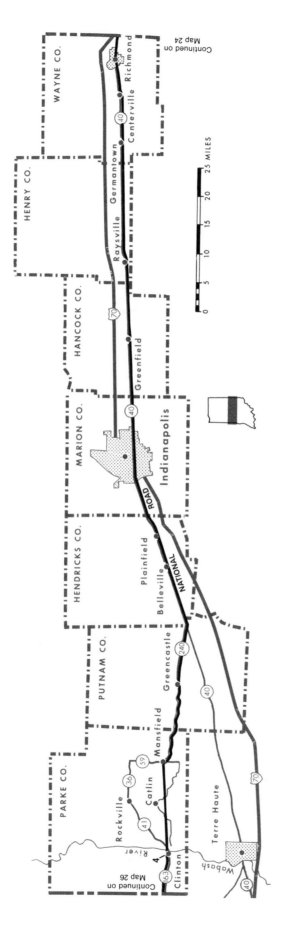

Continued on Map 24

WAYNE CO.

Richmond

Centerville

40

HENRY CO.

Germantown

Raysville

HANCOCK CO.

70

Greenfield

40

MARION CO.

Indianapolis

HENDRICKS CO.

Plainfield

ROAD

Belleville

NATIONAL

PUTNAM CO.

Greencastle

240

Mansfield

40

PARKE CO.

Rockville

36

59

Catlin

41

River

4

70

Terre Haute

Wabash

40

Continued on Map 26

Clinton

63

0 5 10 15 20 25 MILES

Map 25. The Zion's Camp Trail in Indiana, 1834

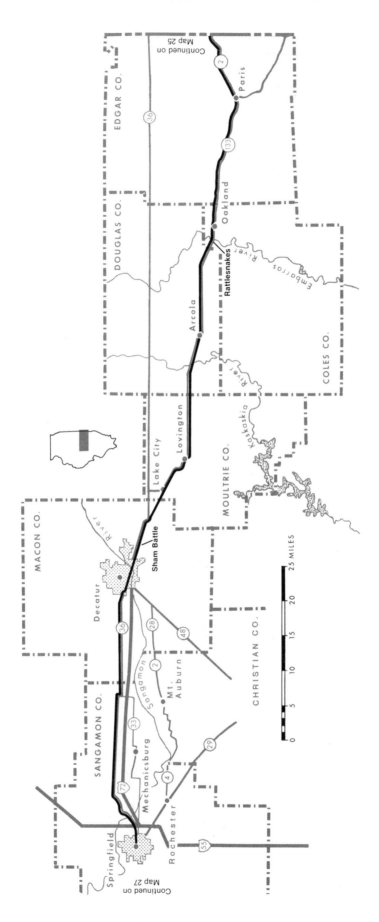

Continued on
Map 25

Paris

Oakland

Rattlesnakes

Embarras River

Arcola

Koskaskia River

Lovington

Lake City

MOULTRIE CO.

EDGAR CO.

DOUGLAS CO.

COLES CO.

MACON CO.

Decatur

Sham Battle

Sangamon River

SANGAMON CO.

Mt. Auburn

Mechanicsburg

CHRISTIAN CO.

Rochester

Springfield

Continued on Map 27

25 MILES

0   5   10   15   20   25

Map 26. The Zion's Camp Trail in eastern Illinois, 1834

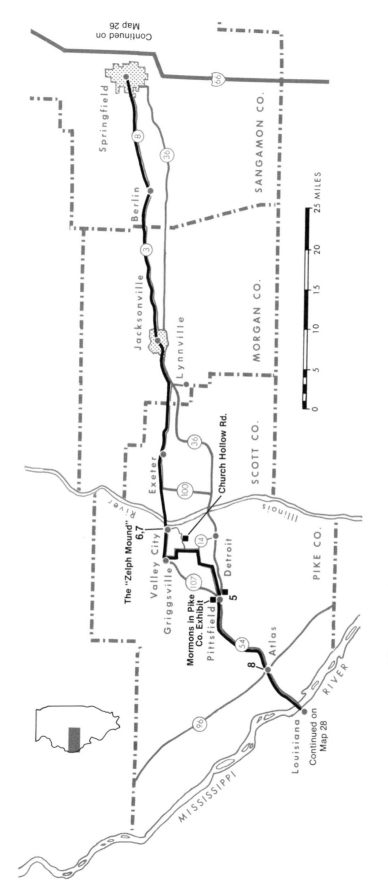

Map 27. The Zion's Camp Trail in western Illinois, 1834

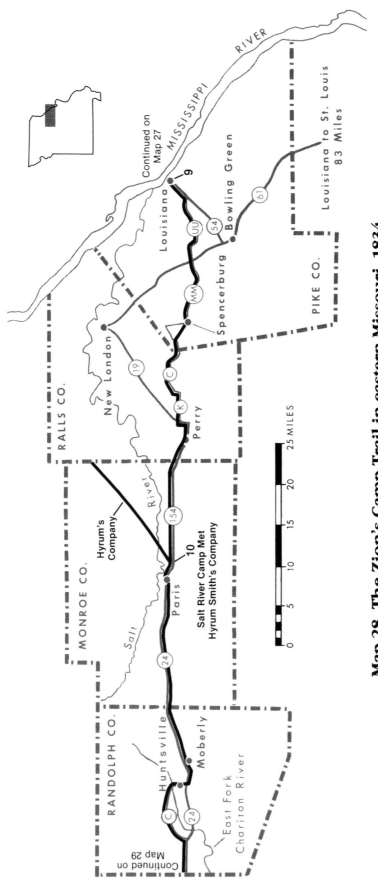

Map 28. The Zion's Camp Trail in eastern Missouri, 1834

MISSISSIPPI RIVER

Continued on Map 27

Louisiana

Louisiana to St. Louis
83 Miles

9

UU

54

Bowling Green

61

Spencerburg

MM

PIKE CO.

New London

19

RALLS CO.

C

K

Perry

154

MONROE CO.

Hyrum's Company

Salt River

10

Paris

Salt River Camp Met
Hyrum Smith's Company

24

RANDOLPH CO.

Huntsville

C

24

Moberly

East Fork
Chariton River

Continued on Map 29

Salt

25 MILES

0 5 10 15 20 25

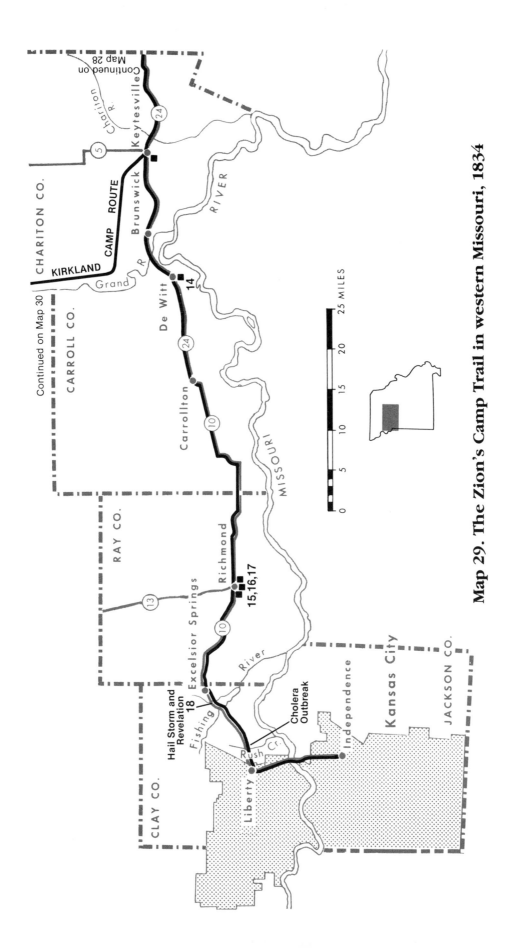

Map 29. The Zion's Camp Trail in western Missouri, 1834

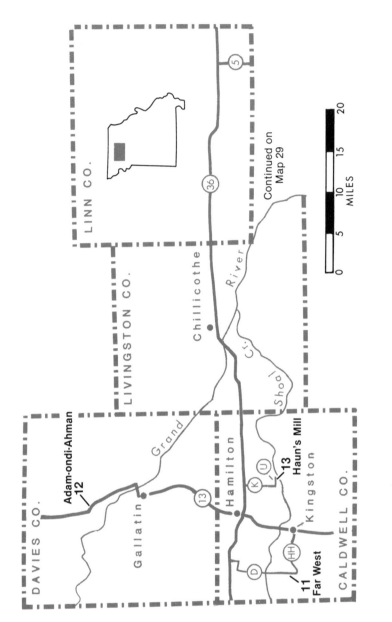

DAVIES CO.

LINN CO.

Adam-ondi-Ahman
12

Gallatin

LIVINGSTON CO.

Grand

Chillicothe

36

River

5

Hamilton

Shoal

Cr.

13

Continued on
Map 29

K

U

13

Haun's Mill

D

Kingston

HH

11

Far West

CALDWELL CO.

0   5   10   15   20
MILES

Map 30. The Kirtland Camp Route supplement in Ohio, 1838

XXIX

The Mormon Zion's Camp March of 1834 and the Kirtland Camp March of 1838 in Ohio, Indiana, Illinois, and Missouri

The nearly 900-mile march of Zion's Camp from Kirtland, Ohio, to Jackson County, Missouri, during the spring of 1834 gave the Mormons their first practical experience in moving large groups of people and materials over long distances, helping prepare them for the much greater exodus of 1846–48. The purpose of this small army, which originally consisted of only 130 men and eventually numbered 205 men (plus 11 women and 7 children), was to help some Missouri Mormons regain their Jackson County lands from which they had been driven by mobs earlier that same year. Joseph Smith led the march, and almost all the leading Mormons of that day participated.

Later, in 1838, after Smith himself had moved from Ohio to new church headquarters in Far West, Caldwell County, Missouri, most of the Mormons in Ohio followed. One group of about 550 people came to be known as the Kirtland Camp, and they generally followed the same route of Zion's Camp with a few important differences. Here the emphasis will be placed on Zion's Camp with occasional references to the Kirtland Camp, especially where the routes were not the same.

This trail (really road) of 1834 and 1838 is perhaps the easiest of all routes that nineteenth-century Mormons used. This is because both camps mainly passed through settled areas where established roads existed, roads which still exist. Furthermore, almost all of the communities along the line of march today existed in 1834 and 1838.

Ohio
(see maps 23 and 24)

---

1 ## Kirtland Historic Site

Kirtland, Lake County

After the Mormons left western New York in 1831 (see trail XXVIII), Kirtland, Ohio, became church headquarters until 1838 and there is much history in the area. The most important things for the traveler to see is the Kirtland Temple on Chillicothe Road, which is well maintained by the RLDS church and open to visitors. Other points of interest are the old cemetery just north of the temple and the recently restored Newel K. Whitney store at Four Corners. Literature regarding the whole Kirtland area may be obtained free at the Whitney store.

On or about the first of May 1834, Zion's Camp started west from Kirtland to its staging ground at New Portage, where there was a branch of the church, about 50 miles to the south on the Ohio Canal.

2 ## New Portage Staging Ground Historic Site

Barberton, Summit County

To reach this area, now known as Barberton, from Kirtland take Highway 306 due south for 27 miles to Streetsboro, via Chester Center, Russell Center, Bainridge, and Aurora where Highway 306 becomes Highway 43.

From Streetsboro take Highway 303 west for 5 miles to Hudson, then via Stow go south on Highway 91 for 10 miles to Talmadge. From Talmadge it is 13 miles of greater Akron urban sprawl to Barberton. Perhaps the best way to reach Barberton is to go west from Talmadge to an expressway bearing the number 8, then south to I-277 (which becomes I-76) to the Barberton exit.

The Zion's Camp march proper began at New Portage, probably near the old town square, on May 9 and proceeded without incident through open, rolling hill country. Days began at sunrise, followed by prayer and breakfast; animals were rested about every two hours. A noon stop was brief; they camped before dark and averaged about 25 miles per day.

From New Portage the old route went southwest about 25 miles to Wooster via Doylestown and Chippeway (modern Easton). This is Highway 585 today. From here take Highway 30-A some 30 miles west to Mansfield via the old towns of Jefferson, Reedsburg, Jeromesville, Hayesville, and Mifflen.

From Mansfield take Highway 430 and U.S. 30 for 25 miles west to Bucyrus as the Mormons did. On July 16, 1838, several members of the Kirtland Camp were arrested near Mansfield for passing some paper money that had been printed by the Mormons in Kirtland, but they were released the next day.

From Bucyrus both groups of Mormons had two choices to reach Bellefontaine, Logan County, some 50 miles to the southwest. Old maps show clearly that the main road went by way of Upper Sandusky and Kenton, but the account of the Kirtland Camp makes it equally clear that they did *not* go that way. Unfortunately it is not clear which route Zion's Camp took. I will, therefore, give both routings. The first is easy enough for in early times main roads went from one county seat to another. Today take U.S. 30 for 15 miles from Bucyrus to Upper Sandusky, Wyandot County, then 23 miles southwest on Highway 67 to Kenton, Hardin County, then 20 miles south on U.S. 68 to Bellefontaine, Logan County.

Those who wish to follow the 1838 routing of the Kirtland Camp can do so via county roads. From Bucyrus take the Wyandot Road southwest 10 miles to Wyandot and turn west on Highway 294 for 13 miles to Brownstown, then turn southwest 2 miles on Highway 67 to Marseilles, Wyandot County.

Here at Marseilles pick up county road 142, (which very soon becomes county road 265) and drive 7 miles to Pfeiffer, Hardin County. Continue along 265 for another 11 miles to a merging with Highway 273. In about 1 mile Highway 273 turns sharply west and Highway 274 continues southwest. Take Highway 274 for 4 miles to Rushsylvania, Logan County, where county road 9 begins and in 8 miles you will be in Bellefontaine, Logan County, and back again on U.S. 68, the route of Zion's Camp. From Bellefontaine the road goes straight south for 31 miles to Springfield, via West Liberty and Urbana. Just 3 miles south of Urbana watch for a road sign marking Hickory Grove Road, which will cross U.S. 68 at right angles. This intersection marks what once was known as Donavin's Hill—one of the few elevations in central Ohio. From here one obtains a beautiful view of the surrounding countryside, especially to the south. Take a moment to enjoy it because you will not have such an opportunity again along this trail in Ohio.

3   Springfield-Dayton Turnpike Historic Site

Along Highway 444 in Bath Township, Green County

Avoid downtown Springfield. U.S. 68 is a bypass that crosses the Mad River, as the Mormons did. Take the U.S. 40 exit and ask directions to the Dayton-Springfield Road near Limestone City. Take this road for 8 miles to the Green County line where it becomes Highway 444, which in 13 miles will bring you to Dayton.

Just inside Green County, an interesting event in the march of the Kirtland Camp took place. Somewhere along the 6 miles of Highway 444 that pass through Bath Township and to the east of the Wright-Patterson Air Force Base, the Kirtland Camp contracted (to earn some much-needed traveling funds) to grade one-half mile of the Springfield and Dayton Turnpike, then under construction. To do so they camped about one-quarter of a mile from the Mad River and worked from July 31 through August 22. During this layover three children died and were buried there.

At Dayton both camps crossed the Miami River and proceeded due west along what is now U.S. 35 for 16 miles to Eaton, Preble County. Then they traveled 11 miles northwest on U.S. 35 to the Indiana state line.

Indiana
(see map 25)

On May 17, 1834, Zion's Camp reached the Indiana state line just east of Richmond and picked up the famous National Road (today's U.S. 40), which is still marked National Road. While still far from complete in 1834, it was the first and only "interstate" of its day and far preferable to other roads in Indiana. In 1811 it started in Cumberland, Maryland, eventually reaching San Diego. For both camps the march across Indiana was generally uneventful.

Both camps stayed on the National Road most of the way across the state via Centerville, Germantown, Dublin, Raysville, Knightstown, and

Greenfield, 66 miles to Indianapolis. From Indianapolis they continued west 30 miles on modern U.S. 40 to Highway 240. Here, from the intersection of U.S. 40 and Highway 240 the two camps followed different routes to Paris, Illinois, some 55 miles due west.

Wabash River Historic Crossing 4

Clinton, Parke County

Zion's Camp took a route in western Indiana that is today quite difficult to follow, one which certainly should not be attempted without Putnam and Parke counties' maps. Even with these maps I asked directions half a dozen times before I drove the short distance of only 30 miles between Greencastle, Putnam County, and Clinton, Parke County. If one insists on going this way I recommend taking Highway 240 for 11 miles west to Greencastle, then take Highway 231 north for 9 miles to U.S. 36, then drive 19 miles west to Rockville, Parke County, then another 12 miles to Clinton on U.S. 41. At Clinton, Zion's Camp ferried the Wabash River and took what is today Highway 163 due west for 6 miles to the Illinois state line. There they headed up what is today's Highway 2 for 10 miles to Paris, Edgar County, Illinois.

A much easier, and just as historic way to Paris, Illinois, is to follow the Kirtland Camp that simply stayed on the National Road (U.S. 40) all the way to Terre Haute. From West Terre Haute the modern traveler can pick up a county road and take it about 5 miles northwest along Sugar Creek to the Illinois state line and continue on Highway 4 for 13 miles to Paris and once again join the Zion's Camp route.

Illinois
(see maps 26 and 27)

From Paris, Illinois, both camps made their way another 200 miles pretty much straight west across central Illinois on established roads, and the old route can be followed quite closely today. I know of only two markers along the entire route in Illinois that refer in any way to the Mormons. One is near Pittsfield, the other is in Pittsfield.

From Paris take Highway 133 (the Old Springfield Road) west for 53 miles to Lovington, Moultrie County, via Oakland, the Embarras River crossing, and Arcola. Then take Highway 32 for 8 miles north to U.S. 36 and go west about 10 miles to Decatur, Macon County, near where in 1834 Zion's Camp fought a sham battle to test their military preparedness before reaching Missouri.

West from Decatur to Springfield the old road generally follows the Sangamon River valley. To do so today take Highway 48 for 4 miles southwest to Highway 28 and turn due west 7 miles to the Christian County line, where the road becomes Highway 2; continue west for 16 miles via Mt. Auburn and Roby to the Sangamon County line, where the road becomes Highway 4 and continues west 12 miles to Springfield via Rochester, Sangamon County. For some 10 miles the road west from Decatur is also part of the Lincoln Heritage Trail and the Lincoln Trail Homestead State Park is 1.2 miles north of the road on the Sangamon River. Watch for signs.

Clear Springfield traffic as best you can, heading towards Washington Park on the west side of the city. Near this park pick up Highway 8 (the Old Jacksonville Road) and continue west some 10 miles to Berlin (pronounced BERlin in these parts).

From Berlin stay on the same road west for 4 miles to the Morgan County line (where the road becomes Highway 3) and continue 12 miles to Jacksonville. From Jacksonville west, for 22 miles to the Illinois River, the historic route is along twisting country roads via Lynnville and Exeter. To reach Lynnville take U.S. 36 southwest from Jacksonville for 5 miles. Lynnville lies 0.5 mile south of U.S. 36 on a county road. Return north to U.S. 36 and take a section-line road due west for 10 miles to Exeter.

From Exeter the gravel road winds some 4 miles down through some pretty bluffs to Highway 100 on the edge of the Illinois River floodplain. From these bluffs you can see some 3 miles west to the Illinois River, where both camps crossed the river at Valley City. Various farm roads lead down to the river, but there is nothing to be seen.

Since there is no ferry or bridge across the Illinois River at Valley City, take a long 30-mile detour via Pittsfield and Griggsville to reach Valley City and again pick up the old route. Take Highway 100 south for 6.5 miles to U.S. 36, turn west for 12 miles to Pittsfield, then take Highway 107 for 8 miles north to Griggsville, then for 3.5 miles east on a blacktop to Valley City. (There is a shorter way, only 16 miles long, using twisting county roads. Take a dirt road north from Detroit, which is just 4 miles west of the Illinois River on Highway 100, go north 2 miles to a tee intersection, turn west for 1 mile, then straight north for 4 miles to the blacktop and go east for 2.5 miles to Valley City.)

Mormon Town Historic Site / Marker   5

On U.S. 6, 2 miles east of Pittsfield, Pike County

Before picking up the trail at Valley City, stop about 2 miles east of Pittsfield on U.S. 36, north of the road, at the site of Old Mormon Town. This is were some Mormons, driven from Missouri during the winter of 1838–39, temporarily settled before Nauvoo, Illinois, became the new gathering place. The site is marked by a white, wooden sign.

> The SITE of EARLY "MORMONTOWN" / FOUNDED 1839 / By 1845 there were 300 voters. A few / years later some returned to Missouri, / others went to Nauvoo. Polygamy was / not practiced here. / PIKE COUNTY HISTORICAL SOCIETY.

No visible trace of the Mormon Town remains, although at one time there were supposed to have been gravestones there. The old East School of Pittsfield is now a Pike County museum, which has on exhibit a large map illustrating Mormon history in early Pike County.

Phillips Ferry and Zelph Mound Historic Sites   6, 7

Near Valley City, Pike County

Today Valley City is the location of the Phillips Ferry which both camps used to cross the Illinois River. One mile south of Valley City on a dirt road along the river the famous Zelph Mound is west of the road. On June 3, 1834, some of Zion's Camp dug into an Indian burial site atop this river bluff and uncovered a skeleton. Joesph Smith later declared that it was the remains of "a white Lamanite [Indian] . . . whose name was Zelph." The site is on private ground and permission to visit the mound must be obtained.

From the Zelph Mound there is much dispute regarding the route Zion's Camp took to Pittsfield, which is 13 miles to the southwest. The easy way, the way the Kirtland Camp took, is to return to Valley City, then southwest on Highway 107 to Pittsfield via Griggsville.

A much prettier (and more difficult) way is via Church Hollow, a rough twisting 2-mile cut up through the bluffs from the river bank. The entrance to the hollow is approximately 0.7 mile south of Valley City on the same riverside road used to reach the Zelph Mound. The cut bears west up through the bluff. The easy way to Pittsfield from the Hollow is to take the first road west as one emerges from the hollow, go west for 2 miles, then north for 0.8 mile, then west for 2 miles to Highway 107, and follow it 7 miles southwest to Pittsfield.

8   Atlas Historic Site / Markers

Atlas, Pike County

The next point of interest is 12 miles west of Pittsfield at Atlas. Take U.S. 36 west of Pittsfield, then U.S. 54 southwest. On the northwest corner the intersection of U.S. 54 and Highway 96 in Atlas is an old, two-story brick building (restored) and two markers. One refers to the building.

> Oldest Building / in Pike County / Built 1823 for / trading post on / trail between / Keokuk and St. Louis / Pike County Historical Society.

The other refers to Atlas:

> Atlas / Site of the / first permanent / Seat of Justice / in / Pike County / DAR 1935.

When the Mormons were driven out of Missouri during the winter of 1838–39 Brigham Young and his family stayed in this two-story brick home, or trading post, in Atlas for a few weeks. Part of the Heber C. Kimball family also sought refuge in this community at the same time. Other Mormons went east of Pittsfield to Mormon Town (see site 5, above).

From Atlas U.S. 54 follows the old route closely for 5 miles to the Mississippi River, where both camps ferried across to Louisiana, Missouri.

Missouri
(see maps 28 and 29)

The old route went almost straight west across Missouri about 190 miles between Louisiana on the Missouri River and Liberty, near Kansas City.

Most of the route followed by the Zion's Camp March of 1834 passed through settled areas and the modern traveler can follow their route easily. *See trail XXIX.*

Donavin's Hill, Ohio, is one of the few elevations in central Ohio. The Zion's Camp March passed this way in 1834. *See trail XXIX, 2.*

Old Mormon Town, Illinois, is marked by this sign, but no visible trace of the town remains. *See trail XXIX, 5.*

Louisiana Ferry Historic Site   9

Louisiana, Pike County

Louisiana, a Mississippi River port since at least 1817, was a prominent supply stop for pioneers into the Salt River Country. Zion's Camp was heading for this Salt River Country because there was a small Mormon settlement somewhere near Paris, Monroe County, which was then known as the Allred Settlement.

Lousiana is situated where it is because the Noix Creek valley provides a gentle grade up through the high river bluffs into the interior of Missouri. There is a historical marker just west of town telling the history of Louisiana. The first 55 miles of the old road in Missouri, from Lousiana to Paris, is some of the most difficult to follow along the entire 900-mile length of the old road. Beyond Paris, however, the old road is quite easy to follow.

The easy way to Paris is to take U.S. 54 west from Lousiana for 22 miles, then follow Highway 154 the rest of the way. The more historic route through pretty valleys and past old cemeteries, via Spencerburg, Madisonville, and Florida, is quite difficult to follow and Pike, Ralls, and Monroe counties' maps are necessary. For those who wish to try this way, the following comments might be helpful.

Take U.S. 54 up the Noix Creek valley southwest from Lousiana. In 4 miles turn due west on UU; in 6 miles UU turns south, but you stay west for 2.5 miles until an intersection with Highway 61, cross over and take U and MM to Spencerburg, in the cemetery of which are tombstones dating from the early 1830s. From Spencerburg take a dirt road north for 4 miles to C and turn west; with a good many turns this road will bring you to Madisonville. From Madisonville county roads C, P, and K bring the traveler to Perry.

From Perry the old road goes west to Florida. To do this take J north from Perry for 4 miles to BB, which goes due west for 6.5 miles to Florida, birthplace of Mark Twain. Then take U for 6 miles west to where U turns due north and curves around to the south into Paris. The old trail does not turn north here, but meanders 5 more miles west to Paris—with a Monroe County map travelers can do the same thing. This twisting road is very pretty, being part of the old Paris to Florida Road. It enters Paris from the east on a bridge across the Middle Fork of the Salt River on Hill Street. The bridge is where the original ford was located.

10 Junction of the Two Contigents of Zion's Camp

Near Paris, Monroe County

Here, just east of Paris on the Salt River, at what was then known as the Allred Settlement, the main part of Zion's Camp rendezvoused on June 8, 1834, with a smaller contigent from Michigan Territory led by Joseph's brother, Hyrum. (This group marched via Pontiac, Ann Arbor, Jacksonborough, Spring Arbor, and Constantine, Michigan; Elkhart and Laporte, Indiana; Ottawa, Peking, and Quincy, Illinois; and Palmyra, Missouri.)

From Paris the old road proceeds due west for 30 miles to Huntsville via Moberly, both of which are in Randolph County. There is nothing to see in Huntsville, which is today off the main road, U.S. 24. The purist, however, may wish to go that way, for this is where both camps (Zion's and Kirtland) crossed the Chariton River. To do so take county road C, 5 miles west of Moberly, to Huntsville and either return to U.S. 24 or ask directions on how to follow dirt roads and circle westward back to U.S. 24. Twenty-seven miles west of Moberly is Keytesville, Chariton County, through which both camps passed (see map 29). Here is a Missouri historical marker telling the history of Keytesville and just west of Keytesville is a similar marker commemorating old Fort Orleans of 1723, the westernmost outpost of the old French Empire in what is now Missouri.

11–13 Historic Sites North of the Zion's Camp Line of March

(see map 30)

At Keytesville, Chariton County, the Kirtland Camp turned north off the State Road and went up the east side of the Grand River to Chillicothe, Livingston County, then southwest to Far West, Caldwell County—the end of their march. Almost all of this old road has disappeared. The modern traveler may as well drive the most direct way to Chillicothe by taking Highway 5 north from Keytesville for 25 miles to U.S. 36, then turn west for 32 miles to Chillicothe; stay on U.S. 36 for 20 miles to Hamilton, Caldwell County, then south for 8 miles on Highway 13 to Kingston. Drive west again on Highway HH for 5.5 miles to D, then north for 2.5 miles to the site of Far West, which is well marked today by the fenced-off area of the old Far West Temple site. Within this area are several markers and information signs about the history of this old Mormon church headquarters.

Once travelers have reached Far West, it is convenient and important to visit two other related historic sites near by—Adam-ondi-Ahman and Haun's Mill.

To reach Adam-ondi-Aham, "where Adam shall come to visit his people," continue north on D for 5 miles to U.S. 36, turn east to Hamilton for 7 miles, then take Highway 13 for 13 miles north to Gallatin. Go 6 more miles north on 13 to the first of several highway markers giving instructions to this site, where other information signs present its history.

To reach Haun's Mill, where seventeen Mormons were killed by a Missouri mob in October 1838, return south to U.S. 36 at Hamilton, then east 7 miles on U.S. 36 to road K, then south for 3.3 miles to U, then about 1 mile east to a two-story white farm house, then 1 mile south, then 0.5 mile east to some markers regarding the area.

To rejoin the Zion's Camp route, return to Highway 13 at Hamilton and drive south for 32 miles to Richmond there turn east on Highways 10 and 24 for some 65 miles back to Keytesville.

De Witt Historic Site / Marker   14

De Witt, Carroll County

From Keytesville it is 17 miles west on U.S. 24 to the tiny community of De Witt, Carroll County, founded by the Mormons in 1838. It has nothing to do with either Zion's Camp or the Kirtland Camp, but since it is right on the way it should be noted. In town center is a bicentennial flagpole and marker telling the story of De Witt.

THE MORMONS

In 1838, members of the Church of Jesus Christ of the Latter-day Saints (Mormons) living at Far West in Caldwell County, Missouri, were encouraged to settle at DeWitt by several landowners. Land was purchased near this location in June, and within a few months several hundred Mormons had created a village of tents and wagons. Land was cleared, crops were planted, and homes were built. However, the persistent misunderstandings which had followed the Mormons soon reached Carroll County. By October DeWitt was held in a virtual state of seige by non-Mormons from surrounding communities. To avoid further violence on October 11, 1838, the Latter-day Saints loaded their possessions into seventy wagons and departed.

This marker was presented to the people of DeWitt, by the Church of Jesus Christ of Latter-day Saints, July 4, 1976.

Seventeen miles beyond De Witt, near Carrollton, take Highway 10 which follows the old trail closely 30 more miles west to Richmond, Ray County.

15–17   Richmond Historic Site / Markers

Richmond, Ray County

In Richmond the most important historic site is the monument to the Three Witnesses, in Pioneer Cemetery at the intersection of Highway 13 and Crispin Street on the north end of town. Here, among others, is the grave of Oliver Cowdery, one of the Three Witnesses to the Book of Mormon. On Court House Square is a statue to General W. A. Doniphan, who defended the Mormons during the Missouri presecutions. And in the City Cemetery west of town on Highway 10 is the David Whitmer grave. Whitmer was also one of the Three Witnesses. His grave is located on the east side of the cemetery, on top of the hill and next to a large tree. It is rectangular and about four feet tall.

18   Fishing River Historic Site

West of Excelsior Springs, Clay County, south of Highway 10

From Richmond continue west on Highway 10 for about 11 miles to Excelsior Springs, a one-time famous health spa. Just beyond Excelsior Springs is the hamlet of Prathersville nestled between the branches of the Fishing River. It was here, somewhere on relatively high ground between the river branches, that Zion's Camp was attacked by a Missouri mob. The attack, however, was foiled by a sudden storm that raised the level of the water in the river so high that the Mormons were in effect protected by a moat and the mob dispersed. During the height of the storm, some of the Mormons took shelter in a near by Baptist meeting house. This meeting house was just west of Highway 10 in Prathersville, in the northeast quarter of sec. 15, T52N, R30W.

This aborted attack was the only military action Zion's Camp saw. The next day they pushed on some 10 miles west to Rush Creek, which Highway 10 crosses just east of Liberty, Clay County, where they camped and disbanded without having achieved their goal of reinstating their fellow Mormons on their Jackson County lands. Camp members then returned as they pleased to Kirtland, Ohio, where the march had commenced.

While travelers are near Liberty and Independence, Missouri, they should visit Mormon historic sites in those communities. In Liberty is the Liberty Jail Bureau of Information near the intersection of Main and Mississippi Streets. Here Joseph Smith and five companions were imprisoned from November 1838 to April 1839. The old jail has been restored in a cut-away fashion and completely enclosed by the bureau. Here a guide to the historic sites in near by Independence may be secured.

In Independence the best place to start a tour is at the LDS visitors' center at Walnut and River streets, where information about other historic sites in the area may be obtained. One should also visit the RLDS Auditorium just across the street from the visitors' center.

In the 1840s and 1850s many Mormons and other emigrants traveled west from Independence along the Oregon-California Trail (see trail XI) and the Santa Fe Trail and its variants (see trail XXIV).

Appendix

Museums and Historical Societies along Western Trails

There is a museum or historical exhibit in almost every important city and in almost every county seat through which the trails described in this book pass. For the convenience of the reader, the addresses of selected, recommended points of interest are listed below.

Arizona

San Pedro Valley Historical Society
142 S. San Pedro
Benson 85602

California

Mormon Battalion Memorial and
  Visitors Center
2501 Juan Street
San Diego 92110

San Luis Rey Mission
San Luis Rey 92068

Vallecito Stage Station
Vallecito 95251

Colorado

Baca-Bloom House
300 East Main Street
Trinidad 81082

Bent's Old Fort National Historic Site
Box 581
La Junta 81050

Depo Museum
202 West First Street
Julesburg 80737

Fort Collins Museum
200 Matthews
Fort Collins 80524

Kit Carson Museum
425 Carson
Las Animas 81054

Longmont Museum
375 Kimbark
Longmont 80501

Loveland Museum
503 Lincoln
Loveland 80537

Old Fort Vasquez
13412 U.S. Highway 85
Platteville 80651

Overland Trail Museum
Junction I-76 and Highway 6
Sterling 80751

Pioneer Museum
215 S. Tejon
Colorado Springs 80903

Illinois

Nauvoo Restoration, Inc.
Young and Partridge Streets
Nauvoo 62354

Joseph Smith Historic Center
Water Street
Nauvoo 62354

Pike County Museum
P.O. Box 44
Old East High School
Pittsfield 62363

Iowa

Johnson County Historical Society
310 Fifth Street
Coralville 52241

Keokuk Museum
Foot of Johnson Street
Keokuk 52632

Lucas County Museum
17th Street and Braden Avenue
Chariton 50151

Pella Historical Society
507 Franklin
Pella 50219

Wayne County Historical Museum
Highway 2
Corydon 50060

Kansas

Fort Larned National Historic Site
Route 3
Larned 67550

Fort Leavenworth Museum
Reynolds and Gibbon Avenues
Fort Leavenworth 66027

Grant County Museum
300 East U.S. Highway 160
Ulysses 67880

Hamilton County Museum
U.S. 50
Syracuse 67878

Hollenburg Pony Express Station
Hanover 66945

Kaw Mission Museum
500 N. Mission
Council Grove 66846-1433

Old Castle Museum
515 Fifth
Baldwin 66002

Pony Express Museum
809 North Street
Marysville 66508

Rice County Historical Society
221 East Avenue South
Lyons 67554

Rock Creek Valley Historical
    Museum
Westmorland 66549

Santa Fe Trail Center
Route 3
Larned 67550

Santa Fe Trail Museum
Ingalls 67853

Wyandotte County Museum
631 N. 126th Street
Bonner Springs 66012

Missouri

Fort Osage
Old Selby (north of Buckner on
Highway 20 E and follow signs)

Jefferson National Expansion
    Museum
11 N. Fourth Street
St. Louis 63102

Mormon Visitors Center
937 W. Walnut Street
Independence 64080

Patee House Museum
1202 Penn Street
St. Joseph 65402

Pony Express Museum-Stables
914 Penn Street
St. Joseph 65401

Raytown Historical Museum
9705 East 63rd Street
Raytown 64133

Rocheport Museum
Moniteau Street
Rocheport 65279

Nebraska

Ash Hollow State Historical Park
    Visitors Center
Box A
Lewellen 69147

Buffalo County Historical Society
710 W. Eleventh Street
Kearney 68847

Dawson County Historical Society
805 N. Taft
Lexington 68850

Hastings Museum
1330 N. Burlington
Hastings 68901

Fontenelle Forest Nature Center
1111 Bellevue Boulevard
Bellevue 68005

Fort Kearny State Historical Park
R.R. 4
Kearney 68847

Fort McPherson National Cemetery
Maxwell 69151

Lincoln County Historical Society
2403 N. Buffalo
North Platte 69101

Mormon Pioneer Cemetery and
    Information Center
State Street and N. Ridge Drive
Omaha 68112

Old Fort Atkinson
Box 237
Fort Calhoun 68023

Pioneer Trail Museum
Highway 385/92
Bridgeport 69336

Pony Express Station
Ehmer Park
Gothenburg 69138

Rock Creek Station State Historical
    Site
Rt. 4
Fairbury 68352

Sarpy County Historical Society
2402 Clay Street
Bellevue 68005

Scotts Bluff National Monument
Box 427
Gering 69341

Stuhr Museum of the Prairie Pioneer
3133 W. Highway 34
Grand Island 68801

Union Pacific Museum
1416 Dodge Street
Omaha 68179

New Mexico

Fort Union National Monument
Watrous 87753

Governor's Palace
The Plaza
Santa Fe 87501

T. Roosevelt Rough Riders and City
    Museum
731 Grand Avenue
Las Vegas 87701

Old Mill Museum
Cimarron 87714

Pecos National Monument
P.O. Drawer 11
Pecos 87535

Philmont Museum
Philmont Scout Ranch
Cimarron 87714

New York

E. B. Grandin Print Shop
Main Street
Palmyra 14522

Martin Harris Home Visitors Center
Highway 21
Palmyra 14522

Peter Whitmer Farm
Highway 96
Fayette 13065

Ohio

Kirtland Temple
9020 Chillicothe
Kirtland 44094

Newell K. Whitney Store
Highway 306
Kirtland 44094

Utah

Daughters of Utah Pioneers Museum
300 N. Main Street
Salt Lake City 84103

Museum of Church History and Art
45 North West Temple
Salt Lake City 84150

Pioneer Monument State Park
1084 N. Redwood Road
Salt Lake City 84116-1555

Sons of Utah Pioneers
3301 East 2920 South
Salt Lake City 84109

Wyoming

Fort Bridger State Historical Site
  Museum
Fort Bridger 82933

Fort Laramie National Historical Site
Fort Laramie 82212

Guernsey State Park Museum
Guernsey State Park
Guernsey 82214

Old Fort Caspar Museum
14 Fort Caspar Road
Caspar 82604

South Pass City State Historic Site
Rt. 66, Box 164
South Pass City 82520

Bibliography

There is a vast literature on western trails, consisting of books, monographs, guides of all kinds, federal, state, and local publications, popular and scholarly articles, and hundreds of what librarians call ephemera and fugitive publications. This selected bibliography of suggested readings is restricted mainly to recent publications readily available to travelers and to students of the transportation frontier of the United States and is presented in the same order as the trails appear in this book.

For the Mormon Trail system, I recommend several of my own publications, including *The Traveler's Guide to Historic Mormon America*, 16th ed. (Bookcraft, Salt Lake City, 1986); *111 Days to Zion*, with Hal Knight (Deseret News Press, Salt Lake City, 1979); *Discovering Mormon Trails: 1831–1868, New York to California* (Deseret Book Co., Salt Lake City, 1970); *The Latter-Day Saints' Emigrants' Guide by W. Clayton* (Patrice Press, Gerald, MO., 1983); "The Iowa Trek of 1846: The Brigham Young Route from Nauvoo to Winter Quarters," *The Ensign* (June 1972):35–36; "The Mormon Trail Network in Iowa, 1838–63: A New Look," *Brigham Young University Studies* 21 (1981):417–30; "The Mormon Trail Network in Nebraska, 1846–1868: A New Look," *Brigham Young University Studies* 24 (1984):321–36.

The Dragoon Trail is described in my "The Mormon Trail Network in Iowa." For the Golden Road in Utah, see my "The Golden Road: 1848-1980," *The Pioneer* (Nov.–Dec. 1980):11, 15, 17, 20. The Mormon Handcart Trail is treated in my *Discovering Mormon Trails*; in LeRoy Hafen and Ann W. Hafen, *Handcarts to Zion: 1856–1860* (Arthur H. Clark Co., Glendale, CA., 1960); and in William J. Petersen, "Mormon Trails in Iowa," *The Palimpsest* 47 (1966):353–84. For a general treatment of the Mormon Trail, you can also consult Preston Nibley, *Exodus to Greatness* (Deseret News Press, Salt Lake City, 1947).

For the Oregon-California Trail system, I recommend Gregory M. Franzwa, *The Oregon Trail Revisited*, 3d ed. (Patrice Press, Gerald, MO., 1983); Gregory M. Franzwa, *Maps of the Oregon Trail*, 2d ed. (Patrice Press, Gerald, MO., 1982); Aubrey L. Haines, *Historic Sites along the Oregon Trail*, 2d ed. (Patrice Press, Gerald, MO., 1983); Merrill J. Mattes, *The Great Platte River Road* (Nebraska State Historical Society, Lincoln, 1969); Irene D. Paden, *The Wake of the Prairie Schooner* (Southern Illinois University Press, Carbondale, 1970); William E. Hill, *The California Trail Yesterday & Today* (Pruett Publishing, Boulder, CO.,

305

1986); and Margaret Long, *The Oregon Trail* (W. H. Kistler Stationery Co., Denver, 1954).

One of the best studies of the Nebraska City Cutoff and Ox-Bow trails is William E. Lass, *From the Missouri to the Great Salt Lake: An Account of Overland Freighting* (Nebraska State Historical Society, Lincoln, 1972). The best sources for information on the Wyoming (Mormon) variant of the Nebraska City Cutoff Trail are Helen Roberta Williams, "Old Wyoming," *Nebraska History Magazine* 27 (1936):79–80; and Andrew Jenson, "Latter-Day Saints Emigration from Wyoming, Nebraska: 1864–1866," *Nebraska History Magazine* 27 (1936):113–27.

For the Overland–Bridger Pass Trail, the best study I have seen is John E. Burns, "The Overland Trail," in the now-defunct *Popular Off-Roading* (Sept. 1972):26–31 and (Oct. 1972):42–49. See also my "Rediscovering Another Mormon Trail: The Overland Trail, 1847–1868," *The Ensign* (June 1984):34–35.

For all trails in Colorado presented in this book, I strongly recommend Margaret Long, *The Smoky Hill Trail*, (W. H. Kistler Stationery Co., Denver, 1947); Doris Monohan, *Destination Denver City: The South Platte Trail* (Swallow Press, Chicago, 1985); and Lillian Rice Brigham, *Historical Guide to Colorado* (Colorado Society of the DAR, Denver, 1931). There is not much on the interesting Jimmy Camp Trail, but the reader will find the following useful: Janet Lecompte, *Pueblo, Hardscrabble, Greenhorn: The Upper Arkansas, 1832–1856* (Oklahoma University Press, Norman, 1978); and C. F. Mathews, *The Jimmy Camp Trail* (Privately printed, Colorado Springs, CO., 1946).

There is an extensive literature on the Santa Fe Trail, and the key to it is Jack D. Rittenhouse, *The Santa Fe Trail: A Historical Bibliography* (Jack D. Rittenhouse, Albuquerque, 1986). The best general and indespensible study of the Santa Fe Trail is Marc Simmons, *Following the Santa Fe Trail: A Guide for Modern Travelers*, rev. ed. (Ancient City Press, Santa Fe, 1986).

For the Mormon Battalion march from Iowa to California, see my *Discovering Mormon Trails* and several older studies, such as Frank Alfred Golder, *The March of the Mormon Battalion from Council Bluffs to California, Taken from the Journal of Henry Standage* (Century, New York, 1928); and Daniel Tyler, *A Concise History of the Mormon Battalion in the Mexican War* (Rio Grand Classic, Chicago, 1964). Especially useful is Charles S. Peterson et al., *Mormon Battalion Trail Guide* (Utah State Historical Society, Salt Lake City, 1972).

For the Boonslick Trail and the Santa Fe Trail in Missouri, see Nancy Short et al., *Milestones in Missouri's Past* (Missouri Daughters of the DAR, 1976); and my *Discovering Mormon Trails*.

BIBLIOGRAPHY

There is scarcely anything published on the Mormons' First Road West other than what is in my *Discovering Mormon Trails*. By far the best study of Zion's Camp is Robert D. Launius, *Zion's Camp* (Herald Publishing House, Independence, MO., 1984). See also my *Discovering Mormon Trails*.

There is also a publication by the Western Writers of America, *Pioneer Trails West* (Caxton Printers, Caldwell, Idaho, 1985), and of further interest is *The Overland Journal* (1983–   ) of the Oregon-California Trails Association. For all trails in Kansas, Louise Barry, *The Beginning of the West: Annals of the American West, 1540–1854* (Kansas State Historical Society, Topeka, 1972) is a must. Also very useful is George R. Steward's *California Trail* (University of Nebraska Press, Lincoln, 1983). See also the journals published by the state historical societies of the states considered in this book, for specialized articles on trails in their area.

Index

Note: Individual sites and markers are listed as subentries by state. Major river systems are listed as subentries under "Rivers, streams, and springs."

A Note on the Author

Stanley B. Kimball is a great-great-grandson of Heber C. Kimball, a Mormon apostle-pioneer and John W. Hess, a member of the Mormon Battalion. He spent his early childhood in Utah. In 1960 he received his Ph.D. from Columbia University and is currently professor of history at Southern Illinois University at Edwardsville, where he has taught for twenty-seven years. He is historian of the Mormon Pioneer Trail Foundation, a founding director of the Oregon-California Trails Association, and a member of the Sante Fe Trail Council.

Professor Kimball has written five books of Mormon history, four books of East European history, and over sixty articles on these subjects; his previous book from the University of Illinois Press is *Heber C. Kimball* (1981), which won the Best Book Award of the Mormon History Association. For his work on western trails, the Department of the Interior in 1974 awarded him the Outdoor Recreation Achievement Award, and in 1982 he received a Special Commendation from the National Park Service.